Psychic & The Sidekick

SHIRLEY J. SMITH

DEDICATION

I dedicate this book to my husband Patrick Cox, who named me his Favorite Person. If one could believe they would have married the perfect match, then Patrick was that. He knew me to the depth of my soul without even having to ask. All he had to do was look at me and I knew things were right. We would survive. Our love would survive. Together the world would be a better place. He always encouraged me to follow my dreams and heartened me to be the true free-spirited person I loved to be. Patrick made me a whole person. I miss him so, but he taught me there were things to look forward to without his being there. He filled my holes, cast away my doubts, brought love and joy into every living minute we were together. Even now, I can hear him talking to me. My guide on the earth has now become my spiritual guide forever. This Favorite Person loves you.

Psychic & The Sidekick

Copyright 10/20/2014

Shirley J. Smith

ISBN 978-1-66782-778-0

ISBN eBook 978-1-66782-779-7

Universal Love Productions

Shirleyjsmith.com

The Universe exists in perfect harmony, and all is in common with the energy. Once you understand apply and align yourself with Universal Love, you will experience transformation in every area of your life beyond anything you have ever dared to imagine.

Front cover illustration by Max Fairbanks

ACKNOWLEDGEMENTS

So many people influenced this book that it would be impossible to mention them all. But I must say special thanks to Toni Harper, Karrie Biggs, and Maxx Fairbanks

TABLE OF CONTENTS

Chapter 1-Two Comets..1

Chapter 2-The Mystery of History 24

Chapter 3-Face to Face 35

Chapter 4-Leon Speaks.. 47

Chapter 5-Mother Nature Has Her Way 60

Chapter 6-Lesson Learned 75

Chapter 7-Memories Are Nice 88

Chapter 8-Shirley's Surprise...103

Chapter 9-Australia-Bound 113

Chapter 10-At the Falls...125

Chapter 11-Dream Time 134

Chapter 12-Life Is Fun 145

Chapter 13-The Muir Woods...150

Chapter 14-Hawaii 164

Chapter 15-Electrifying Changes 182

Chapter 16-A Texas Wonder...190

Chapter 17-Science v. Spiritual....................................197

Chapter 18-Enchanting Times......................................207

Chapter 19-Learning A New Way 215

Chapter 20-The Self's Evolution 221

Chapter 21-Earth's Beauty..226

Chapter 22-Here They Go 235

Chapter 23-Wyoming Power 244

CHAPTER 1

Two Comets

"At that moment, the impact of finding this unexplainable
file caused a shiver down my spine."

When feeling sad, I would usually go to one of my many trunks. They always comforted me. To the contemporary eyes, there was something about an old trunk that captures one's imagination. This black trunk had a brass-plated spring lock with two vintage brass oblong catches on each side. There were leather straps attached by brass holders on each side for carrying. This trunk, filled with my life treasures. I filled it with automatic writings, family and travel pictures, journals, cards, letters, scrapbooks, newspaper articles, Universal Love Seminar materials, souvenirs of little rocks from around the world, and memoires. I called it my Love Trunk. It was always uplifting to look inside, and I wondered what the "feeling better" mystery for the trunk opening this time would be.

As I opened the aged trunk lid, a simple musty smell filled my senses. I at once felt an empowering love. I looked down and gasped at seeing a large aged red Hallmark Valentine's card Patrick had given me.

With a shaky hand, I picked up the card and held it close to my heart. I felt like placing it there would make me feel closer to Patrick. Tearfully I read, "To My Favorite Person. I will always love you. No matter where we are or what we are doing, my love will always be with you."

I sat very still for a few moments, letting feelings take over me.

Very seldom did Patrick call me Shirley. I was always referred to as "Favorite Person." Inside the card was a dried rose from the bouquet he had given me. I never knew when Patrick would shower me with beautiful bouquets, sometimes for no reason. It did not have to be a birthday or holiday for flowers to show up at the door. He said I deserved it.

I was grieving on the inside but believed that I could hide my sorrow from friends and family. I was always one of those people that anyone could read easily. They could see it in my eyes, my movements, and my drooping posture. There was a time in my life when I expressed my feelings in a true way, but I felt I couldn't go on like that. I couldn't keep crying like a baby; I needed to get a grip on my mind and stop cramming my feelings inside my chest. The problem was the space was getting too full, so much harder to ignore. Inner pain is difficult to bare. My wish was to get these emotions out instead of bottling them up. How do I defuse this bomb without triggering the damage I look to avoid?

As I clinched the card to my chest, the tears in my soul became tears in my eyes. With blurred vision, I looked down and saw a file labeled *Psychic & the Sidekick*. I wondered where that came from. I was shocked yet delighted to find these typed pages filled with Patrick's words of when we met and what we were doing at that time. I had no idea when Patrick had typed it or how it got in the trunk. This trunk had locks and only I knew where the keys were hidden. Patrick was never interested in looking at my trunk's treasurers. It was baffling how the file got in my trunk. I had never seen it before. At that moment, the impact of finding this unexplainable file caused a surprising quiver down my spine.

Love transcends all barriers. Patrick had managed to comfort me from the other side. As I started reading his writings from the trunk, my sad heart once again became happy.

~~~

How Patrick and I met can only be explained as if it were like two comets hurling themselves through space, unusual, accidental, exciting, unlikely, but true, with all the drama that comets smashing together would cause. Looking back and remembering, I saw myself happy, self-assured, at the top of my game with a successful career and exciting friends. I had never been happier or less in need of a companion. I loved my life! I barely had enough hours in the day to take it all in; I was just so happy and content. I would never have met Patrick if I weren't so diligent about keeping ties with my friends.

I had always considered my friends as jewels. Everyone was precious and essential in their own way. I cherished them all, and still do. I had always made time with a quick note or cards or phone calls to all the people who had enriched my life. Giving love to friends and receiving was its reward. It had always made me stronger in my feelings of self.

Before telling about the end, I reminisced from the beginning. I do not know why; I just knew this is what presented itself.

~~~

When Patrick, my love, died a few years ago after a long, hard battle with cancer, it made me feel as though there was a never-ending dark void that consumed everything. I was left feeling nothing. Empty. Nothing to subside my hollow soul. I chose to stay away from other human life because my emptiness was so consuming. I could not pretend that everything was okay. Moments of emptiness still come like an ambush, yet in the company of a true friend, a real smile can return, a real laugh and real warmth.

All around the walls were pictures of Patrick, of his golf champions and of us. I closed my eyes, letting my mind fill with his voice. I could hear him teasing me like he is just a few feet away; my mind filled with witty jibes he could never say. I wanted to call him softly to see if he could step out of the dusty frame. The power of his picture was expressing truth at this moment, to talk with my soul so personally, in a way that volumes of words cannot. The emotional reunion is told in the soul connection of our eyes, in the sweet touch, in the strength of such a long-anticipated hug. For in that moment is the sweet release, the relief, the chance for joy to take us center stage to dance.

The day had come when I was home alone with my friend, Susan Fry. It was one afternoon, and we were sitting on a sofa that faced a large veranda. The sun was slowly giving out the warm rays of light. Susan had been chatting softly, trying to say all the things a good friend says when they are trying to get their friend through a difficult place. I appreciated her efforts, but I could hardly hear Susan as I sat, holding Patrick's favorite shirt. I had purposely not laundered it because it smelled like him.

Susan said, "In your heart…"

I raised my hand in mid-sentence. "My heart?" I repeated the words back to Susan. "My heart hurts, Susan. It misses Patrick's physical touch. I know he is in a much better place, but my human side wants to touch him. We made each other question things. I found parts of me I didn't know existed and in him was a love I thought no longer was real."

Susan asked, "What do you mean your love is with him. He died; he's gone."

Susan sat quietly while I explained about my love being with Patrick.

"Patrick's physical body, the necessary vehicle he had to carry while living on earth deteriorated and stopped functioning, so it died. But his soul and spirit moved on, carrying all his love and life data with it. Now that Patrick is on the 'other side,' some call it the 'spirit world,' he will continue to work on behalf of Universal Love. The universe exists in perfect harmony. You know, Susan, all is in common with the spiritual love energy vibrating in the universe. Once we understand, apply, and align with Universal Love, we will experience transformation."

By the look and appearance of her smile, I could tell she didn't understand. "Susan, open your mind but remember to filter and make connections with concepts. A tidy brain is your blessing," I said.

Susan nodded her head yes and smiled. I continued, "The All is Mind. The Universe is Mental. Everything we see and experience in our physical world has its origin in the invisible mental realm. It tells us there is a single Universal Consciousness. The Universal Mind, from which all things manifest, the All energy and matter at all levels is created by and is subordinate to present everywhere at the same time."

The Universe's energy is all about the mind, our thoughts are what we create on heaven and earth.

Susan, brushing her hair from her face, says, "I love talking to you; you give me inspiration and your information is usually something I never even thought about. I need freedom to move in any direction in search of real solutions. We have the same powerful brains as the ancient Greeks, but we let them decay with junk. Every conversation I have revolves around the topics of the day—fear, terrorism, money, petty disagreements—no one ever focuses on the real puzzles of the universe. I want to talk to someone who knows our intellectual walls are artificial. 'All is Mind,' in the Universe is new to me, but I do understand. What Patrick thinks now is what he gets."

I crossed my legs and said, "Where he calls home, I'm sure his soul will be filled with passion. There is a solace in feeling the goodness of one's soul, in the gentle certainty that one was born to absorb and reflect heaven's love. Patrick's thoughts now create where and whatever he desires, it will quickly manifest."

Sometimes, it's difficult for people on earth to realize this, but I know it, and that helps me to understand where Patrick is now. God gives everyone eternal life. When we have a physical death, it is only a passage into the real place from which one comes from.

Life is more than hearing, seeing, or even touching; it is eternal. Patrick's soul now exists and stays somewhere in the heaven, and he will advance to where he chooses and understands. It is knowing everything is done by our thoughts on Earth and the Other Side. Our God-given free will, the ability to choose gives us freedom in life forever and ever. There is scientific proof that everything in life is our choice of creation, our manifestation. If you do not like what you have around you, then with your God-given free will, just change it. Nothing is etched in stone. You can make changes with your thoughts."

Susan gave a long sigh and asked, "Wouldn't it be wonderful if everyone on Earth had that same kind of love for each other?"

I told her this was what I was working to teach in my seminars. Then I continued, "Patrick's meditations were with colors so wherever he is, he will learn more about colors. It's his soul's desire leading him to the right place for better understanding."

Susan stopped me and asked, "So is this what it means when we love someone with all our heart and soul?"

"You're right! Our soul is the receptacle that holds our data and lives in our heart, the essence of our God part. When we are born with the first breath of life, the Holy Spirit directs our soul into the physical body. Our soul will then program our brain's subconscious with all its past data. The spirit is really called our emotional energy. It is our get-up-and-go for our physical body. It's the energy that keeps the physical body alive. Just like a car, it takes gasoline to make it run. Our physical bodies have emotions that keep us moving."

"Isn't that the truth?" Susan came back. "That's why little kids run around at Christmas time. It is the energy or spirit in their soul that keeps them moving, flowing within and out to others," I replied, "You know, Susan, many times, Patrick told me he would go first. He would clear the path for me. I always countered by saying I would be the first. After all, I was the oldest. He would laughingly give me a big hug, like he knew something that I didn't."

Susan sighed, "I have witnessed the closeness you and Patrick had. It is like the two of you were connected at the hip. But I never understood why. I want a relationship like that."

I answered, "Breathe; you will. I promise. Patrick and I are Soul Mate Matches. Some people call it Twin Flames, but do not allow yourself to be confused about the differences of Twin Flames and Soulmates. The idea is that some believe Twin Flames are one soul split into two bodies. Soulmate is a soul that has divided into two bodies, and they are connected to their other half's data and has a strong fiery love connection. The true meaning of Twin Flames is a 'Fire Energy' (reason for name twin flames). It is a love energy each soul feels especially when meeting their soulmate. The twin flames' connection between two souls is extremely powerful and extraordinary."

"At its heart, meeting your soulmate is a love about spiritual growth, and its purpose is to be awakened. The purpose of meeting your soulmate is to speed up growth, to release wounds, remove blockages, and lead you to true self-love. Soulmate is the other half of you, it's your mirror."

I continued, "Soulmate relationships can be incredibly challenging because they shine a light on your insecurities and your deepest fears for that spiritual growth to happen, and that can be challenging to face. The things you don't want to deal with, the doubts you have, the inadequacy you see in yourself, will all come up through their existence. In truth, this relationship is designed to test and develop your very understanding of yourself and your energy. The reason for the soul to split is because each half wants to learn more through life's experiences to evolve higher into the Universe's love and light energy. So, you see, the more you learn, the higher evolved you are. Patrick and I being a Soulmate Match, together on earth wasn't to be a challenge; we came together to teach Universal Love. "

"Slow down and let me absorb," Susan replied.

After a while Susan said, "I understand that now; tell me more."

I got up and started walking around just like Maggy used to when she was teaching me.

"When one of the halves of the soul comes to earth and meets, each half brings their knowledge, data, and wisdom that they have learned from their past lives. It helps them reunite for illumination like spiritual knowledge, love, compassion, and understanding. You know, all those positive feelings and the way we treat others," I said.

I could tell that Susan was thinking about what I had just said.

I nodded my head.

"We need more of that in the world; that's for sure," Susan replied.

"Ready for more?" I asked.

"Not quite. I need to absorb all of this some more. Let's go out into your backyard and just sit and soak up nature. Then can we continue from there? Your yard just brings me so much peace."

I responded that I would love to do just that, and I would brew some tea. We sat in contemplative silence for a while. I loved it out there. I just did not get going for me in the mornings until I had my 'backyard time.'

The flower that had been a tight bud only days ago had begun to open, already had a deeper blush of pink. The winter should have still been in force but already spring has pushed it back to moderate temperatures and the kind of gentle breeze you do not notice unless you stop and be present in the moment. Susan walked over to the flowerpot and stretched out her fingers to touch the silky pink petals; they were smoother than she thought. She tried to will it to open faster, to see the beauty she knew was inside. But nature has its way, its timing, and the flower was not ready yet. A few more days of warmth and it would bloom; Susan just had to wait.

"Ready now? 3-2-1…Let's go!" Susan said with calmness but excitement at the same time.

"Soul mates are two hearts learning separately, and if one creates any karma, then they will not be a match for living or working on earth.

Earth is our schoolhouse, and we can learn faster here. We choose earth to learn and pay off our karma for evolvement of higher enlightenment.

"Patrick and I chose to meet on earth to teach people to better love and understand themselves."

"What do you mean by chose? How can you choose to meet someone you don't know?"

I got all excited and told Susan my dreams about Patrick three months before meeting him. I explained that everyone with their free will can manifest their dreams. "When you meet your other half, even if you are complete as an individual, there is a sense that you still add up to one, as if 1 +1 somehow equaled 1. Meeting someone new is a divine pleasure. Regardless of how things turn out, I love the dance of meeting someone." I continued, "I will miss Patrick's physical touch, but we will still work together. He is just on a different dimension while I remain on earth. Patrick always had a way of bringing me back to basics. He had a playful way to get me out of any funk. Each one of us chooses our fate and what we had was a beautiful unending love that most seek. For twenty-three years, he was my protector, my friend, and my lover."

I blinked briny tears from my red eyes, and they made wet tracks down my face and dripped from my chin. My hands open and closed, rhythmically clenching as if there could be some violent solution to my pain if only, I could find it.

Susan waited a moment and then asked, "How did you learn all this spirituality?"

I took a sip of my tea, which was cold by then, but it did not matter. My recollections made me feel warm and talking with Susan only made me feel warmer. Good thing it was not the heat of summer.

"My Indian friends and Maggy taught me. When science and spirituality meet, then the meaning of true love will be understood. And that is what happened to us. Patrick had three degrees in engineering, and I had the spiritual knowledge. Our twenty-three years together were successful in many ways. Patrick called me his 'Favorite Person' and he was my 'Favorite Person.' Our two hearts meeting and working on earth served its purpose in passing spiritual information and love to many people. Maggy also told me that it would be extraordinary for souls to meet and match on earth. But we did for the sake of teaching Universal Love."

I continued, "At one time Patrick, the engineer, and I, the spiritual knowledge, soon learned regarding energy. Patrick could not imagine light to act as both wave and matter nor that matter and energy were the same thing. But through automatic writings, he soon learned time is not a continuum but another energy transformation, and it is part of what brings the sense of distance and space. For now, Susan, let us think of time as a ball of light, a buzz of energy that we call 'the present.' As such, there really is no past or future, only 'right now.' Yet, what we do with this gift of 'the now' decides the health of our planet in all the moments to come. So, there is a separation to make here. We have what time really is, a ball of energy, and our human concept of it being a continuum from past to future. What I propose is that for our purposes rather than those speaking in the everyday sense, that we use energy-time and imagined-timeline. What was once thought of as one thing becomes two, and so it goes on. This is learning; this is progress."

Susan patted my shoulder while nodding her head as though she knew what I was talking about. I didn't know what else to say. I felt so empty.

"Patrick was a kind-hearted man," chatted Susan. "I felt lucky to have him for a neighbor. Patrick and I became acquainted every day at our mailboxes. We always visited there under the shelter of the spreading branches of my old oak tree. One day, he told me his wife was a renowned psychic and had written a book. I laughed, thinking he was joking until he invited me to your house for an autographed copy. Being around you and Patrick, I always felt calm, happy, relaxed, and it made me want to be around even more. You two made me feel that good."

"Fantastic!" I added. "I am so happy we could give that to you."

By now, tears were falling down my face again. Tears of love, joy, memories, and loss.

I told Susan, "Our love flows like the still waters that run deep especially when one sees the sunshine through the storm."

All my life, I have worked diligently to help people feel good and happy about themselves, and I felt it was necessary to do that for Patrick. But he would not allow it. He made me, his Favorite Person, be the center of everything. Even when others tried to make him the center of attention, especially with my work, he would not allow it. He always walked behind me. There were times I tried to put him in front, but he never allowed it. He always walked behind me. He repeatedly said I was a special person, I deserved whatever made me happy, and I needed more time for myself. I worked seven days a week with long hours. If people needed help at 2:00 a.m., they called, and I answered. I was that devoted. It happened many times. Being a psychic, I worked to keep my personal life to myself. People tried to spread words about our relationship, but they were not truthful. Some people thought they were part of my world, but they were not included, and it was my secret. He was the love of my life although he was not perfect, and I wasn't either, but we were perfect for one another.

Patrick's love energy was extra special to me. He made me happy, safe, and secure.

"I've had that feeling. You get something so special that you want it so private for all the joy it brings to you. You want to share whatever it is with others but treasure it so much that you think by telling others part of your feelings slip away," Susan exhaled softly.

"My happy ending is a happy ending for everyone, and that can only come long after I am gone," I softly said. "So, as it is here in this moment, as it is in those moments to come, to bring such a thing is the teamwork of the divine. It comes from those who believe in love, truth, and goodness."

I was silent for a moment and let Susan take it all in.

Talking with Susan brought back a time etched in my mind. Patrick was in the hospital dying from cancer. It was the early morning phone call on March 27th, 2012, from Katherine, Patrick's nurse, which was not easy to accept.

"Shirley, I'm so sorry, but Patrick has passed away. It happened quickly, not allowing me to call you sooner. I'm so sorry you weren't here." What appeared to me, Katherine's loud words, calling out Patrick had died, was a sign my higher brain just packed its bags and let the hulk version of me start to smash up my loss.

I felt my world was falling apart, even worse than a vast Lego construction that a child had built. Katherine's words caused my mind to flash with a bright light explosion. The atomic bomb had hit. My entire body felt like a breathtaking, beautiful crystal vase being knocked off its stand. One sees all the slivers and pieces of this crystal vase fall to the ground in slow motion. As they fell, my vase shattered into a million pieces. Then there was total silence. It was at that time I realized the vase was not only shattered, but it was gone forever, which took my breath away. There was only dead silence.

I wept. The heartbroken tears were almost silent but were tearing me apart. I knew the bomb was coming. I just didn't know when it was going to hit. It was an earthquake, a hurricane, an erupting volcano shooting out a blinding light all at the same time. Patrick's physical touch, something I totally treasured, was taken away in a split second.

"I know you're hurting. Is there anything I can do to help you?" Susan asked.

"Just sit here with me." Again, we waited in silence. Susan reached over and patted my shoulder. She gave me the time I needed.

"Throughout life, Susan, we sometimes meet someone who is unlike any other. The two of us would talk for hours and never get bored. We were two opposites meeting in a bar generating a Soul Mate Match love story. Patrick had Cherokee blood. You have seen him. He was broad in the shoulders, thighs the size of tree trunks and feet so large and flat it took more than a gale wind to knock him off the earth or change his mind."

I felt this heaviness with the gloom hugging my skin as a protective brother, always bringing a sense of stoic calmness until the light returns.

I remembered the time Patrick thought Detrick, the owner of an oil-and-gas company, was one of his special friends. Patrick had created and worked for a year on a huge oil and gas project worth millions. He was pleased and delighted to have created this big project that would help people in several states. The project was almost completed when Patrick decided to tell Detrick. They were special friends in the same business. Detrick would be pleased because Patrick was carrying out this enormous project.

I tried to tell Patrick that Detrick was not a sincere friend; if Detrick weren't a part of Patrick's new creation, he would do anything to stop it. Patrick would not listen. After their lunch date, Patrick's project came to a screeching halt. There was no resurrecting it, and Detrick had done an excellent job killing it. Later, Detrick and company were arrested for milking investors out of millions of dollars from five different states.

Patrick learned to safely remove the dagger from his heart, only to find that upon the final healing stitch that Detrick had implanted it in between his shoulder blades. He had embraced Detrick to be a friend, yet he was a foe. Patrick's hurt feelings made him realize just how headstrong he was, not listening.

Susan wondered if he'd be like that on the 'Other Side.'

Patrick's inquisitive mind made him a unique exploratory spirit. His healthy curiosity was an excellent key for seeking the truth because the truth is hidden to those who are not inquisitive. Patrick's inquisitive, scientific mind was constantly searching for answers especially when something unexplainable would happen. In my life, that was not unusual. Guides manifesting, automatic writings, or moving objects happened on a regular basis. He always searched until he found enough information he was comfortable with, so he could explain it to others.

"Susan, he told me about a time when he was a little boy, almost nine-years-old. Santa Claus had given him a train set for Christmas. He decided he wanted the train to run faster, so he mixed ingredients with his mother's blue Cheer laundry detergent. While mixing the ingredients, he caused an explosion, blowing out the side of their house. He always said he was still grounded for that experiment."

We both broke out in hysterical laughter. The kind of laughter, a gift of our souls, as pure as ringing bells, causing our hearts to leap with the confidence of a prima ballerina. Laughter is the best medicine, and I was temporarily relieved from my pain.

"I've always heard the truth is hidden to those who are not inquisitive," Susan clapped her hands together in delight knowing she understood all I had said so far. Susan was feeling it then, not just knowing it.

I stared straight ahead, watching a squirrel run up the tree and hide among the branches.

Susan asked, "Are you okay?"

I replied, "I remember living in a home in Thermopolis, Wyoming. I loved that house, but it was haunted."

The haunted house kept its ghosts for the same reason people keep a strong dog, to guard and to love, to ease the lonely hours. Even the key to the spooky house was fashioned from shadows, for ghosts can do that. The spirits can cross over from other realms with a wisp of a dream and hand over a golden key. Every night, we could see and hear spirits moving through the house. A good example was one evening the doorbell rang.

I quickly replied, "It's broken, Patrick," but Patrick didn't believe me and opened the door. No one was there.

Patrick stood as still as the eye of a hurricane and asked, "What the hell is going on here?'

"Check the doorbell wiring," I told him.

Patrick found the wires were cut. He quickly turned to me, "Who did that?"

"It was only Aaron, one of your Guides, being playful and having fun teasing you." I told him.

Patrick, walking away from the door, while shaking his head, "Oh we have a galaxy joker visiting."

One early morning, Patrick was trying to wake me up, his sleepy Favorite Person. I woke up and we were surrounded by all these Guides. They were dressed in long white robes with gold sashes around their waists.

"Do you see them?" Patrick asked. "Do you see all these Guides surrounding us? They're telling me they have a message. They look Biblical, sort of like Jesus."

"Who are they?" Patrick asked, stunned and not stunned at the same time.

Trying to wake up, I rubbed my eyes. "Yes, I see them. They are the Counsel of Twelve. They appear to people who are earnest seekers and want to assist humanity in their forward evolution."

Patrick laughed and said, "You know them better than I do. You talk to them all the time. What do they want?" He was amused. "Tell me now; what message do they have?"

Yawning, I replied, "They are here for you; they have come to talk to you. So be quiet and listen to their messages."

Patrick was one to never keep still. "But but…" There was that inquisitive mind again.

I rolled over and went back to sleep. The next morning, while cooking breakfast, Patrick was excited, but didn't know quite why. He told me the Guides had given him a message. "Show your love for all to see for I am you and you are me."

I replied, "Whoa…that is powerful. It is so beautiful and from your saying it, I feel a glow, along with I really feel it inside too."

I was pleasantly surprised about the respect and efforts Patrick had with his spiritual awakening. This was the same message the Aborigines had given me when I was in Australia.

Susan and I smiled watching that amid the long green ears of the grasses were those of a rabbit family, partaking of their meal.

Susan said, "I noticed there was a clever wisdom the way your hands move, a deft confidence. I am surprised Patrick was even interested in spiritual awakenings."

"He didn't come across that way. By his big burly type ways. One would think he was not that type," Susan continued.

Thrilled, I went on. "Others felt our spark of love. We believed our purpose in life was to love, learn, and experience. That way, we would fulfill our mission of enlightening our souls. He was my mirror reflecting scientific wisdom and empowering love. Patrick knew his science and my spirituality were two separate energies. And these two energies brought balance vibrations into reality."

"Henri Poincare once said, 'It's through science we prove, but through intuition that we discover.' Life is all about energy. Someday, spirituality and science will come together, creating a new world. Science is negative energy and spirituality is the positive frequency. The science of today is the technology of tomorrow. Science without spirituality is lame. Spiritual without science is blind. They are a powerful energy balance. Sadly, we have become a world of the mind and technology we do not really know. They're just the gadgets we think we have to have."

I looked at Susan with doe-like eyes. "Have you heard the saying, 'Ignorance is bliss'? It surely is; the less you understand the more carefree and, therefore, happy you are. Over-thinkers constantly analyze everything happening in their life and beyond. This can be draining at times, especially when you're thinking processes take you to undesirable, frustrating conclusions. It's just easier when you flow with life instead of trying to analyze life.

Turning to look at Susan, I told her about one of my visits at the Hopi reservation. I was told the Earth's modern technology would influence the human brain and overpower people's emotions. Humans would lose the sense of their touch and feel through being disconnected from their natural flow of their physical, mental, emotional, and spiritual self. The children, the future, would be controlled by their brains and would lose their wonderful gifts of being artistic. Their emotions would become confused and they'd lose the insights of learning from their elders.

"Susan, remember this; we must learn that our emotions are an energy that works the entire physical body with the brain at control.

When we follow our hearts, the brain will accept the heart's data through our emotional flow."

"How did Patrick take that thought?" Susan questioned.

I hoped I did not have a female form of Patrick. I had answered plenty of his questions when we were together.

"Brains can get noisy and create static within our body. Emotional, out-of-balance energy will create illness by tearing down our body. Any illness we have is created by an out of balance emotion.

I continued, "You see, Susan, our souls are designed in the Universe, created by God, and existed before this life. The heart is where the soul lives and holds only love and truth. It's the human brain that can play tricks creating difficult learning experiences."

Again, I got up and started walking around like Maggy did when she was teaching. Yes, I was indeed Maggy's student.

"I learned Torah, the Law of God, was revealed to Prophet Moses on Mount Sinai. The God Code articulates specifically how God's name reverberates in the DNA of all life. This code is within every biochemical function in our bodies, especially within the life-giving DNA-RNA. As we learn the connection of our physical body, we can rewire and reconnect changing our DNA. At birth, our souls enter our physical body with the data of The God Code," I continued.

"Okay, stop there," Susan said, "God Code?" She was quiet for a minute and then her eyes lit up with total understanding.

I resumed, "We can tap into that code through colors and tones from the pure loving God energy, or some call it the Universal Love energy. For some reason, we have disconnected ourselves from this code, and it lies dormant within. It is hidden. Meditation revealed this to Moses, and in those days, people were taught by the prophets, by using the name of God. It is reverberated in all creations as the name of God is encoded in our human DNA and the RNA. In fact, it is coded in all living creatures and plant life. Our minds will follow what our hearts tell us to do when following our hearts, not our minds; we will balance our male and female energy."

"Need another break?" I asked, as I was sensing that Susan did.

After we both had been sitting quiet for a while, Susan inquisitively said, "Yes; what you're saying is rather deep and mysterious. I'm not sure what this all means, but I do like hearing you say it."

"It was time to slow life down," I announced. "What's the big hurry anyway? Hurry only creates one to push and then we make mistakes. We must slow down and learn about our energy instead of the world's machine technology."

Susan kindly asked, "What is the answer for earth's future? People appear to be unhappy and frustrated nowadays. I just read that earth has until 2030 to stop this catastrophic climate change."

"According to what I have learned, 'Know Thy Self and Thy Know All,' is the future for Earth's peacefulness," I declared. "Until the masses truly know and love themselves, there will not be any change. The Dalai Lama once said, 'We can never obtain peace in the outer world until we make peace with ourselves.'"

I continued, "You know, it still rings in my heart about an automatic writing I received a few years ago concerning earth's future."

Susan moved her chair closer to me and listened as if my words were golden, perhaps with some solution she had been waiting all her days to hear. I could tell she was thinking very deeply. Then, she asked softly, "What did the writings say?"

"The writings say we must discuss with you there will be major changes on your planet earth with government, religion and corporations. All three are going to have a major shift, creating falsehood and fear worldwide. You must remember you are born with love; you are taught fear. Never allow fear to control you. The media will show the battles, but they are untrue. It continues to talk about China, Tibet, Europe, Germany, Italy, America, and Russia being involved in all the falsehood of what the media will show. It is a warning. It is to happen worldwide due to greed and political votes. It will be a battle of good versus evil. It is like the phoenix, the government, religion, and corporation will burn themselves to the ground rising from the ashes with renewed youth to live a new life creating a new earth.

"When it does happen, people will understand how they have been controlled through religion and politics. That has been the fear of the greedy political leaders because they know they will lose control. It will create people to get back to the basics of life and learn more what their spirituality truly means. The energy is like a free-spirited horse running to its destiny, with its own freedom. When a horse has its freedom, there is nothing to hold it back. People must bring God back into this world and more spirituality permeated with self-awareness. It is the necessary process of infusing the material world with a palpable spiritual presence."

Susan stood up, as I continued, "This makes me feel like I'm in a cage and it's closing in, sealing off any workable exit. I dreamed last night of sitting in church as a masked man painted over every window until every one of them was black. I awoke before the dawn into blackness and my heart almost exploded with fear. The fear was a weight on my ribs and a dull ache in my eyes, unwillingness for my mouth to lift past neutral. I thought I can double down on my efforts for a victory or sit back and be prey, sheep or lion, my choice, my path. I knew I had a choice of living, for in the future I had a life of great happiness."

I leaned back in my chair and said, "I taught Patrick the importance of the colors, tones, and their connection with the physical, emotional, mental, and spiritual energy. I was amazed how he unbiasedly absorbed the information and wanted more."

"So do I," Susan told me. "Give me an example."

I began, "Sometimes, we would go to the pool; he loved to swim. I would put my arms around his neck while he swam, with me floating behind, talking, and teaching. I can't believe I didn't drown while swimming with my mouth open. You know, like never talk when your mouth is full except this time my mouth was full of words. Or, sometimes, we would just sit by the pool or walk in the park. It is more of a natural flow to better understand spiritual information when outside. Mother Nature's energy is always there to help those who are willing to learn. It is a natural way to connect for enlightening the soul."

"Now that you don't have Patrick's physical touch, what brings you comfort?" Susan timidly asked.

"I have a passion to write and knowing where Patrick is; we still communicate. It's only a matter of time until we are reunited," I smiled. "When someone crosses over or as you know it dies, they leave their physical body and, at that moment, or at once before, a sunburst of light appears. This light acts as the doorway to the 'Other Side.' In it, loved ones and Guides of the person appear to take their hand and escort them to the Spirit World. There are various levels where they go, and some choose not to cross over at all. Like those who commit suicide, they can go into a state of limbo. They feel guilty or unworthy of going into the light. Angels or deceased relatives greet them. It is all about your spiritual level of thoughts and love. Our thoughts manifest everything."

While meditating, I saw Patrick choose the high-frequency level of colors and tones. On this level, there is an intense love vibration with a variety of colors and music tones flowing.

"Wait a sec.," Susan interrupted. "I need to catch up." I waited a moment and then Susan said she was ready for me to continue.

"The scenery has crystal mountains with an aura of rainbow colors, rainbow sky, turquoise seas, trees with sparkly rainbow leaves, relaxing flute music, colored waterfalls. Green acres with assorted colored flowers as far as you can see. Everything is in a beautiful deep flow of colors unimaginable to the human mind. It is hard to explain since we don't have those colors on Earth."

"Did you ever experiment with drugs, like LSD?" Susan was kidding but hysterical with laughter. "I wonder why he chose this level?" a dazed Susan asked.

"Patrick was a Spiritual Warrior and always used colors to enhance the power of vibrating the Divine love for healing energy purposes, and he loved to play the flute," I serenely replied. "Rainbow colors are the same as human's chakras, red, orange, yellow, green, blue, indigo, and violet. We always called rainbows a gift from the universe. He understood spiritual wisdom is not merely knowledge applied to a circumstance. It's a skill of seeing beyond the thin surface of how things appear."

Susan was puzzled about all these colors and chakras. She had heard the word before but didn't really know what it meant.

"It takes a wise person who reaches to grasp what is the driving force beyond how things appear. Spiritual wisdom is the truth of insightful guidance and brings success of what needs to be done. Patrick, knowing the importance of this, called it the great energy of truth. Maggy, my mentor, taught that when the two energies unite it will create a new light filled with love and for planet earth."

"Patrick and I daily reminded each other to look inside ourselves. Learning is connected to the goal of eternal life. It is through learning in the direction given to us by God in which we develop into a higher consciousness. There are stages of love, and there are stages in the development of wisdom, which corresponds to different levels of enlightenment."

"Oh, this is why the older we become the more wisdom we have," Susan added.

"Yes, but don't tell that to teenagers. They think they have the answers to everything," I added. We both got a good chuckle about that one.

"The Universe is not outside; it's inside of us. This fire that we call love is strong and is necessary for our souls. We lived life as if everything were in our favor. He was my soul mate and my best friend."

I sat down and waited a few minutes remembering.

"I appreciate your concern, Susan, about Patrick's death, but there is nothing you can do. Even though he is on the Other Side, I know we will always be connected. Our love is that strong. It is just not having the physical touch that is so devastating. There are times I reach over in bed at night to touch him and he is not there. It's such an empty indescribable feeling."

Susan got up, lightly patted my hand, and said gently that it was time for her to leave. She had to pick up her daughter at school and softly walked away. I sat there with Patrick's shirt in my hands and watched the sun surrender to the night and the stars come out. I never bothered to turn a light on or move from my place. I just sat and stared at the stars and held my memories.

I missed Patrick's strong arms holding me while whispering in my ear, "Let me take your little girl on a magic carpet ride." I could feel his breath against my ear, and his deep voice was softly singing.

Then, he would laughingly pick me up and whirl me around while finishing the song. I knew it was time to say goodbye. I had to let him start his journey. Patrick was on a quest, for the reason to find his place on the other side. When the song of creation calls directly to your heart and soul, your journey becomes your source of love and happiness rather than any destination.

I knew what to do. My love for Patrick stays and though they move in new spheres, I feel blessed for the time we had, the love we shared, and the best of him will remain in my heart. So I will travel onward, knowing Patrick's love will be with me.

CHAPTER 2

The Mystery of History

"These men began to relate to Patrick a story of mistrust,
murder, and buried treasure."

While brewing a cup of tea, my thoughts were in suspense as to where and how Patrick's story file had been put in my trunk.

Maggy and I had experienced items to appear like that. We called it a gift from the Universe. Or if we lost something, it was in the Universe's lost and found box. Patrick's gift was like a most melodious sound, sweeter than any musical instrument. It resonated in my mind, dissolving in my heart. I was the only person who had the keys to open any of the trunks. That is how I knew no other person had placed that file in there. Once I picked up the Hallmark card, the file was noticeable and precisely under it. All my life there had been unexplainable things happen, and I loved it. In my thinking, there was no mystery; it was a gift from Patrick.

Slowly, it gave me the softest emotion to Patrick's unexpected gift.

He loved to tease me, and many times would hide things making me look for them. Once on my birthday, he hid my presents all over in our SUV. I had to crawl over and look under seats to find them.

Patrick laughed. "You haven't found all of them yet; you've got more." I could see Patrick up there laughing and taking his energy to place that file for me to find in the trunk.

Patrick was a great cook. Most people called him a chef, and I was his assistant. He would tell me "Favorite Person, you are my chef de partie." On his apron, somewhere beneath his mass of batter smears, was the pattern of a crawdad. He wore it like a battle scar, proudly defiant.

I have good memories of me aiding him and talking about the title for my next book.

Patrick turned with a bell pepper in hand and said, "*Psychic & the Sidekick*. You are the psychic and I have been your sidekick. The guy who totes and fetches."

I was surprised at how perfect the title was. This was going to be it and no other way!

Patrick loved to tell stories, and there they were, from his mysterious file. It began...

~~~

Patrick-February 1990

It was a warm February day when I saw trees blooming along Walnut Hill Lane in North Dallas. Could spring be around the corner? I hoped so. It had been a long, cold, blustery winter in West Texas where I had spent the last three months freezing my..., oh well, it sure was a beautiful day in Big D. I started thinking and remembering...

I was going to meet an old friend as well as a new one, I hoped. An exciting project… I expected my friends would think so. This place, Gershwin's, was not my first pick for this type of meeting. Yuppies were one group that was as useless as teats on a bull I believed. They were as thick as thieves in there.

I walked in and heard, "Hey, Pat, what's all the excitement?"

Mike Rogers was a long-time close friend and business associate who always seemed to be amazed I could fall into a barrel of crap and come out smelling like a rose.

"Well, buddy, you're not going to believe it this time."

We headed for a table that was out of the way, all the time looking to make sure no one was lolling around, much less listening to the yarn I was about to spin. When we were seated, and I was sure no one was listening, I leaned over toward Mike and in a faint voice almost hushed, spoke very deliberately,

"Mike, I've found it!"

"Found what?"

"You remember before Christmas, I told you the story about this buried treasure these guys in Abilene were looking for? Well, I'm sure I've found it!"

As I was about to continue, we looked up to see a tall, swarthy look-ing fellow approaching our table.

"You must be Jerry. Have a seat. This is Mike Rogers." I said.

We began to exchange basic pleasantries and ordered lunch. I thought I must be nuts. How was I going to convince these two men that I needed each of their areas of expertise for free? Unless, of course, if I were right, then it would be worth our weight in gold.

"The reason I called you both here is because you each have a partic-ular area of expertise needed for a project I'm working on near Abilene.

I explained to Mike, "Jerry owns a company that does horizontal road boring. You know, like under roads for cables and such."

"Jerry," I said, turning to Mike, "Mike is my business associate. He also can help in many other ways which will soon become clear."

We were interrupted by the waitress' beautiful smile as she placed our lunch before us. What a welcome beginning! It allowed us to tell various war stories and relax before getting to the business at hand. Bonding completed, and the table cleared, I noticed we were alone as the lunch hour had ended. Now was my time and I was not hesitant at all. I was not one to sit on the fence waiting to make decisions. I knew who I was and watch out if anyone tried to make me anything different. I will make changes in myself when I am ready.

Reaching for my briefcase, I began anew, "Jerry, what I'm about to show you has to remain in the strictest of confidence. Agreed?"

"Agreed."

"Last July, I met two guys, David and Joe, at a bar in the motel I was staying at in Abilene. They knew all about me. Knew I owned some oil wells south of town. Even knew I was an engineer."

While unfolding the series of maps, laying out newspaper and magazine articles, it became clear I had their undivided attention. That must have been enough reason to gain their trust to tell them about what I was about to say.

"These men began to relate to me a story of mistrust, murder, and buried treasure. After three, maybe four, hours of listening to their stories and buying several rounds of drinks, I agreed to look at their location to see if I could be of some help. Frankly, I did not believe much of what they were saying. Oh, I have heard some of these stories in the past, but I never put much faith in them. That is until I met this guy, Dr. Joe."

I gave them an article. "Here, read this article."

I handed Jerry the original article in the *Treasure Hunters* magazine which is a treasure hunter's bible when it comes to finding lost gold. Fumbling through his pile, I found a copy for Mike to read.

I began to speak and looked at them both in the eyes as doing so. "Joe and David, the two guys I met, took me to meet Dr. Joe. Even though he was 96 years old, he was sharp as a tack."

For the next two hours, I told them stories Dr. Joe had related. All the while, Mike and Jerry perused the information I had given them. They may not have been looking at me directly because of what they were reading, but, man, I knew they were listening because neither of them picked up a glass.

"You see, Dr. Joe claims to have some firsthand knowledge of where this treasure is located. He told me he was one of Poncho Villa's bodyguards. Dr. Joe was entrusted to take three wagons of gold bullion and other artifacts to an area between Clyde and Abilene that was known as The Badlands. These artifacts were to be hidden in some cave that Dr. Joe knew of from his childhood. After Poncho Villa escaped, Dr. Joe was to bring him the gold to finance his takeover of Mexico."

"THE Poncho Villa? You're kidding, right? The mean-ass guy with the bullets across his chest?" Mike chided. "I've seen that same picture of him a thousand times. I mean, man, didn't he ever look different or did the camera only work once and then stop? Or maybe, he was so in love with it that he would never let another one be taken."

"No," I said bluntly. "Now listen and let me finish. This was supposed to have occurred in 1922, so it was possible from an age standpoint. What impressed me the most about the guy was his sincerity; he told me how everyone involved in the wagon train had been murdered or disappeared, including some threats to him. He also spoke of these attempts to recover the gold. By the time it was safe for him to retrieve it, the landmarks had changed. New roads had been built, collapsing part of the cave system.

"I had to convince Mike and Jerry that this was true. Anyone who has been to West Texas knew it was highly unlikely, simply from the standpoint of understanding the surface terrain. Most of those little hills around Abilene had been active volcanoes at one time. These volcanoes had to have flue vents for the lava to rise to the surface. These vents were what Dr. Joe described to me as the storage place for the gold. All this made sense to me. With the construction going on things could have changed."

"Wait a minute," Jerry interrupted, "Are you trying to tell me that this group of guys pulled a couple of tons of gold hundreds of miles from Mexico to Abilene. One guy survives to this date, and he's willing to tell you where this buried treasure is located so you can bring it up and spend it? Are you naïve or what? Patrick, I thought you knew better than to believe in stuff like this," Jerry said laughing.

But I knew he was interested and did believe. Everyone knows that in Texas any and everything is possible.

"Not exactly, this is what got my attention. He doesn't want any of the gold for himself. He's got a charity he's going to give it to."

"What's that?" shot Mike.

"Get this. He wants to pay off the national debt."

I thought Mike and Jerry were going to come unglued. "NO, really; everyone involved was taking him very seriously."

"How's that?"

"As you can see from this treasure magazine article, this guy has been incredibly accurate about the directions he has given to other people. But there is one other thing I haven't told you. He's dead."

"Gosh, Patrick. You bring us all this and then tell us the guy is dead. Are we supposed to believe you?" Mike asked.

"Yeah, yeah…. We know it's in the magazine article. So, what's the big deal about a 96-year-old guy kicking off?" retorted Jerry.

"Let me go on, and you'll see." I was patient, unlike myself when it came to things like this. But I knew I had to keep them listening.

"I thought that it wouldn't hurt for me to go check it out. So, one day for lunch, I met Joe and David and followed them across some back roads to a point southwest of Clyde. When I got out of my truck, the first thing I noticed was everyone was carrying guns. I turned to Joe to ask about the guns. With a crooked smile, he mumbled something about damn snakes.

"After the 'snake guards' let me in I saw the biggest abomination I had ever seen. Directly in front of me was a huge hole, 90-feet deep, with two men working a backhoe and bulldozer near the bottom. A third man was working a dragline, peeling the east wall back. Water was seeping from various layers up and down the walls. It could collapse at any time. That's when David ordered everyone up."

The two men were rapt with attention now. I knew they would listen to the end but not entirely positive on how this would all turn out.

"As I walked around surveying this huge crater," I continued, "I thought to myself that greed was more important than safety to these yah-hoos. Halfway through my inspection, I noticed a yellow outline on one side of the wall. Instantly, I looked around for any other yellow stains in the area. I hollered across the expanse of the hole to have Joe get the draggling operator to scrape that section and get me a sample of that yellow stuff. I came around just as they were bringing the bucket up. Breaking off a piece of the mud and yellow stuff, I smelled it and tasted the acrid flavor of hydrogen sulfide. I then told David he'd found his flue vent."

The question then became which way will this go? Were they in or out?

"That's when Joe and David went back to their car and came back with some paper and took me to a large meat packing type scale. They hand wrote an agreement saying that if I helped them get the gold out, I would receive my weight in gold. I got on the scale."

"What did you weigh?" queried Jerry.

"235."

"What, are you going for 250 before you get it out?"

"Cute, Mike. You'd have to roll me back out there."

I was hooked. "They backfilled the hole 50 feet and built a ledge about 45 feet from the surface. We ordered a water well drilling rig to come in and drilled some test holes with the hopes of breaking into a cavity."

That's when Joe brought up what the Pennsylvania psychic told him.

"A psychic?"

"Hey, Mike, you've known me a lot of years. You know I don't believe in that kind of shit, but they do."

Looking skeptically Jerry asked, "Well, go on, what happened?"

"Joe announced to everyone that if we broke into the tunnel two things would happen. We would find gold on the drilling bit, and Dr. Joe would die. I didn't believe for a minute anyone could predict either event was going to happen, I thought. So, I went on moving the rig around as I saw fit."

They all settled back into their chairs and took a drink. I waited to get more of their attention. "All of a sudden, at 48 feet, we broke into a cavern," I reported. "The bit dropped 10 feet before it picked up weight. We drilled two more feet underweight and pressure before we pulled up. David was looking at his watch as we came up."

Mike and Jerry both took a big gulp of their beer. "Well?"

I reached into my pocket, pulled out a small plastic sandwich bag, and threw it on the table. Mike picked it up and slowly raised it to the light. As Mike gently shook the bag from side to side, they all looked at the sunshine through the window causing the gold specks to almost dance.

"We found gold! It sounded like the 4th of July with all the gunfire. Bet we scared every damn snake out of the county." I laughed hard just picturing the scene.

"Okay, you can continue," Jerry said. "Even if you don't have this good of an imagination."

"I looked them both straight in the eyes. Joe swore everyone to secrecy before they left to go to the bar and celebrate. I arrived first not knowing what to expect.

Twenty minutes later, Joe and David walked in, looking nervous. When asked why, David, with a glazed expression, told me Dr. Joe had died that afternoon. Apparently, he had been visiting with some friends when he keeled over. It was obvious that David was upset, but Joe had dollar signs in his beady little eyes."

Mike then posed the million-dollar question, "Patrick, what brought me here? Just what can I do to help?"

"Since the day we had the breakthrough, we've had nothing but problems. Joe and David had been acting strangely. Equipment was breaking down. Hell, I was being followed everywhere I went. Someone was following me. You know my temper, Mike, you would have loved it."

Turning to Jerry, I explained, "Kenny is my pumper on my wells. We were on one of the leases when these two turkeys pulled up by my tank battery where we stored our oil. We could see them, but it was obviously they couldn't see us. I sent Kenny around this hedgerow while I came from the front. Before the two guys in the car could react, I had pulled the driver out and had him slammed against the side of the car. The passenger was reaching for a gun when Kenny told him he was about to make the biggest f*ing mistake of his life. To make a long story short, these idiots were treasury agents assigned to keep an eye on me."

"Yep, Patrick. FBI agents and you. That I can believe for sure," Mike replied sarcastically.

I went on. "Joe and David left for about a month to raise more money. They went back to Abilene just after Thanksgiving. By then, two of the contractors had walked off with their equipment. That left them plenty of time to strategize and figure out their next steps. In the meantime, winter set in; they haven't been able to turn a lick in weeks. Now the weather is clearing, and we need help from Jerry."

"What do you need from me you don't already have?" Mike asked. "Why didn't you call?"

I had to finish telling them the story, so I ignored him.

"We need someone to bore horizontally up to 300 feet to see how far the tunnel went and what direction we needed to take."

"I can do that," Jerry was adamant.

"For your weight in gold?"

I scratched my chin in silence and looked back and forth from Mike to Jerry. I asked if I was doing the right thing.

Finally, he broke the silence, "There is one other thing. Do you guys remember hearing about the treasure ship Atocha that Mel Fisher found off the coast of Florida a few years back?"

"What does that have to do with Clyde, Texas?" That was a reasonable question from Jerry.

"Seems as though one of the Fisher's crewmen was part of our group. Early in the excavation before I got involved, they dug up a dagger that had the exact same markings that Fisher discovered on the Atocha. Strange connection, perhaps, but they found it right where Dr. Joe said it would be. Now if you remember your history, Cortex, De Gama, and many other Spaniards traveled the old Texas trails searching for the Seven Cities of God."

"Patrick, what does that have to do with where Dr. Joe hid his stash? Mike's eyes were extremely intense as he searched my face for the truth.

"Dr. Joe hid his gold in the same cave that some of this plundered gold was hidden in. The dagger that was found matched one that Dr. Joe had taken from the cave when he hid his stash."

"Buddy, what do ya need from me?" Mike was quick to ask. He was ready to go right then and there.

"Mikey, just cover my ass."

Jerry came back, "When do we start?"

"God willing and the creek don't rise, Monday."

"Deal," they both said, and Jerry got up to leave.

But before Jerry left, I gave him the appropriate directions, shook hands, and left. Mike and I continued to talk until he looked at his watch and announced, "Well, buddy it's six o'clock, and I have date in an hour. You going to stay in town over the weekend?"

"Na, got no reason. I think I'll finish this drink and head back to Abilene."

The place was getting crowded again as I moved to the bar and found a seat. "Hit me again, barkeeper."

I swirled my straw around in my scotch and water. I couldn't remember when the last time was, I sat in a bar for four hours with two hairy-legged fellows and no women. I guessed it was with Joe and David. Two hundred- and thirty-five-pounds times 16 ounces times $400 an ounce—this could be a good new year for me.

I was still at the bar, looked at my watch and thought, *Oh well, a good year, good day, or a good month*. I didn't care as long as it was good. I hoped it would be a good night because it was time to get out of here if I was going to return to Abilene at any reasonable hour.

"Barkeeper, it's time to travel. If you give me my tab, I'll be walking."

It was then that my life changed forever.

CHAPTER 3

Face to Face

"If you bring the gold out of that cave, you will die."

Shirley—February 1990

A crescent moon was dancing with the clouds on that February night. I felt this could be a magical night with mysteries and miracles. I was excited to meet Heather and Jackson, two of my psychic friends at Red's Café on Walnut Hill Lane in North Dallas. I hadn't seen them since returning from my three-month journey in Australia. My good friends were excited to hear my outback stories, and I was ready for their big hugs and laughs. Their laughter was always filled with big deep, loud, hearty bursts, the kind they could feel in their lungs, sometimes so hard that it took your breath away. The lack of oxygen didn't matter. All their anguish of the past melted like snowballs in hot water. Their laughter was a blessed relief from any distress, and I always loved it.

Turning towards Red's Restaurant, I couldn't help but smile. Heather, wearing a white leather mini skirt with a low-cut pink satin blouse and black heels, was sitting, legs crossed, on the hood of her black Mercedes. I didn't know what to expect; Heather was always doing something different. Laughingly, clutching her small black handbag, she hopped off her car and walked over to me. Seeing how Heather was dressed, I thought it was to be more casual and wished I had dressed differently. I had chosen slender black cut slacks with boots and a burgundy blouse.

"Red's is under renovation, and they are closed, Shirley. Don't worry about Jackson; I'll call him, but we must decide where to go."

Not knowing North Dallas, I told her to choose the place. Heather named Chinese, a Texas steakhouse, and several other restaurants but she mentioned Gershwin's five different times.

"Must be Gershwin's, Heather."

Heather was explaining that Gershwin's was a five-star restaurant and that since it was in the middle of the week, we shouldn't have any waiting for a table.

We had a forty-five-minute wait and were ushered to the bar. The place was packed, except at the end of the bar there were two empty stools. After we ordered a glass of wine each, I asked Heather, "So, no waiting in the middle of the week, huh?"

Heather laughingly said to me, "So I lied. Really, Shirley, who would have thought this many people would be out on a Wednesday?" Heather was sitting in the position that faced slightly outwards towards the rest of the bar, smiling.

I sipped my wine trying to calm my jittery feelings. I was nervous but didn't know why, so I grabbed my purse and took out photos Leon, my teacher, a Comanche Medicine man, had given me. Heather had always loved his art. I never dreamed Leon's paintings would create my next life's events. I hadn't paid any attention to who was on the other side of me. Instead, I was busy trying to adjust to the place filled with loud people.

Patrick, a man I had never met, was standing at the end of the bar on the other side of me. Turning to leave, Patrick noticed us sitting next to him admiring some pictures. Curiosity got the best of him.

"It's either a disco ball or UFO," he said. At this comment, me being that blonde sitting next to him showing the photographs, turned to face him just as my auburn-haired companion looked up from her drink. Patrick promised himself that he would never forget the blonde's Bambi softness of her eyes, nor would he ever forget the surprised expression they showed.

He stuck out his hand and said, "Hi, I'm Patrick Cox. I'm sorry, but that picture caught my eye."

I replied that I was Shirley Smith, and my friend was Heather.

I thought there stood a good-looking man smiling and twirling a swizzle stick in his drink. The way he was standing made us look directly in each other's eyes. There was smoothness to his appearance, a kind of warmth married to a man with benevolence. It was the look of an honest soul and in that moment, I knew I found a special man.

I was stunned. I felt like I was caught in a time warp. The dreams I had about this man was back in the old days when Indians wore breech-cloths. I thought about past life stuff, and now here he stood beside me in real life.

It was not only the face; it was the whole body. He was a perfect match for the guy in my dreams, instead of wearing a cloth and bare-chested he had on modern dress clothes. He was real!

There was a pleased look in his eye, as if some element of internal peace had alighted within him and begun to sing. I thought he must know about my dreams.

"I've witnessed many UFOs. Do you believe in UFOs?" I asked him.

As I spoke, Patrick was bewitched. My voice was as soft as my eyes.

"Not much, except that I've probably taken thousands of pictures of lights in the sky. I know about Project Blue Book, Majestic 12, plus other government files," Patrick said trying to be nonchalant.

This began a staccato of conversation in which Patrick learned I was a renowned psychic. He noticed that my eyes were glistening with the compassion of wisdom he had never known. Heather was cajoling her friend to talk about UFOs. However, four scotch and waters from Patrick's earlier meeting were beckoning him to the men's room.

As he left, I quickly turned to Heather, "Heather, this man… I've seen him in my dreams while in Australia."

Wide-eyed, Heather brushed her bangs back and asked, "What dreams?"

I had her full attention. I began to tell Heather that it was during my time in Australia. "This man looks exactly like the guy in my dreams. I've dreamed about him for three months, and it's an unsettling feeling."

My mind was whirling in different directions wondering what this dream represented. It almost made me dizzy, and I wasn't a dizzy blonde.

"My dreams always come true, but I thought it had to do with my work. Now I'm not for sure," I said mystified.

"Tell me one of your dreams," Heather was captivated.

I didn't know what or how much to say, but I remembered Heather knew of my abilities and would understand.

"The night I flew out of the LAX airport, the plane was packed so after a meal and a glass of wine, I pushed my seat back and closed my eyes."

I felt excited about meeting the Aborigines and hearing their stories. It would be so rewarding to tell stories at the seminars. I finally fell asleep and dreamed that I was walking out of a teepee where a group of Indian women were weaving baskets and men were sitting around a campfire smoking and passing a pipe around. Suddenly, drums started beating and then a man, who looked exactly like Patrick, came from behind the teepee. The women started chanting:

"The drums are beating from the Warriors in the sky.

They welcome the new one who is spreading the light.

The tom-toms beat and the singers do sing,

For the Mighty New Warrior has been sent your way.

Love and compassion run strong in his veins,

While he fights many battles with little or no pain.

He knows Mother Earth.

He talks to Father Sky.

He communicates with the Masters.

Way up high.

He sensed many a mystery way into the night.

Then looking up above was quite the sight.

A rainbow in the heavens was created that night.

The Warriors were shouting with great delight.

Now the gates are open to those who do seek.

For kindness and love is at your feet.

Thank you, we say to this warrior so brave.

As he goes out again to create another new way.

Universal Love is what you will teach."

"WOW! Just wow!" Heather exclaimed not knowing what else to say, and she wasn't a woman of few words.

I told Heather there was more. I began again telling Heather that I woke up to the smell of coffee and the chitter-chatter of people enjoying the new morning. As the plane flew into the sunrise, I had this uncanny feeling that one phase of my life was ending and another starting. My heart leaped with delightful anticipation.

"You know, a handsome man's beauty starts from his hearty loving soul and radiates from there to create his final form," Heather replied.

He is handsome from the depth of his eyes to the gentle expressions of his voice, I said, while folding my napkin. I knew Patrick had the look that was in my dreams, but I had some questions.

Heather looked over and said, "Same man. Shirley? He looks like a neat guy. Let's invite him to dinner!"

"What will Jackson think?"

"Don't worry about Jackson. He's our friend. Patrick could be a keeper for you!"

Heather had to be right, or I wouldn't have butterflies performing a circus routine in my stomach.

But Patrick stalled from leaving, thinking that there was something about the blonde. Pushing that thought aside he decided that it didn't matter. Abilene would be getting farther and farther away unless he did something right then…like, leave. However, walking down the hall from the men's room, something was tugging at him to listen. To what he didn't know.

I couldn't help myself and glanced at him walking back trying to be nonchalant and not stare at him. Now it was my turn to leave to use the lady's room. I was nervous and excused myself. As I walked into the lady's room, I was thankful it was empty. I planned to calm down and get a grip because I had never felt this way before—like something was getting ready to happen, but I didn't know what. Usually, I could sense what it was going to be.

I passionately believed my Guides from the Universe had opened its gates and brought this handsome, muscular man with a sexy voice to me. I was amazed and wondered if this could be real. I knew I didn't have time for anything but my work. It was my life. I loved my work.

Then a thought came rolling in, *It would be nice not to be alone.* He looked exactly like the man in the dream, but would he accept and respect my work, something I never had before. I wondered if we would have fun, or would he even want to be in my life? After all, meeting someone I had dreamed about has a different phenomenon. And to think if Red's hadn't been closed, we wouldn't have even met.

Shortly, my mind quieted down. I took a deep breath, looked in the mirror, brushed my hair and walked back to the bar. After sitting down, I noticed Patrick had a distinctive look on his face. He took my hand and said, "Heather told me you are a psychic and a very special lady."

I turned, and we stared intently into each other's eyes.

When our hands physically touched, I felt a warm tingling sensation. The kind that warms your heart. Amazement doesn't quite cover it. I felt like someone just took my spark of wonder and poured on kerosene. The smile I showed on the outside couldn't adequately reflect what I felt inside; it's like every neuron of my brain was trying to fire in both directions at once — the best kind of paralysis.

That night, looking into each other's eyes, the person we really were. Although the feeling puzzled him, he still wanted to hold my hand. He knew there was something between us, just that quickly.

I knew it to the core of my being because when his hand touched my hand, I felt this energy in my heart. It was though I had traveled for years and was weary and tired my heart had come home, home at last. This weary traveler had met her soulmate.

Patrick didn't know it quite yet, and I never let on. I knew whatever was going to happen would and I would just let it play out on its own.

Patrick said, "Okay, if you are really a psychic, when is my birthday?"

Before I could say anything, Heather quickly answered "June 23rd." Heather's eyes were dancing as she spoke.

"How did you know that?" Patrick asked bluntly.

He reached for his wallet to make sure it was still in his back pocket. This was funny and we both began to chuckle. Patrick thought to himself these ladies are weird. How could they know so much about him before he had a chance to say anything? He thought they could be up to something, and Patrick didn't want to get involved in it.

Great jokes are something to laugh at, but it seems as though Patrick didn't understand this one. It was at this time that Jackson joined our little group. Both of us gave Jackson a big hug, introduced him, and Heather asked if Patrick would join us for dinner.

I quickly looked down; I didn't want him to know how anxiously I was hoping for a big yes to come out of his mouth.

Patrick had promised himself that he wouldn't say yes if it weren't for the blonde's eyes.

I wondered if he knew what was going on and could he see all those Guides around him.

In silence, we followed the hostess to our table. Looking at the menu, I thought Jackson had no idea what just happened. I needed to change the subject and remembered the three of them knew about this psychic stuff, but they needed to be considerate of Patrick. The dinner conversation was pleasant, although for the life of him Patrick couldn't understand how people got involved with hurricanes, crystals, and UFOs.

It gave Patrick the opportunity to watch me. He always said that watching me was like watching a child with a new toy. Each story I told caused my entire body to move with a gentle persuasiveness never known by mortal man. Patrick was confident of that fact.

I was thinking to myself that he sure didn't talk very much. Most guys bored me to death with their machismo attitudes. He was different. He was listening. I hoped that whatever I said wouldn't blow his mind.

Heather broke my train of thought and spoke to Jackson, "I bet you two are happy to be on land instead of out in the Yucatan Sea?"

Jackson laughed and started telling stories about how we both survived Hurricane Gilbert. I changed the subject by telling stories about Maggy, my mentor. The more I talked the more attention I got from Patrick. He was watching every move and listening closely.

I could tell Jackson was having a problem with Patrick. His lady friends were picked up at the bar by a strange man. Heather also became uncomfortable, moved her chair closer to Jackson, leaned over and whispered something in his ear. Patrick was uneasy and started telling jokes, causing us ladies to laugh, but not Jackson.

Suddenly, Jackson scooted up to the edge of his chair, put his arms on the table, leaned over staring straight at Patrick and said, "Patrick, we don't appreciate your off the wall jokes. I think you owe us an apology."

It shocked me. Jackson was always slightly shy, but he was upset in a restrained way by Patrick's jokes.

"I'm a man who respects everyone, but I don't think it's necessary for me to apologize. My jokes were just that, nothing but jokes to make us laugh."

I leaned toward Patrick in agreement, and Heather patted Jackson's hand.

While Jackson and Heather were visiting, Patrick announced, "I must go. I am working in Abilene on a gold project."

"If you bring that gold out of the ground, you will die," I blurted out. I clamped a hand over my mouth and gasped. I couldn't believe what came out of my mouth. When I am triggered, it is extremely hard to have self-control; I just have to say it.

Patrick immediately responded, "I'm not afraid of death. Besides, I get my weight in gold."

Shaking my head, I answered, "If you take the gold and artifact out of that cave, you will die."

Patrick tossing out his credit card, said, "And if that was to be the case, then my money would go to the Dallas Children's Hospital, where I yearly play Santa Claus."

Shaking my head, no, I cautioned him that with the first poke into that cave, someone would die.

Patrick didn't tell me that had already happened.

I took a sip of my water, thought, *Is he serious, or is he creating karma? Maybe he's just not listening.* I leaned forward and spoke very softly, so quietly he had to keep leaning in closer to hear my spoken words.

"The gold and artifacts buried out there are the gems of times past and buried for a reason, Patrick. It's best to leave them alone. They have energy that mankind must not interfere with."

"Sorry, sports fans. It's been real, but I've got to go. Tomorrow is a big workday." Patrick started to stand up.

I started begging silently that I wished he would walk me out.

"Patrick, will you walk Shirley to her car?" Jackson asked.

"Sure; it would be my honor," he responded with a look of pleasure.

Then, I knew for sure that the Universe was working with me that night. When I thought something would happen, usually it did. What was happening tonight was for real. I hoped he would forgive me for telling him he would die.

We walked to the car in silence. I fumbled in my purse for keys and was hoping he would kiss me. Then I hoped he wasn't picking up on my feelings. I had to stop those thoughts! *Good God*, I thought, *I hope he doesn't see how nervous I am.*

Triumphantly, raising my keys, "Got 'em."

He took my keys, opened the door, and watched as I gracefully settled into my seat. Patrick was thinking to himself if he should take a risk. When I peered into his eyes, that question became a moot point. The first kiss with someone special is always etched indelibly on one's mind, and he gave me a special kiss, the kind all ladies dream of.

I was completely unprepared. In the moment of his kiss, I felt protected in his cocoon. I thought he is a strong and masculine man, yet with such a warm soft kiss, how can he be so gentle. This was even more special to me. It was so unexpected.

"Here's my card, Shirley." I handed him mine. "I'll stay in town tonight and be at my office mid-morning and give you a call."

Turning, he slowly walked away. The slight nip in the February evening air seemed refreshing to him. His train of thought was broken by the sound of a car engine that wouldn't start.

I thought to myself, *Does he know this car is a symbol of my run-away emotions?* I sucked in my breath, slightly overwhelmed by his cute butt and masculine walk. I thought, *Oh my God, of course, everyone knows that their car not starting was like runaway emotions. The car is a symbol of the owner's emotions.*

Suddenly, Patrick wheeled around with his hands on his hips to see me staring sheepishly out my side window. When our eyes met, the car seemed to jump to life. We waved what he hoped was not a permanent goodbye. Hopefully, it was an "I'll see you later wave."

I drove off waving bye, knowing I had enough for the night.

CHAPTER 4

Leon Speaks

*If they don't, there will be a death energy for all who
participate. Man's greed will get the best of them.*

I love my bed. As soon as my head hits the pillow, I always fall asleep. On
this special night, I fluffed my pillow and went right to sleep and into a
dream. My dream showed Maggy and Duke sitting by a babbling brook
in a luscious green forest; a waterfall brought its own music and lacy
white water to the travelling brook. If there ever was a place where magic
flowed in a bed of mossy green, it was there. Their love was evident. I
felt a sensual pleasure, and, like an embrace, was a general delight as I
walked toward them. I felt like a falling star who found its place next to a
unique love constellation having me to sparkle in the presence of Maggy
and Duke's love.

I remembered they raised their heads, watching me slowly walking
toward them.

Maggy spoke to me first, "Patrick is the face you have seen in your
dreams. He is a balance for you and your work."

Duke chimed in. "He is not just a face. You have met a man with emotional warmth, and it shows us, you have met a prince among men. A man who loves and holds compassion and thoughtfulness as his highest values; we will say you have found a treasure of the Earth. So, if you want to be loved as strongly as those storybook princesses... you have found the prince among men. Patrick is a man of good heart, but he doesn't recognize his spiritual potential yet."

I quickly asked what they meant. My query went unanswered.

Buzz! It was the alarm. Bewildered, I rolled over to see my traditional clock radio informing me it was 7:30 on Friday morning. Patrick had not called, and panic began to take hold. Was last night for real and was he going to call? I just wasn't a person to panic. I flung the covers back, leaped out of bed, grabbed my robe, and raced to the kitchen to see if there were any messages on my recorder. As I was Pondering over my next move while fixing my morning tea, the phone rang. It was Heather.

"Hello."

"Heather, he hasn't called yet."

"Shirley, it's not even 8:00! Did he give you his number?"

"Yes."

"Did you give him your number?"

"Yes."

"Give him time to get to work and call! Then give me a call here at work and let me know what happened. This is exciting."

Heather made it sound so easy. Almost too easy. I stared at his card in my hand and said to myself that I should call him to see if this was a real office number. Dialing the number, I was filled with curiosity and wondered if he had been playing me. Instantly, I cast that thought aside because of my dream.

"Hello! Energy Companies," the woman's voice snapped me out of my daydream. I didn't know what to do as I was thinking, *Oh, my god. That's what it says on his card. Now what?*

"Energy Companies." The voice was becoming irritated. "Energy Companies." It was time to speak, but I didn't know what to say. Before I could respond, my question was answered by a click and a dial tone. My panic became sheer terror, thinking, *What next!* This ringing, this insatiable ringing. What was it all about? I was just baffled.

Then Maggy's voice came to me, "It's the phone, Shirley. Answer it."

"Hello."

"Hello, ma'am. My name is Anne, and I'm calling from the *Dallas Morning News*. Would you be interested in subscribing to our paper?"

"Huh…No I don't think so," I said.

Everything was happening so fast. I needed to slow down and get a grip on the reality of this situation. I needed to understand what was and what was not an achievable idea that resembles the actual truth about my life right now. I knew my dreams about Patrick were always in the past days. It was a time when Indians lived in teepees with a creek nearby, campfires, and drums pounding.

My second dream had a scene where I saw an Indian chief stand up and shouted "Howgh," a word meaning, "I have spoken." Then a man who looked like Patrick, wearing only a breechcloth, walked out from behind a teepee. I saw myself as a medicine woman wearing a deerskin dress with turquoise beads around my neck and rushed up, inviting him to my teepee.

Inside, I asked this Indian man, "Oh, where have you been. Tell me your stories." My lips spread with a grin as I turned and saw this man had been through quite the battle. I just knew it to be true. I told him firmly, "I'm your medicine woman to cover and protect while mending your wounds. Something I know I can do."

He told me the stories he remembered so well. The energy battle of the heavens was won, allowing the light to shine once again. Now many warriors could find their light; their path was clear, and the Great Spirit was happy. So, the Indian man was sent back. Universal Love was the key to his heart for he truly knew the Great Spirit's ultimate plan.

I sat quietly and realized those were not dreams. *Are they visions? Visions from our past lives?*

In my research about dreams, doctors said that a person's subconscious creates the dreams that they have each night. Neurologists believe that the neurons in a person's mind fire at random. The images, memories, and thoughts are released, jumbled, and completely random. The story in dreams is put together by the rest of the mind. When a person wakes up, the mind tries to make sense of dreams. This is one possible reason random people appear in dreams. People could have seen them on television or in line behind them at Starbucks. They never consciously noticed them or thought about them, but their image was imprinted into their memory. Because of this, people dream about things and their minds just trying to make sense of the memories later.

However, I had never met Patrick until last tonight. But, in the past, I had dreamed about him. I knew the conclusion. It was not a dream. It was a vision. Now this vision has come into reality. I wondered if this could be trusted for a blissful life.

I loved stepping into a hot shower. Mentally, it was the only time I had during the entire day where I had complete privacy. It was my domain where I was alone with my private thoughts. Emotionally, it was the only time I felt 100% trust, just me and the water. I could trust water. Plus, the sound of water created an ambiance that tended to reinforce this trust. Spiritually is the only time I felt 'holy' clean afterward. Refreshed. No judgment. Clearing off and out the burdens, peeling of the heavy layers. Just clean. While drying off, the phone rang.

~~~

Patrick and Shirley—1990

At the same time as Shirley was in the shower, Patrick was on the phone as he walked into his office. "Hey, Mikey," greeted Patrick.

"I didn't think you were coming in today; what's up?" Mikey replied.

"It got too late, so I spent the night at home. Why don't you grab Mitchem and let's look at that South Texas place of his? Then we'll go to lunch." Patrick glanced at his secretary as he walked to his office, "By the way, Karen, any calls for me?" he asked casually as he was still on the phone.

"Just the usual salesmen."

"Okay. Mike, can you give me about 15 minutes. I got some calls to make."

Patrick picked up the phone and dialed, "Hello, Shirley, this is Patrick."

"Good morning, Patrick!" she was ecstatic as she began walking around.

Patrick thought she sounded so cheerful that early in the morning.

"Did you think I had forgotten about you?" he questioned.

After a slight hesitation, she spoke, "Oh, no, I just figured you were busy doing whatever it is you do. What is it you do anyway? Last night you didn't talk about yourself."

"I didn't think it was necessary. Besides that, it gives me the opportunity to ask you out for tomorrow night, that is, if you're free."

"Well, sure, that would be great."

"Fine, with your permission, I'll call you tonight to work out the details. Okay?"

"Sure."

"Later then."

Shirley knew Heather was going to love this. She felt a taste of triumph as she heard the phone rang.

"Travel Directions, may I help you?"

"Is Heather busy? This is Shirley."

"Hello; it's Heather."

"He called! He absolutely has a company! He is an engineer and works in oil and gas… and get this—we have a date Saturday night!"

We talked for a good hour. That was unusual. Heather was so excited. She put everyone on hold so we could talk.

~~~

Later that evening, Patrick was at the bar playing pool. Patrick turned to Bob and told him he was a dumb ass and if he hadn't scratched on the eight ball, he wouldn't have lost the pool game.

"Set me up again, Marty. Bob's buying as usual."

The musty smell, green felt, and dim lighting reminded Patrick that if this was his home away from home, he needed to change his address.

"Last game, Bob, I've gotta get out of here."

"Why do you always leave when you're winning? C'mon, give me a chance to catch up," Bob said.

"That's why I'm leaving so you can have a chance. 'Sides, I got stuff to do before I head out."

If Bob only knew that the phone call Patrick needed to make was so important, Bob would have doubled the $50. He had won to get out of this bar. Nice man, that Bob; can't say much for his pool shooting abilities.

The game was over. Patrick won again, so he flipped a twenty on the table.

"Buy some drinks for everyone, Bob, I gotta go; I'll give you a chance to get even next time."

As he walked out the door, he heard Bob yelling something about his questionable parentage. Typically, he would have introduced him to his right hook, but there were more important things he felt compelled to do.

At the same time, Shirley was thinking about Patrick saying he would call this evening. It was only 6:00 p.m. She was worried but kept telling herself that surely, he would call soon. She was somewhat serene as she buffed her nails. The phone rang, and it didn't surprise her when it did.

"Hello."

"Hi, Shirley. It's me, Patrick."

It was midnight. Not only had he let her look into his soul the night before, now he had allowed her to understand the type of man he was. Granted, he was somewhat gruff. She thought that was to be expected with his profession. Regardless, he was incredibly open and interested in what she did. Patrick offered to bring groceries and cook her dinner the next night. She knew then she would learn more.

Patrick drove to her house. It was raining the proverbial cats and dogs. He laughed to himself at that. He knew for sure that Shirley was a sweetheart, but she was terrible at giving directions. At last, he found her place.

"You're soaked!"

"Yeah, and so are the groceries."

They walked toward the kitchen.

Patrick said to her, "Don't give directions very often, do you?"

There was silence. He set the grocery bags down and turned to see her strange expression.

It was then he realized what he must have looked like. His clothes were soaked, water dripping down the length of his nose slowly onto the tile floor where it formed a puddle that was growing at a very rapid rate.

"You had better get out of those clothes before you catch a cold," she chided Patrick. The matter-of-fact tone of Shirley's voice let him know she was probably right.

"I've got a change in my truck. If you wouldn't mind taking care of the groceries, I'll get my clothes and be right back!"

Shirley was overjoyed thinking that this was one fantastic way to start an evening. She was hoping to see him without a shirt. She shook her head wondering if his chest looked the same as in her dream because she liked what she saw.

When they finished the incredible meal, Shirley was very curious as to where he learned to cook like that.

"Taught myself, mostly," he replied, but Shirley hadn't asked the question out loud.

"Let me clear the table and then you can show me what you are so excited about."

"What about the mess?"

"I'll clean. You talk."

He began to unfold a story.

Shirley was surprised that it was unreal this type of guy would be involved with her. His presentation showed her he was intelligent, keen, and humorous but also cautious. She didn't know as much about him as she thought she did.

"Patrick. Let me see those drawings again," Shirley insisted, come here; let me show you something."

They walked to her bookcase. Something was not quite right.

"Here, look at this." The drawings were identical.

"Where did you get these books?" he asked.

"My teacher Maggy gave them to me before she made her transition."

"Transition?"

"Yeah, before she died, crossed over to the other side or some call it the spirit world."

"I assume that's another story?" he asked curiously?

"I saw in a vision… you're the only person who can bring out the gold, but something is bothering me about this project of yours. Do you feel danger?"

"Anytime you're dealing inside the earth, there is always a danger," he warned her. "There are traces of hydrogen sulfide outlining what I think is the chamber, but we've taken precautions. We should be relatively safe from the toxic fumes."

Shirley responded to him nervously, "I'm not so sure. Can you leave me some of this material and I'll check into what's going on for you?"

His mind wandered to the dig while walking across the room, wondering, and hoping she would investigate this for him.

"I was hoping you would look into this for me, so I made an extra copy of everything." Handing the information to her, "I don't mean to be a party pooper, but I have a lot of organizing to do before Monday," he murmured.

Her eyes had a longing sadness as he continued, "I promise every-thing will be okay. You could certainly make things easier if you could give me an 'I'll see you later kiss.'"

Shirley retorted, "You better believe I'll see you later. Nothing could keep me away from you now."

Patrick leaned in a little closer, their foreheads touching. Dear god, she couldn't fight against the thoughts that were going through her. His very smell was flooding her senses. His lips brushed not innocently, like a tease but hot, fiery, passionate. She felt him pulling away at this moment and he walked out the door.

She was so aware that Patrick was a strong man, full of purpose. She was afraid that this project might be his undoing. Even though she was falling in love, it had to be his learning lesson. "Oh, Maggy and Duke, don't let it be a severe one," she spoke silently while looking up.

Watching out the window as Patrick drove down the rain-slick street, she couldn't help pondering over the mortality of these kinds of men and why they do things the way they do.

"He will be alright, this time," Maggy's voice came to her, but it was not reassuring.

She felt disconcerted about Patrick's project and decided to get some words of wisdom from Leon, her Cheyenne medicine man friend.

After she told Patrick's story, there was a long silence before she finally heard him take a deep breath and said, "Girl," (Leon called her girl more than Shirley) "Patrick has gotten himself into something way over his head. I know about the Aspermont map with its etchings and the mystery of the spider rock and the artifacts. I know where and what he is attempting to do and it can be deadly."

Leon continued, "This is all about Mother Earth's energy. My belief is the living people are intimately connected with the souls and spirits. Our spirituality featured in practices is based on communication with the spirit world through mediums, known as a spiritual warrior and healer. I can only explain by describing the beliefs, ceremonies, and rituals that feature prominently in our belief system about spiritual energy that Patrick's project is about."

Leon paused, knowing that his pause was a pivotal part to see how carefully Shirley was listening to understand.

He continued, "There were ceremonies and practices of rituals long ago when they placed the artifacts in that cave. The gold was placed later. It was all done by our people to help balance our great planet, Mother Earth. We believe the great mountains breathe; the cornstalks are alive. These are a significant part as symbols of the spirits, which give them form and life. The spiritual forms are manifestations of the one supreme creative power that fills them with meaning. There is One Power, which provides the movement with earthly journeys and seasonal cycles. All this, with the union of the constellations in the night sky, the lunar, and the solar observation. Their truth is deeply and utterly part of us, our ceremonialism and our every way of life."

Shirley took a deep breath and thought, *There is strong energy into his words.* "I don't understand why Patrick removing the artifacts and gold would upset the planet? It was placed by man," she softly said.

"My people and I believe the land are sacred and life is sacred," Leon explained in his low resounding voice, stating facts. "The land has an intrinsic spiritual and cultural value and does not require manmade infrastructure or improvements. Earth is alive, it has energy and its more than just heat, cold and seasons. There are vortexes of swirling energy, and they exist at the intersections of lines of natural energy that make up the Earth's electromagnetic field. They contain powerful spiritual properties to be highly conducive to earth's activities. It's vital to keep earth in balance. For Patrick or anyone to disturb the area can be extremely dangerous.

"Although the mystery of sacred rituals may seem confusing, the esoteric beauty of the ceremonies will touch hearts. This creation is all about energy. These artifacts were put there with ceremonies and rituals to help the earth and must be left alone. If they don't, there will be death energy for all who participate. Man's greed will get the best of them."

Leon's deep masculine voice came rolling out, making Shirley feel secure, "So much faith and perfection are put into our ceremonies that even one slip of the tongue in a recitation, one omission of a word, one stumble in a dance can discredit and bring misfortune for the entire project. If that happens then all is in vain and ancient wisdom is wasted. Even wrong thoughts, evil thinking, will be known to the spirit beings and all is lost."

"Oh my god, one little misfortune?" This reminds me of the Rock Bible and the Yucatan trip finding the crystal and its bowl. We didn't get to complete our mission to help earth because of greed," Shirley said.

Leon's gruff but caring, deep, voice was enunciating through the phone. Shirley held the phone tightly to her ear so not to miss a word.

"Girl, the truth about those artifacts is within your heart and your efforts were strong. You did your best to help Mother Earth's energy. So much you put your life in danger. You are a sensitive woman but not educated enough in relation to energy. Your automatic writings are from pure energy with correct and positive messages. They are like our ceremonies. Everything must be done correctly. If followed as they are written, then everything works perfectly. The negative energy has taken control over Earth's balance and created fighting, greed, and fear. It has created all sorts of things to happen with our beautiful planet. Earth is a living, loving and reproduction planet, but humans have changed it into a battlefield. We are now at a time to learn and love ourselves, and in doing so, it allows time to create a new earth's loving energy balance."

Leon continued, "Everything on this planet creates a balance. The trees, oceans, flowers, animals, everything, including people. All have energy, and my people believe that everything on earth is sacred. It is because of people's greed that we must balance earth again. People must learn earth does not belong to them. They are only here for a short visit.

We believe that the Great Spirit has given everything to survive on earth and it is not necessary to charge for it. Our ancients told us someday mankind would have to pay for water, air, fuel, everything we know to be free and plentiful. Earth is being depleted, and our rituals help balance, and through this balance, there is blissful energy, like Earth used to be."

"You must give my words to Patrick," Leon said. "I know for I have seen Patrick is a man of heart and I saw in my vision he is not greedy. It is a lack of spiritual knowledge. Help him, Shirley. Help him remember the warrior he was before this lifetime. You must help him to awaken and soon. He needs to wake up and walk away from this project. If he doesn't, Earth will spring back and reboot in a few years, but it will start from scratch again. That is the only scary part I'm allowed to tell you; it falls under earth's galactic rules of "fair warning."

Shirley only had one question; "Will Patrick change his mind?"

Leon loudly replied, "No, the only question is will he follow his mind or his heart? Only a wise man changes his mind, a fool never does. It is Patrick's choice and I see he has heart."

Shirley nervously responded; "We need all the help we can get to save our planet. I will do my best to help Patrick with his spiritual awakening."

Shirley stood holding the phone against her chest, feeling the sound of her heartbeat she wondered if Patrick would be a man to change his mind. Would he embrace her news or just question everything?

CHAPTER 5

Mother Nature Has Her Way

Shirley could hear Maggy's voice as she
whispered in her ear,
"There will be no more warnings. Get him out of there!"

Patrick—1990

As I was driving and humming along to the radio, the light mist seemed to dance in the headlights. Mile marker after mile marker whizzed by signaling that I was closing in on my destination. I thought that Abilene, Texas, could never be mistaken for anything other than what it is. It's a dry, arid, one-horse town that could blow away in the strong west Texas winds. An Air Force base, a prison being built, and a dying oil industry seemed to be meager means to support a town of 100,000. Maybe that's why the churches preach fire and brimstone on Sundays, but during the week all hell breaks loose with everyone trying to stab each other in the back with one hand as they steal each other's wallets with the other. It doesn't matter, in the overall scheme, what one thinks of the populace. All that matters is the adventure of finding this lost treasure and the oil wells.

The drizzle had stopped long before I pulled into the dimly lit motel parking lot. Interstate 40 had been desolated but not nearly as much as Highway 83 on the outskirts of Abilene. It didn't appear that it had rained much, if any, as I strode assuredly across the grass courtyard and into my room. I knew this was good and that it wouldn't be too wet to begin what I hoped was my final thrust into the unknown on Monday. The clock radio was the only light piercing the darkness as I stretched across the bed. Closing my eyes to the all-encompassing darkness, I couldn't help but wonder about Shirley's worried expression when I was leaving. She was being overprotective. I liked that in a way because it showed that she cared for me. *Oh, heck, I'm in love with her and I haven't given away my heart to anyone like this.*

The banging at the door could only be one thing. It was time for me to roll out of bed to meet Joe and David for breakfast.

"Yeah, yeah, yeah. I'll be down in a minute," I yelled, not really thinking but knowing that if I didn't act, they would pound on the door until hell froze over. Refreshed after a quick shower, I joined Joe and David as they were finishing breakfast.

"How was Big D?" David always had a smile on his face. Albeit a little crooked, it was still genuine.

"We thought you were coming back three days ago. What happened? Did you get thrown in jail?" Joe's smile was more like a gash that ran half-way across his broad face.

I was wondering why Joe couldn't talk unless he was looking sideways with his arms folded across his massive girth. I chuckled to myself hoping Joe wouldn't ask me what was so funny.

"No, but you know me. It was a possibility, but I did meet an interesting woman who just so happens to be a renowned well-respected psychic."

"Oh really? In Dallas?"

"Yeah, really. She's in Fort Worth. She did say we're remarkably close to the gold, but we could be in for some trouble."

"You're the one that's supposed to keep us out of trouble."

"I know, Joe. Sometimes I'm good at that and other times not so good. At any rate, she said she would look into what's happening and keep in touch. Now for more important things. The road-boring crew will be on location Monday morning. Jerry is willing to cut a deal with you for a piece of the pie; but he's only going to give us three days."

"Is that enough?" David asked.

"I doubt it, David, but it should at least give us a direction to go. As far as I'm concerned, that's good enough for me. That's up to you guys to decide."

They nodded in agreement.

"I've got to go repair some busted belts on a couple of my wells down south. It'll be late when I get in, so I'll plan on seeing you on location in the morning."

Joe and David always invited me to go with them on Sundays. I never did. This time it was certain I wouldn't because I was going to stretch a thirty-minute job of changing two belts into an all-day affair, which was more interesting to me than whatever it was they were doing.

The morning star was still brighter than the first rays of the breaking dawn as I pulled up to the location. Joe, David, Larry, and the whole crew were all ready to get started. Normally, a person couldn't wake those three with an atom bomb this time in the morning. But the sense that something special could happen today was evident in all their collective expressions.

Then Joe spoke. "Where the hell is this crew of yours?"

"Asshole; it's only 6:00 a.m. They got a six-hour drive from Dallas to get here. They'll be here. Now you put yourselves to work and get this equipment out of the way, so they'll have some room to work."

With that, everyone snapped to reality and the men began to prepare for the day's events. Joe and David took up their respective supervisory positions, which meant they went to sit in their car and drink coffee. I just looked at them, sighed and went about doing the things that needed to be done. I thought that if they were going to be like this, I should get twice my weight in gold. But I was a fair and generous man.

Within the hour, all four of us could see the headlights of the big semi tractor-trailer rigs as they came around the bend a quarter mile from where we were. I recognized Jerry as he climbed out of the passenger side of the lead truck. As Joe and David led Jerry to the same scale they had used on me. He directed the three big rigs onto the site and set to the task of unloading and setting the equipment where they wanted to begin.

The closer it got to midday, the hotter the February sun began to feel. I learned long ago that in this neck of the woods if you get heat early in the morning this time of year, you could be in for heavy rains by late afternoon. No way was I going to let that bother me. We were ready to start drilling the first test hole.

"All right men, we're gonna drill five holes horizontally into this wall. Each hole will be thirty feet deep and twenty feet apart. Let's see if we can figure out which way this sucker runs."

We were partially through drilling the third hole when the clouds began to boil in the north. Not breaking through into a cavern had not surprised me, what did was when Jerry came over and told me to shut it down.

"Why?"

"Look, Patrick, if that storm comes down on us, it could wash that sludge into the hole, and then we'd be in deep shit. Let's pull out and wait for the storm to pass. Then we'll see how much light we have and how wet it may be. I see you got lights and a generator. If we must, we can work at night."

"Okay, Jerry, I just don't have a good feeling about this weather," I proclaimed. I knew to pay attention to my feelings but didn't always. This time I did.

"Me neither. Okay, guys pull that pipe in and get that sludge out of there."

No sooner had they pulled the 80-ton sludge to the top of the hole than it began to rain. A typical west Texas frog-choker complete with lightning, hail, and a small funnel cloud. It made for a beautiful sunset although it had cut their workday short. No one minded the fact that their day had been cut short. Spirits were high as they headed into town to have the obligatory cocktails, dinner, and plan their next day's strategy. On the drive back to Abilene, even Jerry's small talk didn't distract me thinking about Shirley and the need to phone her as soon as I could.

I was getting a little curious and worried. It had been over two hours since the first busy signal. I just didn't know what it is women found to talk about for so long. Men said what they needed to and moved along to other things. I remembered that Shirley had told me about her counseling sessions and how she did them at all times of the day or night, but this was ridiculous. My last thoughts before I drifted into a deep much needed sleep were how much I needed to speak to her, for more reasons than one.

The only hint of the previous day's storm was the trickle of water flowing down the north face of the gigantic crater. Rainbows were forming along the path the water was gouging. Mother Earth does marvelous work. I again thought about Shirley and wondered what she thought of my work. Roaring diesel engines snapped my mind back to the project at hand. I turned to see the crews beginning to put the equipment in place to begin their day's labors.

As I approached the crew, Joe spoke first. "I spoke to your psychic friend for a couple of hours last night. She tells me you're the only one who can find the gold."

Anger, wrath, and rage all rolled into… One wasn't the appropriate word for what I felt. "Where the hell did you get her phone number?" I took a step toward Joe and yelled furiously.

A look of malice came across Joe's face. "I got it out of your room, where else?" Joe was taunting me.

The thud in the mud was the aftermath of the right hook across Joe's face. Obviously groggy, Joe tried to stumble to his feet. By now, three crewmen had grabbed me.

"If you ever speak to Shirley again, I'll rip your face off and spit into the hole it leaves."

"Cool it, guys," David seemed to be the voice of reason as he stood between the two of us. "Now calm down. We got more important things to do than fight over a woman. Now apologize to each other. Geez, it's dangerous enough around here without you two throwing punches at each other."

"Joe, I don't like you now; I never have, and I never will," I snarled as I pushed Joe aside. "Now get your ass out of my way. I've got work to do." I turned my back and stomped off heavily.

The heat and the humidity began to take its toll as the day progressed. With each turn of the bit, the tensions from the morning confrontation became more apparent. Frustration began to take hold.

"Breakthrough! We're into something!"

The words pierced through the muggy atmosphere. Twenty men gathered around the sludge as the drill pipe bounced its vibrating signal.

"How far in are we?"

The driller measured the amount of stem protruding from the edifice, adding that to his calculations, "Twenty-four feet, six inches."

"Push on through. Let's see what we got."

As they put more weight on the bit, forcing it, I began to calculate where they were.

"We got four feet of the cavity," shouted the driller over the roar of the engines.

"Pull out," came my reply.

"How come?" David's voice sounded puzzled and pissed off.

"Let me show you where we're," I said and rolled my maps out fully and pointed to a sight David didn't want to see. "If the cavern runs the direction, and I think it does, then we'll be crossing onto someone else's property. We'd better drill a diagonal hole at this point, so we can see which way it runs. You'd better hope it doesn't go, or we're in for problems."

"What kind of problems?" David was concerned. "If we must cross under someone else's property, we don't have the right to retrieve anything unless we have a lease. Believe me, if you think there's gold under his property that lease will cost a fortune."

Joe's voice was gruff. "You don't know what you're talking about," he announced like he knew it all.

"Listen, mister!" I turned and lunged toward Joe. "I've been drilling oil wells in this state for over twenty-five years. That's the law, and I, for one, don't intend to break it for anyone no matter what it's worth. You'd better hope for two things to happen. First, you'd better hope I'm off on my directions, or you better hope you can negotiate with that landowner." I wasn't going to give Joe any other choices and Joe sensed that. He turned away.

A nerve-racking two hours passed as they drilled the confirmation hole. My worst fears came to pass. The cavern got wider as they approached the neighboring lease line. The flue vent was about eight feet wide and four feet high. It ran for approximately one mile to the base. I knew that it was an extinct volcano. This is one question I couldn't answer and that was why they hadn't hit anything solid drilling horizontally, but that had done so vertically. I was so ensconced into my work that I forgot all about Shirley.

"Well, boys, maybe we had better back off for the day and figure out what our next steps should be," Jerry recommended.

"I agree, Jerry. It's bad enough working under these conditions without having our neighbor and the sheriff down our throats." I hoped Joe would be sensible about this. For some reason, he was.

That night, at their bull session, it was decided to do things the right way. I understood the money pinch that Joe was in; however, Jerry, David, and I convinced Joe that in the long run, this was the right thing. If there was as much gold as estimated, it would be worthwhile to do things in an orderly way that we could control instead of running about half-cocked with a forty-five in one hand and a bottle of whiskey in the other, daring anyone to have a crack at us.

When we finished, I called Shirley. "Shirley, I'm on my way back to Dallas. Would you like to spend some time together?" I was trying to act cool about asking her out, let alone 'some time.' I hadn't made this much of a serious and honest request to a woman since I was about fourteen years old, and my testosterone was starting to kick in.

"Patrick, I've been concerned since I spoke with Joe. Are you okay?"

"Yeah, everything's fine," I caught myself thinking that with that statement I should never lie to a psychic, much less Shirley.

"Are you sure?" Shirley sensed there was something I wasn't telling her.

"We'll talk later. Let me get back to the office, go by my house and grab some clean clothes, and I'll see you tomorrow night, okay?" Again, I wondered why I was a little unsure of her response.

"Okay; tomorrow night is fine if you wait until after seven."

"See you then!"

Shirley knew there were problems and was consumed with the fact that I wouldn't tell her.

I thought she didn't need to worry about me. I could take care of myself.

When I arrived, I broke out into a huge grin, grabbed her, gave her a kiss, and spun her around. "It's good to see you, Shirley!"

"You, too. Can I get you something?"

"Na; just grab a jacket, and we'll go get some Chinese."

Over dinner, I related the entire series of events that occurred. Shirley never really looked at me during my tale. Rather, she looked around me as if she saw something that no one else could.

"That's where we are, Shirley. Two days from now, we'll be back at it. Got any advice?"

Shirley had a strange look on her face. She seemed nervous. "Don't do it!" Her tone of voice was one that I had never heard before. It was like she didn't have a filter between her brain and mouth. She just couldn't understand what was happening to her. She felt out of control.

She immediately declared, "Patrick, if you break into that cavern, you or someone else will die immediately."

"Why?" I couldn't and didn't want to believe what she was saying. I had no idea what was happening. I didn't want to examine what she just said.

"The artifacts were placed in that cavern eons ago by what we term The Ancients to help balance the planet."

"Who are these ancients?" I was puzzled.

"They were a race, long since gone, that worked with the planet to keep it in balance. They used ceremonies to keep harmony and peace. If you enter that cavern, you'll die." There she went again, proclaiming something that strong to a man she barely knew.

"Look, Shirley; I don't believe in curses or the boogie man or for that matter anything I can't see. Now, I'm an extremely cautious man when it comes to safety. We're prepared for any eventuality." I took her hand and said self-assuredly, "If anything should happen to me, my share will go to Children's Hospital in Dallas where it'll do some good."

Shirley was thinking about what good it would do for earth. "Patrick, what you're doing will be harmful to more people than just you and your crew!" Now she was serious.

"Shirley, there's no turning back. Our minds are made up. We're going forward."

The rest of the dinner and the drive home were conducted in an eerie silence. Shirley was distant to the point that I wondered if we would ever see each other again. She felt it was her mission to protect me and Earth.

At the door, I held her close, looked into her eyes and spoke. "I'll see you soon."

"No, you won't, if you go back out there," warned Shirley. It was a warning I did not expect. I got in my truck and drove off very slowly. Shirley wondered if she would ever see me again.

The next day, with my windows down, rock and roll blasting from my radio, the miles flew by on the warm spring-like day. At 75 mph, the Dodge Ram purred like a tiger, pacified but ready for more. Womp! Something hit me hard on the left side of the face.

Instinctively, I looked in the outside left rear-view mirror. The small inset mirror was gone. Glancing around the truck, it was nowhere in sight. *This is impossible*, I thought. Out loud, the words took on an even more unbelievable meaning. *Here's my exit; I'll pull over and figure out what happened.*

Thud, bang wop, wop, wop! "What the hell?" I hung on as the Dodge Ram careened wildly toward the exit ramp. Finally gaining control, I pulled over to the shoulder of the ramp. "First things first." Now I thought that I was a realistic man, and nothing was going to stop me from getting my job done. "I'll get this figured out."

The search of the interior turned up no mirror. However, the interior mirror showed I had a nice little mouse developing under my left eye from the crash. Next, I had to determine what happened to my right front tire. The tires barely had one thousand miles on them. I thought that I must have run over something.

The service station at the bottom of the ramp was empty when I pulled in. The attendant was able to check the tire out immediately. "Nothin' wrong with this tire, Mac."

"You sure?"

"Mac, I do this all day every day. Ain't nothin' wrong with this tire!"

"Weird" was not the correct verbiage I used. It was more like, "What the hell," but it was weird enough. I was driving through Clyde, Texas, when thump, my right rear tire had gone flat, directly in front of the last gas station in town. Same results; there was absolutely nothing wrong with that tire.

Doubled up with uncertainty, I headed down the winding, dirt path over the last eighteen miles to the location. I was the man who was never uncertain. I may have appeared to be, but I was soft and kind, so much on the inside that I had learned to protect this part of myself. Kirby's general store was the last building in the middle of nowhere before my last turn. It looked almost comical, the expression on old George's face, as I headed straight for the porch and his rocking chair. The left rear tire had gone the way of its predecessors. At twenty miles per hour, on a caliche road, with a flat tire on the driver's side, I could understand why old George's eyes were as big as saucers when I finally reigned in the truck just inches shy of his porch. I, this self-assured man, needed some help.

"Who taught you how to drive, boy! Damn city slickers!"

"Sorry, George, but I gotta flat."

I was not surprised when they couldn't find anything wrong with the tire. Nor was I surprised when old George told me that his crew had gone home for the day. After the tire was back on, I cut across the country road to the interstate. This gave me time to review the series of events that led to being late and losing another day and I didn't like to lose anything.

When a person comes into Abilene from the south headed north on 83/84, they are on a six-lane highway with just a center stripe for a divider. Across the highway, on the southern edge of town was a railroad crossing. As I approached the crossing, the arms began to descend. Being in the inside lane, toward the center strip, held a significance for which I would soon find out why.

The arms raised, the cars lurched forward, and then it happened. The crossing arms initially crashing through my windshield sent shattered glass shards everywhere. Temporarily blinded by the exploding glass caused me to leap from the truck into the oncoming traffic. Fortunately for me, a department of public service officer saw the incident. He pulled a U-turn, hit his emergency lights and siren, leaped from his car, and tackled me before I stepped in front of an oncoming semi.

"Hey buddy, don't struggle. I'm a police officer. Open your eyes. Can you see me?"

Fortunately, when something foreign enters your eyes, they begin to water to clean out the debris. When I tried to open my eyes all I could see was blood, tears, and an extremely fuzzy vision.

"Can you see anything? How many fingers am I holding?"

"Oh my god! Is he deaf!" I could hear a lady ask.

"No, lady; I just can't see shit." I didn't know if I was actually speaking or thinking. I could just barely hear the ambulance's siren over the roar that was emanating from my brain.

"Step back, everyone. Give the attendants some room."

"Sir, did you hit your head?"

"I don't think so."

"Did you go through the windshield?"

"What's your blood type?"

"Are you hurt anywhere else?" I could hear questions from around me.

This entire racket was giving me one hell of a headache. Opening my eyes for the first time, I began to see shapes. Gradually, my focus began to return.

"I'm all right; just get me something to get this blood off my face," I said.

My eyes burned, as the solution forced blood, sweat, and tears down my grime covered face and on to my shirt. For the first time, I could focus on my truck and what damage there might have been.

The crossing arm had dissected my windshield like a scalpel. Through the open door, I could see the front compartment was covered in broken glass. My hair, face, hands, shirt, and blue jeans were filled with slivers. I guessed it could have been worse.

During the next half hour, while the attendants continued to flush my eyes, I couldn't help but wonder about my last conversation with Shirley. Did she have anything to do with this? Thoughts raced through my mind thinking that she is some sort of a witch. Or was she truly worried about me? There was an unseen force at work there.

"Mr. Cox, I've contacted the railroad; they'll take care of your truck."

"Thank you, officer."

"Mr. Cox, if you'll come this way, we'll take you to the hospital."

"No, I'll be fine."

"Suit yourself, but as hard as you were hit, you could have some serious brain injuries. At least, let us take you overnight for observation. If nothing shows up, I'm sure the doctors will let you go tomorrow or the next day."

I knew I didn't have any brain injuries. I just felt that Shirley was right there beside me, watching over me. It was an eerie feeling. *Damn the feeling,* I thought.

"Officer, where's this shop?"

"Are you sure you can drive?"

"Yeah, lead the way."

While they began to replace the windshield, I called Shirley. "Shirley, what the hell are you doing to me?"

Anger was the sole emotion, and Shirley was the recipient.

"What do you mean?" It was obvious from the break in her voice she was on the verge of tears.

Shirley knew something had been wrong all day; something just wasn't right with me. Her thoughts were, *Well I have always been a giver, warm and loving person, but I feel empty, cold and drained.* Her senses were letting her know something had happened to me. If someone were to ask, she would have said an accident. She had this bad feeling about her but didn't know what had happened. She just knew I had been in an accident.

I related, step by step, the day's occurrences. Her laughter was unsettling.

"What are you laughing at? This was dangerous," I was unsettled.

"Patrick, I always laugh when I'm nervous. You need to come home."

"Shirley, I've never walked off a job, and I'm not going to start now."

Shirley could hear Maggy's voice as she whispered in her ear, "There will be no more warnings! Get him out of there!"

I was insistent. "Shirley, I'm going to finish what I started if it chaps the devil's ass."

Stern and precise, Shirley's response was direct and straightforward, "There will be no more warnings!"

The silence was deafening. The click of the receiver and the ensuing dial tone meant business. I stood there, phone in hand, staring at the push buttons. Ma Bell's phone somehow held the answer. It just wasn't like me to be so muddled.

The phone rang, and it was Shirley. "Patrick, again there will be no more warnings. It's time for you to come home. I love you." She was surprised that "I love you" came flying out of her mouth. She thought real love is a protector, a defender, a ride-or-die connection that stays with you in quietness and is your comfort. Real love will celebrate with you and raise you up. Love will be okay with your sadness and kiss the scars you hide from others. It is rare. Treasure it, for real love is the greatest blessing heaven can give. She was very private.

"Hmmm, well I don't know about that love stuff," I replied hesitantly.

Shirley immediately started explaining to me, "There are all kinds of love. Caring love, passionate love, sweet love, etc. Love is love, and I love everything. I love my home, my planets, my work. Love is the most powerful energy there is. Now, goodbye." She was firm.

That little voice inside me spoke, telling me to listen to her. I knew that little voice. Everyone has it and it has never lied to me before.

The solution was simple. I called a cab company and sent Joe and David information. When my truck was finished, I began my trek back to Dallas. I had never quit a job so close to completion, but for some very strange reason I was peaceful. I looked in my rearview mirror at the setting sun over Abilene.

CHAPTER 6

Lesson Learned

Sitting in front of the fireplace with a snifter of brandy could be romantic unless Shirley had something important to discuss.

Shirley—1990

"All I know, Heather, is that he had some sort of accident and he's on his way back from Abilene."

Heather asked, "You warned him before he left, didn't you?"

"Yes, but he wouldn't listen. He thinks that he should never quit anything he has started, even if it could kill him."

"Well, Shirley, like you always say, everyone's got to learn their own lessons. It's just that some people like Patrick have to learn some things the hard way."

Shortly after I hung up the phone, it rang again. It sounded extra loud, and it made me feel jumpy. I quickly grabbed the phone thinking it was Patrick.

"Hello."

"Hi, Shirley; this is Mike," he spoke, while clearing his throat, "I need to talk to you about something."

His voice made me nervous, and I immediately thought, *Patrick is hurt?*

Quickly, he continued, "Shirley, my buddy Patrick, well, he's been hurt by other women and I'm worried." Clearing his throat again, like he always does when he is nervous, he added, "My buddy Patrick, well, he is in love with you. I'm asking is this love one way? How do you feel about him?"

Before I could say anything, he swiftly continued, "I must say I'm surprised how fast it happened. Why, only three weeks ago, you two met. If this love is only one way, then I need to start talking to him like yesterday. You know Patrick and I have been through a lot, and I don't want him hurt. He is a good man and I really care about him."

"So, what do you think, Shirley?" he added.

My thoughts were running wild; *What a great friend Patrick has.* I answered. "Mike, no worries; I agree it's been fast, but I dreamed about him for three months before we meet, and it just lets me know its natural and meant to be. I love Patrick, so it is a two-way love."

Mike sighed and said, "This is music to my ears. I only want what is best for my friend. Enjoy the rest of your day, Shirley' I'm going to."

~~~

Patrick—1990

"Boy, are the guys gonna' be surprised when I show up empty-handed."

I thought that I would stop at Shirley's, spend the night, and go in tomorrow. I was being presumptuous. Besides, I was my own man. If they didn't like it, they could just shove it where the sun….

As I pulled through the front gate at Shirley's apartment complex, I was surprised to see the guard recognize me. I was hoping Shirley wouldn't be too surprised at how I looked. I was a big mess.

Shirley opened the door. "Oh no! Patrick, you look awful. What's that on your face and in your hair?"

"Glass."

"Come on. Let's get you in the shower." A weak smile crossed her face as she continued. "I bet we can shine you up real nice."

"But we gotta'…," I started.

"We don't gotta' do nothing until you are taken care of. Now do as I say or I'll…"

"Okay, okay! I'm on my way." Seeing this tiny little woman feign anger was curiously funny. I wondered if she could get really angry. "But first a kiss," I was assertive. I had to have that kiss! Shirley wanted that kiss too.

Sitting in front of the fireplace with a snifter of brandy could be romantic, unless Shirley has something to say, and I sensed Shirley had something important to say. Most people found it fascinating to listen to her marvelous stories, and I was no exception.

"Patrick, you know why you didn't want to quit that job?"

I asked, "Is this a trick question? Yeah, for the money."

"No, Patrick," Shirley continued with a deep sigh. "It was your ego. It wouldn't let you give up. You must understand what ego really is. I like to describe ego as a little Pac-man that runs around in front of your chest trying to protect your heart from what you don't understand. Most people, when they don't understand something, they either become very offensive or they shut themselves off not wanting to believe what they are faced with is real."

I let Shirley see my self-pride in my posture, allowing my positive sense of self-worth diffuse into all that my family and I were. I knew communication can be from the body to the consciousness as much as the other way around and said, "You and Leon are spiritually aware. With me being Cherokee, you think I am too. I haven't thought about it until now.

"My Granny had taught me at a young age that in 1838, Cherokee people were forcibly taken from their homes, incarcerated in stockades, forced to walk more than a thousand miles, and removed to Indian Territory, now Oklahoma. More than 4,000 died and many were buried in unmarked graves along "The Trail of Tears."

"The Cherokee's resisted their Removal by creating their own newspaper, *The Cherokee Phoenix*, as a platform for their views. They sent their educated young men on speaking tours throughout the United States. They lobbied Congress and created a petition with more than 15,000 Cherokee signatures against Removal. They took their case to the U.S. Supreme Court, which ruled that they were a sovereign nation. However, Granny said that the old swindler, President Jackson, ignored the Supreme Court decision, enforced his Indian Removal Act of 1830, and pushed through the Treaty of New Echota.

"My granny said that Cherokees believe Earth must have balance, harmony, cooperation, and respect within the community along with people and the rest of nature. Dad told me Cherokee myths and legends taught the lessons and practices necessary to maintain natural balance, harmony, and health.

"My Cherokee family stories are…my great-great grandmother— she walked The Trails of Tears. My granny Ethel Mae Jones Cox was born

February 28, 1900, in Brown Prairie, Indian Territory, a daughter of James Jones and Lourena Jones. Her nickname was Lucy. It was terrible when the Government took their Indian Territory land adding it to the Oklahoma reservation."

"I was educated during the Golden Age the Cherokees' educational system expanded and improved for the first time since White Americans were introduced into the Cherokee culture. They revived a tribal newspaper and began to publish books and pamphlets in the Cherokee language. The Cherokee established college level education and public schools. Cherokees were not just the farmer and working class. My dad didn't want his kids to go through what he had. In his day, Indians had a curfew; they were scorned on and laughed at, and men constantly picked fights. I didn't live on the reservation; I didn't learn their traditional ways. I was educated to be in the business world. Granny Ethel told me stories, trying to teach me their ways, but I didn't pay any attention. She called me a Spiritual Warrior, but I was young and didn't listen. When Granny told me stories, it stirred something inside me, a feeling of something running hot but I've never figured it out. It feels like something old that needs to be released like energy knowledge or wisdom of some sort, I don't know, and it makes me anxious. If I can figure it out, then I could release the anxiety.

"I have always trusted myself by following my gut hunch. You know the old saying, 'Trust your gut and you can't go wrong.'

"Guess I wasn't to learn about my spirituality. Learning was easy for me, but the catholic school was strict; I had the feeling just give me the freedom to learn by my own errors without judgement and I will school myself faster than you can ever teach.

"In my high school days, early in the football season I sustained a severe fracture of my femur in my right leg. I had to be hospitalized for four months, practically the whole first semester. My dad didn't want me to miss any school, so he managed for me to "attend" classes by means of an inter-communication system arranged by him with the Telephone

Company. So, lying in my hospital bed six miles from the hospital, I listened to all my classes, absorbing explanations, and asking questions when necessary. I got to listen to Mr. Pizzetta's explanation of the theorem in geometry, my favorite subject. My math teacher, Sister Dolores, Priest Warren, visited me daily along with my family. I was glad Mr. Emrick, my coach, came for a visit too.

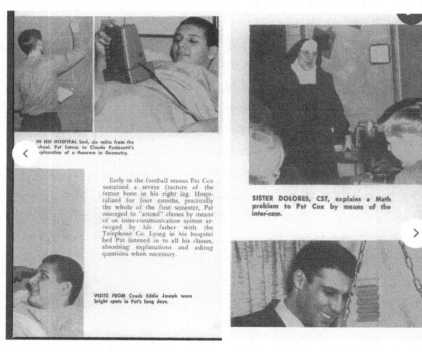

IN HIS HOSPITAL bed, six miles from the school, Pat listens to Claude Panizzutti's explanation of a theorem in Geometry.

Early in the football season Pat Cox sustained a severe fracture of the femur bone in his right leg. Hospitalized for four months, practically the whole of the first semester, Pat managed to "attend" classes by means of an inter-communication system arranged by his father with the Telephone Co. Lying in his hospital bed Pat listened in to all his classes, absorbing explanations and asking questions when necessary.

VISITS FROM Coach Eddie Joseph were bright spots in Pat's long days.

SISTER DOLORES, CST, explains a Math problem to Pat Cox by means of the inter-com.

"Granny Ethel was the only family member to try and teach me Cherokee. She called me her spiritual warrior and I would dance around and make her laugh."

Then Shirley asked, "Spiritual Warrior? I'm not for sure what you mean?"

I continued, "The meaning of being a warrior has changed, and the actions have changed, but the Cherokee word still has the old meaning, describing what people did when they went to war. When using old words in modern times, it's important to know their true meanings, so that they can be applied correctly. Or else, Cherokee becomes like English, where 'warrior' is just a label, without any real meaning. With the old meanings, the language stays alive and connected to the past. I haven't learned my spiritual being, so I feel I'm not a full Warrior. My heart has this strong desire to learn what is inside me and it's ready to come out."

By the look and appearance of Shirley's smile, I could tell she was understanding it all.

Sometimes, Shirley's smile would put a lilt in her voice, and this was one of those times.

"Your friends tell me you go into a bar looking for a fight. Is that true?"

I replied, "I've been known to start a few. I like to fight."

Shirley replied, "You don't necessarily try to offend people as much as you become aggressive with your point of view. Your ego is a great God-given device if you understand its true purpose."

"I don't understand. What's wrong with being aggressive? Being aggressive gives me an advantage."

"If you understand the balance to aggression, then it is just that, pure aggression."

"What's good about that?" I quickly asked.

"You just make people fear you and I don't think you want people to think that's all you are. When we each win our inner battles there won't be any out there," Shirley responded.

"Okay, I give up. I need to learn to be more non-aggressive. You wouldn't believe the number of fights I've gotten into," I continued. "When it comes to a fight, there's no honor, no code. All that matters is the win and I take nothing for granted. I'll offer the other person peace first, a chance to surrender on my terms, something they, of course, refuse. Then the first blow comes, a single sniper shot to their head. Next the negotiation restarts with the second in command. I always leaned toward short and brutal to curb the fatalities, maximize the fear and thus my power base. What's the point of winning if there's no-one left to subjugate?"

Shirley told me if I continued to fight, she would just walk out of my life. It was then I made her a promise never to fight again.

Shirley was strong in her beliefs and continued, "Passiveness allows the ego to become quiet, so your senses can determine if what you're faced with requires the ego to enter into the moment. When you quieten the mind and body, you have the opportunity to listen to all your senses at the same time."

I vowed to learn how to silent my mind instead of fighting. I didn't know what quieting my mind was, let alone how to do it. I wasn't sure if this was a good thing or not. The engineer in me just kept asking questions but I decided to listen to see what she said next.

"This flow gives you the time to determine when you are faced with something to ask yourself if this is truly a challenge or if it's just energy that can be dismissed without a second thought."

I came back, "I'm an engineer not a physicist. I had promised myself I would never take a physics course after the one I was forced to take in high school. I knew there were mysteries out there, but I just left them to the scientists to figure them out. I wasn't the least bit interested in it and felt strange about it. I told you before that I never stopped asking why this or why that. I drove my teacher crazy and some of my friends too. They all learned to ignore me when I started asking. In the second grade, I asked my teacher why blades of grass didn't fall over and if God were in the sky what would happen if a helicopter got too close. She sent me to the principal's office. I never got my answers from him either."

Shirley firmly spoke, "Being emotionally disciplined means that you are competent to stay calm in challenging situations and overpower your own negative emotions. You can then deal with any difficult situation, without making it worse. You do not have to be at the mercy of your emotions. You can control them, direct them into constructive channels. Emotional discipline is not a one-size-fits-all technique. Rather, you can develop and customize it to your own needs. It sets up the capacity to deal with current and future challenges.

I calmly said, "But what if I want to fight?"

She continued, "Raging anger or fear provoked by emotions is a roller coaster ride and can lead you to crash and land in heaps of trouble. Learning the emotional discipline of your self is to learn you are valuable and become a positive thinker. You will not want to waste your energy on negative thoughts, and you will want to remedy any existing problems. You learn every day; life is our teacher."

I was thinking there was all that philosophy, and I hadn't majored in that either. But I knew what free will was. I had paid attention to it in school and learned what the difference was between free will and predestination.

Shirley had to cut me short from getting off the subject. "Remember, if something does not meet your understanding you have the free will to accept or reject whatever that is at any time."

"Where did you get that information?"

Shirley explained, "Through automatic writings." She sensed I was a little puzzled about what she was saying. I knew what automatic meant and what writings meant but I just couldn't put the two together. I trusted that she was innately right.

"Before you ask. I have done automatic writings for years. Come, let me show you." I was wondering who this irrational woman was. I followed her into the bedroom where Shirley kept the numerous notebooks filled with writings in a bookcase. Bedroom? I had to clear those thoughts from my mind. I knew Shirley could read them.

"What is the meaning of automatic writings?"

Shirley willingly explained, "Automatic writing is when someone starts writing without conscious thought typically using spontaneous free association as a medium for information on the other side. An automatic writer can get information from Guides and master's to access higher intelligence for information."

"Guides teach through their messages."

"You've seen Maggy's pictures hanging on my wall. She and her soulmate Duke wrote information to help teach people about loving themselves. Also, I get writings from many others on the other side too."

I then knew this woman intrigued me. We sat on the edge of the bed and Shirley handed me a notebook. I slowly opened the book with a sense of a mission as I started reading. Shirley noticed my serious expression as I turned the page.

"Do you realize what you have here? This writing has very precise information; it holds data that could save our world."

"Not really but the writings told me someone would come along and explain it.

"I have three degrees in engineering, and this notebook has formulas for new technology." I was more than impressed.

"Well, someday we can talk more about this. Right now, you need to understand more about your ego." Remembering Leon's warning, Shirley continued "Patrick, you really do. It could be your undoing."

I had this look of one with a soul intact yet hiding from something I did not understand. While walking to the living room, I thought I did not have a big ego; I didn't think I was the smartest person on earth, or only thought only of myself. I did like to fight so maybe that was the ego she was talking about.

We sat at her dining room wooden table with rainbow in browns, the kind that brought sweet memories up for air. Reading my face, Shirley could tell she had my undivided attention.

Shirley went on, "There is a simple equation to help you understand; it's 3+2=1.

I replied, "It's 3+2=1? You must be kidding, right?"

Shirley answered, the 3 is mind, body and soul being in a vibrational tune with the balance of your positive and negative energy, which equals the 2. Then you become in a vibrational tune with your "Oneness" with God and the Universe that represents the 1.

"Your emotions are your get up and go like the electricity to your computer. It's your ego that protects your heart and soul. If your ego energy is out of control, you will have aggressive energy fighting to protect your heart," she said.

By this time, I was very curious. I knew this woman was telling me something but what, I didn't know yet.

"I'm going back into the bedroom," I declared. "You just stay here; I need time by myself."

Shirley was reading in the living room, I called out, "Shirley. Shirley, can you come here? I need you." I recalled that normally I didn't need anyone.

Shirley walked back into the bedroom, and I asked, "Do you see that dragon on the wall?"

Shirley replied, "No, but you do, and that is all that matters. Dragon is a sign of your ego."

I thought this was another puzzle. I dismissed her again saying, "Okay, leave me and this dragon alone."

Shirley noticed my eyes reflected anger. The soul translation of angry eyes is "I have activated my emotional indifference. I could kill and not care one bit. So back off."

Shirley heard a noise like someone does while practicing martial arts. A few minutes later, I walked out smiling.

"I just slew that dragon. So, I don't have an ego anymore," I announced proudly hoping for her approval.

Shirley cried, "Oh NO... everyone must have an ego. It's our God-given gift for protecting our heart. What you have done is put your ego in harmony. Have you studied martial arts? The noise you were making sounded like those kinds of sounds."

"Yes, I have a black belt in karate. Also, I have studied I Ching and Kung Fu; that's how I slayed the dragon." I started to demonstrate it.

Shirley saw me as complicated. I leaned over and my foot went sailing past her head.

"You could have hurt me!" Shirley shouted.

"No, I had no intention to hit you. Just wanted to show you; that's all."

Shirley was upset, so I continued, "Martial arts, I Ching, and Kung Fu teach discipline, patience, and energy. I knew with my energy focused on my foot it would go directly where I wanted it to and not hurt you."

Shirley wondered what else this man knew that she didn't know. She generally knew who people were right away.

I was a highly educated man and eager to study more about myself.

"How do I learn more about myself?" I asked then.

Shirley loved hearing my words. "'How do I learn more about myself?' It's a remarkably simple question, but it's difficult for many to ask. Meditation is a must for you first to start learning," Shirley emphasized. "When you experience the benefits of your meditation, it will become the best part of your day. It will quiet your brain and relax your body. To find your within 'Mind Emptiness' is necessary; then your person within connection will allow the feeling of wholeness to appear. It is then you can love who you are and will feel the deeper sense of yourself. It is knowing the connection within yourself that allows you to trust and genuinely love others.

"At my seminars, meditation with colors was the beginning for everyone. Everything has color, including inside our bodies. To flow, your colors enhance everything to flow significantly."

I said, "Lets slow down; explanations of most aspects of life can only make real sense if they are emotionally intelligent. Because a divided self will, in time, bring a divided world. What is within will manifest externally. Win me versus me and all will begin to fix itself. I think I need a break."

Shirley got up from sitting on the bed and started explaining more about color meditation.

"Let's take a break and go eat dinner. I'm starving. But this time, you pick the place."

Shirley would say Texas Live, but that was noisy. She wanted some place quiet so we could just talk. She didn't mean McDonalds.

I replied, "Ready for a drive? There is the best Italian restaurant in the world but it's in Dallas. It's Bugatti's and will give us more of a chance to get to talk about our pasts. You know, really get to know each other."

I took her hand and twirled her out the door.

CHAPTER 7

Memories Are Nice

They looked at each other in quiet silence.
The world stopped moving.

Shirley—1990

Arriving back at my place, we sat on the sofa and looked out the sliding glass door. We gazed at those bright friends of the moon and their pattern that seems so fixed and yet ever-changing, distant lights to call their hearts, to inspire dreams of other worlds. But for now, with my head on Patrick's shoulder, the starlight kept its familiar pattern. The constellations, who had witnessed centuries and millennia just the same, watched over this tiny moment.

I sensed my feelings towards him and thought feelings were like temperatures. "Attraction is warm, and curiosity is warmer. Anger is boiling. Hate can torch, but it can also freeze. Love... Well, that's a temperature best left under neutral."

He put his arm around my shoulders, giving me a kiss. In this kiss, I was home, and it created a static that crackled in the air. It was enough to make the baby hairs on the back of my neck stand up. We both jumped.

Patrick said, "Okay teacher, let us continue with me finding myself."

I knew a good teacher was an igniter, a fire-starter, always ready to provide fuel for the blazes they set in, and I was ready.

"It's time to continue aura teachings. Even at night, you can see colors. Auras don't go away," I declared. "Everything has an aura. Every substance on the planet has a certain field of colored energy around. It's a scientific fact that the Earth's whole existence is energy. One part of the energy manifested itself into a certain level of vibration, which makes it a physical form. Another part of the colored energy does not manifest itself into a physical form, but it still has a form."

"Hold on for a sec," he implored.

I waited until I saw his body relax just a little bit. "So, a form which is not yet physical still maintains a form, and is called an aura, like in the four forms, liquid, solid, gas, and plasma. Bet you didn't think I knew plasma is now considered a form."

"Shirley, you need to give yourself more credit. You are an incredible woman with lots of knowledge. That's why I love you. Oops, like you. Like you."

"It's okay to say love. There are three kinds, philia like Philadelphia the city of brotherly love or friends. Agape love is universal love—love for friends, strangers, and nature. The third one is Eros...now we don't have to go there. We all know what erotic is," I said.

I now knew he was unique and had to have more. He looked at me intensely to keep me talking. However, he was intrigued and wanted to understand my passions about this. After all, if he was falling in love with me, he had to pay close attention to get to know me, really know me.

I cleared my throat and continued, "Auras are of many kinds. Essentially the physical, mental, emotional and energy status of who you are right now in a certain way is represented by your aura, or it's visible through the aura. Aura is the periphery of a person. It shows all around them. Once you can see people's auras, you know what they truly are as a person."

"You know, Shirley, there is this off-the-wall guy that I have worked with that no matter what he did, I just wanted to punch him. What color of aura is that?" Patrick asked.

"An aura is an emanation of energy surrounding one's body, and it changes depending on the experiences the person has and the emotions they feel. I would say his aura was probably cloudy green or yellow green, which represents jealousy or envy. Inside our body, we have colored chakras, and when flowing properly, they help to create a brighter aura," I explained.

"Okay; in my college days I had never heard the word chakra. What is that? Remember I could not have cared less about all that inner truth stuff. I could not keep it straight if Aristotle taught Plato or Socrates or if it was the other way. I'm not sure they even lived at the same time. I know they are dead. I never could keep those guys apart," Patrick said.

I laughed. Patrick could make me do that so quickly. I couldn't remember a time I laughed so easily.

"Chakra is the Sanskrit word for wheel. Do you know what Sanskrit is? I'm sure you've at least heard the word. The human body is a complex energy form and has seven basic chakras. There are 114 in the body, and it has 72,000 energy channels, which are vital energy."

"Okay; hold on. I need to do the math, and this is a bit tricky for me to do it without a calculator though I know I can," he interrupted.

"Ready? You are getting this all very quickly. I knew you were smart."

"Yep, smart-alecky," he replied. "You can teach an old dog new tricks, but I'm not an old dog."

We both laughed, and he got up and gave me a huge hug and started kissing me.

"Wait," I said, "I'm not finished."

I stopped myself because I sounded like an elementary teacher telling a student to spit out his gum. But this was harder than that because it was something you could not see. It was an abstract concept. I felt he was ready to learn more.

"The seven chakras inside our bodies are in a straight line with your spine; this line runs down the center of our body from the top of our head to the base of our spine. Each chakra is an energy center and is represented with its unique color. Color meditation involves focusing on each of your chakras and their color vibration to bring about balance in your mind and body, promoting healing and peace of mind. Each of the chakras relates to the elements of the earth, air, fire, and water. The seven chakras and their color associations are

'1. Red: This color represents the root chakra, or some call it sacral chakra, which is located at the base of your spine. This is your life force and represents stability. Your sacral chakra is the center of emotions and feelings and stimulates pleasure. It plays an active role in your sexuality and expression of your sexual needs and desires.

Physically, red is the color that stimulates your body and mind and increases your circulation."

Patrick jumped right in, "I understand about the red. I must have a lot of it because my mind never stops."

"Yes," I nodded.

"2. Orange," I went on. "This color represents the sacral chakra, located in the area two inches below your navel. Focusing on orange and your sacral chakra will help with issues involving sensuality, relationships, physical pleasure, emotional self-expression, and creativity. Physically, orange is the color that stimulates your nervous system."

He interrupted again. "Orange is my ability to express myself and to be sensual. Sensual equals physical pleasure. I do not mean just sex. I mean like a good workout too."

"You are on the right track.

"3. Yellow: This color represents the solar plexus chakra, located just below your breastbone. Focusing on yellow our solar plexus chakra will affect your happiness, optimism, and thought processes. Physically, yellow is the color that helps increase your overall vitality, mental alertness, and analytical thought."

"Is this why everyone should go outside, first thing in the morning and soak up the sun? After all, when we were kids, we drew a yellow sun. I know I have yellow," he added in.

"The next is 4, and it is green," I added. "This color represents the heart chakra, located in the center of your chest. Focusing on green and your heart chakra stimulates peace, love, and nurturing. Physically, green is the color that induces healing."

He jumped up and went to the window and was pointing outside. "Green trees make me serene. I feel loved. You should wear green all the time, but you don't need to because I feel loved already."

"Now, Patrick… Anyway, green symbolizes growth, healing, and the promise of eternity. Green also represents the eco in ecosystem or money. 5. Blue: is the color of the throat chakra. It symbolizes self-expression, expression of truth, creative expression, communication, perfect form, and patterns. Focusing on blue your throat chakra helps with self-expression and confidence. Physically, blue is the color that controls your thyroid gland, lymphatic system, and affects your throat, neck, and voice.

"6. Indigo: This color represents the third eye chakra, located in the middle of your forehead. Focusing on the color indigo and your third eye chakra increases your intuition and your peace of mind. Physically, indigo is the color that affects your endocrine system.

"7. Gold: It circles your forehead. Gold is associated with higher ideals, wisdom enlightenment and understanding. It inspires spiritual knowledge and a deep understanding of yourself and soul.

Then there is the crown chakra, number 8. It is white, flowing out of the top of your head. This color of the crown chakra is associated with the universal connection with spiritual consciousness. The color white flows out the top of your head and then flows colors around your entire body forming your aura."

"Our bodies are unique," he resumed, "Like Earth's colors are enchanting after a rain, making everything a bit more beautiful, akin to God had polished the world anew. How could we resent those blessed drops? For with them came the greenery, the flowers, and every other bit of life we so adore fills with more color. In the darkness their cuddles feel like a little touch of heaven, right?"

I nodded my head.

Patrick continued, "Your cuddles are the only medicine I need; they are the light in the darkness, a lone star in an otherwise empty sky."

We looked at each other in quiet silence. The world stopped moving.

I broke the silence by quietly speaking almost a whisper and calmly saying, "Now please lie down on the bed. I will help you with your first meditation. Take three deep breaths through your nostrils and exhale out your mouth slowly. While taking your deep breath through your nose with mouth closed, you are breathing in God's powerful energy. As you blow it out through your mouth you are blowing out old unhealthy energy. God is our healer."

Patrick did just that.

"Visualize the colors pink and blue flowing from your toes to the top of your head. Pink and blue are your balance colors. Pink is your feminine energy and blue is your masculine. Now visualize your heart beating pink and blue flowing out from your heart connecting with the universal colors. You are relaxed, feeling the vibrations in your heart and out into the universe like a symphony orchestra playing its music. Your heartbeat is the drums playing in tune with the universal orchestra. Relax as you tune into this incredible universal vibration that exists within and around you. Your vibrations are being transmitted throughout the entire body, through your heart as it vibrates out into the Universe Love. You are now a universal antenna that will receive and feel more love and light. Now enjoy this great love experience." Saying so, I left the room.

Forty-five minutes later, Patrick walked into the living room.

"Well, that was an invigorating experience. I saw colors vibrating into each other like a never-ending ocean wave. Then I heard this voice say 'All answers to all questions are within.' And... 'Show your love for all to see, for I am you and you are me.'"

He was pleased with himself as I explained that he had made a connection with one of his 'Guides'. The message truly carries a powerful energy. With love, we truly are all equal.

Sitting back down in what was now his favorite chair, Patrick said, "You're a lady who has ventured many miles to visit with the Indian, and to think my blood is Cherokee. Maybe it's no coincidence we met in that bar. When do I get to hear about your Australia trip?"

"It's a long story, but you asked." I warned.

"Hey, I'm comfortable; bring it on," Patrick replied.

"How I got to Australia all started in January. It was a cold, windy night and it felt good sitting by the fireplace and relaxing while reading some of my automatic writings. The writing always came in fast, and once they were completed, I constantly dated and placed them in a notebook or in my trunk for safe keeping. Since they still came in with such high energy, the only way to know what was next was to read after each journey was completed.

My automatic writings were always accurate, and I never knew what was written at the time. Listen to this. It's date June 20, 1989, at 1:00 am. "You will take a trip to Australia where the Southern Light shines its lights. They are expecting you. It is something to look at and formulate."

"That was an exciting message," he cheerfully said.

"Now wait till we read what happened next," I replied. "The phone rang. I laid the notebook down to answer the phone.

Heather called saying that Kenny, her husband, was on a film festival business trip in New York and she called me to get caught up with my news.

I began explaining to Heather that she was reading the automatic writings about her last traveling, the Yucatan trip, and now they said there is to be an Australian trip. I didn't know anyone there, let alone have the money. Not for sure how this message was going to be played out.

Then Heather's other line rang. She asked me to hold. I knew it was from Kenny. She didn't even have to tell me. I just knew it. After a few minutes, she came back and said that it was Kenny, and I was going to be surprised and not believe why he called. Kenny had told Heather that he had invited a man, Cyrus, from Australia to stay with them while he was in Dallas on business. I paused from my story and said, "Now, Patrick, guess what Cyrus' business is?"

I waited and then could not wait any longer. "Patrick, he's in movies," I blurted out. "He produces and directs movies and has got his first book published out of New York. Kenny told him about my book, and he's interested in meeting me. He believes in reincarnation, enough that he has filmed a documentary proving it. Kenny said he would call me tomorrow and set up a lunch date.

"I was excited. I'd been waiting for someone to come in my life to film Maggy's story."

Patrick smiled with his eyes even though his lips were still.

I continued my story. "Two days later, I pulled into the valet parking at the Palm Café in West Dallas to have lunch with Kenny and Cyrus. Being the first to arrive, I sat at the bar and ordered a glass wine as the men walked in. Kenny rushed over, gave me a big, brotherly hug, and then introduced me to Cyrus. I hugged Cyrus and felt his uncomfortableness. Kenny immediately explained that I hugged everybody. It is my nature and I have never met a stranger. You should have seen him. He relaxed so much it looked like a wet noodle."

"I know what he's talking about you relaxing people. Honestly, Favorite Person, being around you brings me so much energy and relaxation at the same time," Patrick said.

I jumped up and hugged him. "I just wanted to do that right now. Anyway, while we were eating lunch, he explained to Cyrus about how great it was that I didn't let my abilities distract me from everyday life. But sometimes I wish they did. Then I wouldn't have to clean the house," I said laughing. "So, Cyrus talked about his reincarnation video and how important it was to get this information out to the world. Kenny was the Executive Vice President in Marketing with International Broadcast Systems, and they agreed to represent Cyrus internationally for his video and book.

"Kenny glanced at his watch and said that it was time to get back to the office and that he would see me later. Cyrus asks if we could go someplace and talk more.

I asked him where he wanted to go, and he answered because he had been spending so much time at business meetings or hotels that he wanted to be outside with nature.

We sat on the grassy knoll and the trees were filled with chirping birds. He turned to me and asked to hear my story. I told him it was important that I get my teachings out to others. When I started talking to him about Maggy, he looked up at the sky as visualizing her life. He kept looking up and told me that my story is golden in the film business."

"What a love story! And to think of a woman who lived during the era of horse and buggy to the jet set using her intuition to keep her head on straight. It makes an award-winning story. What's the title?"

"An Angel with Muddy Feet," I told Cyrus. "Would you like to see Maggy's Vaudeville pictures and scrapbooks? I have them at my place."

"Being a man behind the camera, it's easy to visualize with pictures. I would like that," he answered.

I was ecstatic to have the opportunity to show him Maggy's material. I knew he would like her story and the history it had to offer."

"I bet you were. Tell me more what happened, Patrick said as he got up and stretched.

"We sat in the living room as he looked at Maggy's pictures. I could tell Cyrus was sensitive." I continued.

Cyrus said, "A woman of wisdom filled with spiritual experiences like Maggy will show people what life is all about."

Patrick took a deep breath, "It is amazing how everything came together for you."

"Let me go on. There's lots more." I spoke.

"Sure, Favorite Person." He said with a smile on his face.

I continued, "The phone rang, and it was Kenny. He wanted us to meet him for 'Happy Hour' at a bar near his office."

Patrick jumped in, "Oh, that's interesting Kenny stopped your presentations?"

I nodded my head yes.

"Kenny met us at the door. We were standing at the bar, sipping our wine, Cyrus told us he had a meeting with Bill Saunders, the president of 20th Century Fox in Los Angeles. I sensed Cyrus was dreading the meeting and said something to him about it."

"I don't know my way around LA and for some reason he felt there was a negative energy."

"He asked me if I would go with him and if I would, he would pay my way. He knew I would enhance the meeting with energy. Then I heard Maggy's message, "This Australian has a message for you," and I told him yes."

"Kenny thought I was crazy but loved the idea. Heather and I want you to join us for pizza. Kenny and Heather had a beautiful home in Rockwall, Texas, about a half hour's drive from Dallas. They chose this area because of the horse farms, making it handy to board their horses. It was also by Lake Ray Hubbard where the three of us went boating many times. It was a beautiful drive with views for Cyrus to see in this part of Texas.

"Heather cheerfully welcomed us at the door. Kenny showed Cyrus to his room while Heather and I ordered pizza.

"While we were eating, Kenny told us he had a telescope to look at the nightly skies. Their backyard was a perfect setting to see everything clearly. He went on and told us that there had been numerous UFO reports over the lake, and he was hoping they could show Cyrus some of their action.

Kenny went outside. Once the telescope was in place, he yelled for us to come out. Heather and Cyrus didn't want to go, so I did. I couldn't understand why they were staying inside, so I went back in to check.

"Cyrus said that he wanted to stay and talk with Heather. He didn't want to go out and watch for UFOs. Heather's energy was something he had never felt before, so he preferred to stay with her. He had taken breathing classes, and they sensitized his energy.

"I understood what Cyrus was saying. I had taught breathing classes in my seminars. It's a spiritual practice that is dynamic. It eases stress and anxiety and helps with concentration and sleep. It's a very relaxing technique. But I didn't understand what he was saying about Heather's energy. Kenny was upset, and I didn't know what to do."

Patrick intervened, "Oh that would not be comfortable?"

I told Patrick that I excused myself and left to prepare for the next day's trip to Los Angeles. Before leaving, Kenny gave me a good night hug and whispered in my ear, "The automatic writings said after the Yucatán trip next would-be Australia. So here you go, Shirley. You're Australia bound."

~~~

I continued with the story about how the early morning sun woke me up while lying under the covers in my comfortable bed. How I started thinking about how exciting it would be to go to LA. What an opportunity to visit more with Cyrus and visit the 20th Century Fox Studio. So, I jumped out of bed and started packing.

"Bobby, a dear friend, drove me to the airport. Bobby drilled me with questions like, 'Why would you go to Los Angles with a guy you just met last night? You don't know this guy. You never know, Shirley; he could be a gangster or connected with the Australia Mob.'"

I said I understood where Bobby was coming from. I didn't know this guy. Even Kenny had just met him. But I knew he was legitimate and answered Bobby nervously.

When we met Cyrus at the ticket counter, Bobby, a lady of 5'2" immediately walked over and took Cyrus's arm, pulled his 6'1" body down so they were face to face and told him he'd better be good to Shirley. She told him that I was an extraordinary, exceptional person, and he must treat me with great respect, or they'll come after him—they didn't care where he lived. They would fly to Australia if necessary.

After a big hug, Bobby left yelling, "Call me, Shirley, when you get back."

Cyrus strengthened his tie and said, "She sure is a spunky little thing, isn't she?"

My friends were very protective.

Arriving at the hotel in Santa Monica, Cyrus suggested a walk to a nearby bookstore. Entering the store, we went separate ways. I heard Cyrus calling my name. I finally found him standing with the book *Pre-Destined Love* by Dick Sutphen.

"You're already famous, Shirley. I pulled this book out and turned to the page that reads 'Shirley J. Smith, a psychic in Arlington, Texas,'" Cyrus said.

I felt embarrassed because the store was big with lots of people staring at me.

"Famous only means a lot of people know you. Yes, I worked with Dick and Gloria with this book about love and reincarnation," I quietly said.

Cyrus said excitedly, "But don't you see? I did a video proving reincarnation. The video had people going through past life regressions and saw where they lived before in other countries in different lifetimes. Then we traveled to the location and proved what they saw was true. It proved reincarnation."

Then he asked, "Can you introduce me to Shirley McClain? That's the lady I need to know, and she would help me with this information."

"I'm not acquainted with Shirley. I'm friends with Belva Bloomer, her corresponding secretary, but that's all," I replied.

Patrick stopped Shirley from talking. "I can see through this guy. He wants to use you; any way, that is what I think."

I looked at him like I already understood something he didn't at the time. I continued. "Sitting across the table from Cyrus in the Casa Del Mar Restaurant at the Santa Monica Pier was pleasant. While pouring our wine, the waiter told us how he saw rainbows over our table.

"Cyrus began the conversation by saying he was married. His wife was a petite redhead who played the cello at the Australia Opera House and was playing in New York now. The reason he was there with her was because a New York publisher had published his book and New York was hosting a film distribution festival. That was where he and Kenny met. He was hiring Kenny to distribute his video that proves reincarnation.

"He went on to say that he had given it some thought and felt it would be a good idea for us to work together with Maggy's book and movies. I would need to be in Australia for three months and could stay with him and his wife, Brigitte.

"I said to him, 'I don't have *An Angel with Muddy Feet* completed. I have many stories to add.'"

"Taking a sip of wine, Cyrus said, 'You come to Australia for three months; we'll have your book completed, and then we'll start on the movie script. I will make sure my New York publisher publishes your book. I have always wanted to make a movie in the United States. Brigitte and I want to move here. Will you help me look for an office while I'm here? I can take pamphlets to show Brigitte. I will pay your expenses. There is another reason we want you to visit Australia. Wanda, Brigitte's mother, has lung cancer, and I think you could help the family cope with this ordeal. Brigitte family is a close-knit family, and the thought of their mother dying horrifies them. Brigitte's dad, Luke, and her sister Anna and son Owen needed spiritual guidance. They need help with someone like you who understands about the other side,' Cyrus added."

"I continued about how my writings about Australia were manifesting quickly. I felt a little overwhelmed with all this happening so quickly. I told him that I must take care of my clients first. Cyrus had told me March would be the best month for both of us."

"With your abilities, we'll be traveling worldwide. I have some great ideas about what to do with you and your work. So, get prepared,' Cyrus said."

"Think Mr. Cyrus is a little pushy?" Patrick snapped.

I started again, "Morning came fast, and I hurried to meet Cyrus for breakfast. I saw him sitting in a booth reading a newspaper while drinking his coffee. The restaurant was full, and it was obvious everyone was in a hurry. After eating, Cyrus asked if I was ready to help with his work. I told him of course. I'm always ready. Then we both laughed.

"After Cyrus's meeting at Fox, he boarded a plane for Australia, and I boarded another plane for Texas with the plan that in March I would arrive in Australia.

"I was home unpacking when the phone rang. It was Kenny saying that he had talked with Cyrus, and he was excited about me coming to Australia."

Patrick walked to his jacket slumped on the chair and said that he was tired. "Shirley, hold on to your Australian story, we will finish when my mind is clearer. It's one in the morning and I'm starting not to hear your words. I will be the loudest 'cry-baby' in the world if I miss any part of your story. I do not want that so give me a good night's kiss and I'll see you soon."

CHAPTER 8

Shirley's Surprise

*The crowd gasped, paused a moment in shock,
and then broke into applause.*

Shirley—1990

I drove up to the restaurant, parked and then took a moment to look in the mirror making sure my hair and makeup looked good. I knew Patrick was waiting for me inside. I had just returned from a seminar tour in Louisiana, Mississippi, and Colorado. I felt like being home was the hug my soul had been calling for. I thought it would be a good idea to stay home and relax with a bath and maybe get caught up on some sleep. But, over the phone, Patrick sounded so mysterious. He had something important to talk about. He had a lot of work to do, but this restaurant was close to his office making it easy for him to be there at 8:00.

"While you were gone, I thought of some things we have to talk about. Like now. And I must tell you in person. Would you meet me tonight?" Patrick asked.

My thoughts were filled with wonder. Usually, I can pick up on what's going on but not tonight. It was due to me being so tired.

The young valet opened my car door. I stepped out when a big flash of lightning along with a loud crashing thunder literally shook the ground. I smiled and thought what could be so earth-shaking that Patrick had to tell me. I hoped the Texas thunderstorm would be over by the time I drove home.

I walked in, scanned the room, and thought that this must not be the place. I almost decided to leave when I saw Patrick waving from a table for two in the corner of the restaurant. I put on a brave smile and steadily walked across the room toward him, chin held high, as usual. Patrick immediately jumped up and pulled out a chair. As he slid the chair out from the table, he very slightly brushed his hand across my back, quite by accident. But in that one briefest of brief touches, he stopped, flickered his eyes somewhat perplexed, quickly sat me down, and returned to his chair. It was the strangest thing. Patrick felt as if he had been shocked. I felt it too, though it was very brief; only I wasn't perplexed. I knew what had happened and I was still taking it in. *Oh! My!* I thought to myself, *OH! My!*

Patrick then motioned for a waiter who hurriedly arrived. Patrick ordered dinner for us after asking me politely which entrée I preferred. He chose the wine as I was sure he always did. After he ordered, he looked up at me, staring very intently and stated, "Shirley, I want you to answer a question for me."

"It would be my pleasure to answer," I replied, turning full face to look him in the eyes.

He then said, "I like a woman with principles, who knows her mind and isn't afraid to say so." He continued smiling at me.

I looked down coyly through my lashes, lifted my chin and replied. "Well, I've been told by many people that I say what I think and mean what I say!"

He reached ever so shyly and put one hand over mine.

"I like you, Shirley Smith. I like you a lot. Would you spend some time with me? I have oil well sites I must check on throughout the state of Texas and thought you would like to see some of the areas. For example, Paint Rock has pictographs. Thought you would like to see them since you've visited many Indian reservations."

"Oh, I would love to," I replied, "but I am starting another ten-day seminar tour."

"You're a busy girl," he laughed. "Don't stay in one place very long, do you?"

"No, I am about to start a lengthy tour and won't have any time until I arrive in San Francisco."

To my surprise, he said to call him, and he would fly out. My heart skipped a beat as he told me he had to see me again, even if I was making it extremely hard to be dated. I laughed like a schoolgirl; it was so much fun.

I said, "I'm a gal who loves nature and traveling has caused me to be in busy cities for many days. Patrick, if you have the time, would you like to get next to nature with me? We could go to the Fort Worth Botanic Gardens. I've been told it's a sanctuary for the senses, and my senses are ready." Laughingly, I continued, "Would you like to enlighten your senses?"

"Me and my senses are ready," Patrick answered playfully. "I will pick you up tomorrow at 10:00."

When two people fall in love, every day is a fun adventure. There is no such thing as an ordinary life when you achieve this feeling! It makes the world your playground with all things seeming new again. I don't think we would have met if I hadn't come to a place in my life when I had truly found myself. I was content, successful, and happy just being myself. After my divorce, I had worked long hours to accomplish being strong, independent, and emotionally balanced. I honestly did love myself. I knew I had to before I could love someone else. I had been blindsided by this love when I least expected it. I had been looking forward to nothing more than a fun night with some old friends, and then that comet hit! Patrick was his own man, and he lived his life to the fullest. He made decisions on his time, and the world seemed to follow.

He had made dinner reservations at one of his favorite places in Dallas when the night turned into an event I had not seen coming. He never did things quite by the book. He always kept surprising me. We had talked for what seemed like hours, heads close, oblivious to everyone but each other. He talked rapidly, and I hung on every word.

He said, "I make fast decisions; I live in the present. I enjoy every day. I tolerate fools poorly, can't stand rules, and do as I please. If you want a white picket fence and a lot of children, leave now. I'm not your boy, but if you're like me, and I'm fairly sure you are, then come along for the ride. You may not always be happy, but I promise you, you will never be bored. I hate society dictating my life and I can tell you hate it too. That is the bond we share, isn't it Shirley J. Smith?"

He reached for my hand. I let him. He said, "Are you in for the ride?"

I covered his hand with my other hand and said quickly "I'm in. I'm your girl."

He smiled so wide I couldn't believe it. He stood up, grabbed my waist, and guided me toward the piano bar. I thought he meant to dance, but he merely took the microphone from the startled pianist and said into the open mic. "People, may I have your attention? I want you all to meet my fiancée Shirley J. Smith, who has flown in today and is going to help me pick out a ring!" The crowd gasped, paused a moment in shock, and then broke into applause. I smiled like a muse, stunned, and thrilled at the same time. He whispered into my ear.

"Go with it—we can always split up if it doesn't work."

I giggled, nodded, and smiled as everyone came up to us. We left the restaurant together that evening—Mr. Cox and his fiancée.

It seemed like a dream, but it was real. It was raw, sweet, and shocking, and I loved it! We did indeed buy a ring the next day as he slid the beautiful stone on my finger.

He said, "A perfect size five. I've waited for this hand all my life."

I had waited for him too. It was like a thrilling roller coaster ride of emotions, a modern-day magic carpet ride. I loved it, and I loved him. We always discussed how different our meeting was. Funny how people never know how each day will end. I loved this breathtaking ride. I was up for it then as I was today.

~~~

I hummed a little tune as I washed my hair and showered the next morning. I hoped Patrick would understand the importance of Mother Nature that the Indians had taught me. "Nature is the mother with her kitchen balancing scales, for she is wisdom and endurance, the immortal soul of the ages, the one who knows the recipe of life itself."

I wondered that since he was a city boy, he might not understand some of the things I did. The doorbell rang, and the clock struck ten. He was right on time. Opening the door, giving him a good morning kiss, I grabbed my tote bag and blanket, and we charged out.

Together, we spread the colorful knitted blanket. The knitted blanket is a glorious expression of my granny's soul; it was the colors of her dreams woven with delicate and loving hands. I told Patrick, "Granny would sit in her old rocking chair, hands moving, brain at peace, and from those delicate fingers would come the blankets. As a child, I saw her as a magician of sorts, and we played long games as rainbow-ghosts with her creations."

The Earth's energy felt calming sitting on the blanket with the soft green grass beneath. I watched the grass move as a heaven-weaved quilt of the earth, as if by root and stem it stood in protection of what mattered. A man close by was playing music on a Hammered Dulcimer that echoed a rhythm of peacefulness in the air. Such a magical place displaying nature's species. My body senses were feeling a new penetration of peaceful energy. I turned to look at Patrick stretched out with his arms under his head and eyes closed. I wondered if he felt as relaxed as I did. I whispered to him just that.

He said reassuringly, "It's invigorating. Glad you talked me into it."

I began telling him stories about my Indian friends and what they had taught me. "Mother Earth is a beautiful planet. It's alive, and we are some of Earth's living life cells. Instead of respecting and taking good care of her, we sell, cut, dig, clear, and then build for control and greed. This hurts Earth and all the living species including animals that need to survive on it."

Patrick immediately thought to himself that he was probably one of those people and promised to himself not to be anymore.

"Humans are working to take animals and make them domestic," I continued. "Animals have their instincts and need to live their way, not the human way. I was told the only way to make decent changes to help everything on this planet is to teach people how to understand and love themselves. Once they learn to love themselves, there will be no need for hate, greed, or fear. They will feel a stronger independence and be a happy person. Someday, people will learn there can never be a love affair as great as that between environmental and humans.

"Now, what do you think of that J. Patrick?" I asked teasingly.

"I understand what you're saying," Patrick declared. "My Cherokee blood runs deep in my veins with a fiery desire to help Mother Earth. Anything I can do to help with your mission, let me know. I will be glad to do so." Then, he stood up and declared, "Let's go for a walk and continue our talk."

"I'd love to walk, especially in the Japanese Garden. They say it's like entering a new world of mystery and enchantment. It has exotic Imperial Carp or Koi that will get your attention. Stone, earth, leaf, and water become one in this land of wonder. The Kyoto style landscape features Cherry trees, Japanese maples, several bridges, and a traditional tea house. The summerhouse, a Japanese Garden pavilion, and moon viewing deck. I love bridges and waterfalls."

I spotted a tree and rushed over to it with Patrick following behind me. "Let's hug this tree. When you put your ear next to it, you can hear it breathe, and trees like to be hugged." Laughing, Patrick indulged me, and put his arms around it and so did I. We couldn't reach all the way around, but that was okay. Patrick babbled, "Let's see what happens when we sing to it."

I responded, "I'm not a singer, but let's give it a try."

With Patrick leading the song we began, "We love you, Mr. Tree. We love you, Mr. Tree. Hi Ho, the Dearie Oh, we love you, Mr. Tree. We love your energy." We stopped.

"Put your ear next to the tree, Patrick. Can you hear the tree breathing?"

"Why, yes, I can," Patrick quickly responded. "Never done this before. It does show that everything is alive."

People were looking oddly at the two of us, but we didn't care.

Halfway across the round-shaped Japanese bridge, we stopped and looked at the large colorful Koi swimming in slow motion as though they owned the world.

"Leon taught me about the spirit totem of a Koi," I said. "It's a sign of good luck and prosperity. You must look for new opportunities and take advantage of them. The Koi brings you the opportunity for transformation through meditation. They bring changes in your life of golden wealth and prosperity."

"Can you be my Koi?" Patrick asked as he pulled me close to him.

"Well," I replied with a smile, "they teach us to streamline our lives. They also signal when one of your senses is being awakened and be prepared to have visions and prophetic dreams. Your clairvoyance will become strong. You will have greater contact with the spiritual realm. Their signals are powerful. Now is the time to have faith and dream big, Patrick. I'd love to be your Koi, but the real symbol of them is more than I would be."

"Who is this Leon fellow?" Patrick acted a little jealous, but he wasn't. He was only pretending to be. He loved everyone who loved me.

"Leon Overbay, Comanche medicine man, my first Indian teacher. I met him and his wife, Mary, in Cottonwood, AZ. They recently sold their business and moved to Maui. After being taught by him, I was sent to the Hopi Reservation. From there, I was sent to Mexico and met a Mayan teacher, Abbot. Then off to Santa Fe to meet Richard, another Mayan teacher and from there I was sent to the Aborigines in Australia." I took a deep breath and blew it out. "Whew, that does make me sound like the world traveler. I never really thought of myself like that. I was just a woman on a mission."

Patrick, as a rule, tried to hide his emotions, but the smile that cracked his face showed his excitement, "Let's go visit Leon in Maui. I think he could also teach me. Let me fly you to Hawaii? Do you think it would be possible for your work? I can arrange my schedule."

"I first must keep my seminar commitments," I murmured. "It's my job. I'll finish this tour in San Francisco. Would you like to meet me there? I can teach you 'The Awakening' a private seminar?"

"You bet! Just let me know when," Patrick answered.

By the time we got back to my house, night had fallen and enveloped the city in a blanket of darkness. I invited him in thinking we would talk more about a trip to visit Leon. We walked into the living room, and Patrick sat down heavily on the couch. He seemed almost to fall into it. Like everything else in the living room, the couch told a story, a testimony to my personality. It was a piece made for comfort, moderately priced copy of some supremely talented designer. Its beige color made it essential to have a blank slate around on which to build the rest of the room's décor. My throw pillows were beautiful art creating a botanical themed design in shades of green, sand, and crimson for the printed pillows. A coffee table was sitting in front of the couch was a big trunk with two multicolor Kachina Dolls, a silver round spaceship with etchings on one side saying "UFO-Noah." The other side appeared to be Egyptian hieroglyphs, and a crystal sitting in the center. On the wall was a big painting of women wrapped in their blanket with long, flowing hair riding on the horseback. It dominated the wall by its colors of pinkish mauve and light turquoise with such precise lines.

"Is the artist a friend?" asked Patrick.

"That is a special gift from one of my clients. It's a 'Bonny' painting from the Houshang Gallery in Dallas. The painting takes me far away to another lifetime. It makes me feel like I'm in this painting, one of those Indian women on a horse. I love it."

I sat beside Patrick and asked if I could get him anything. Patrick shifted his seating making himself more comfortable as he put his arm around my shoulder. "I'd like for you to finish telling me about your Australia adventures. That is what I want."

CHAPTER 9

Australia-Bound

Shirley opened her eyes and sat up wondering what that was all about. She thought her dreams always came true, and then thought about what this man looked like climbing off his horse.

Shirley—1990

I happily started telling Patrick about my trip to Australia.

"When I boarded Qantas Airlines for my Australian flight, the flight attendants passed out pillows, blankets, and a glass of wine before our fifteen-hour flight. After takeoff and drinking my wine, I snuggled down for a good night's sleep. The captain's voice across the intercom woke me out of a dream.

"Oh," so you even had dreams to help you with your journey? Patrick interrupted. "Let's go out on the patio while you tell me more about your dream."

We sat down on the patio chairs, and I chuckled. The breeze we felt existed, but the wind was calm. It did feel nice out there.

Once we got settled in, I began again to tell Patrick more. "In my dream, I had seen a Palomino Stallion with an Indian man riding bareback. This beautiful horse had dark-skin, flaxen mane, and tail with a dark golden body color flowing freely as he ran through the sky. Suddenly a white lightning bolt snaked through the sky followed by a loud thunderclap that shook the air."

"Lighting is a great mystery, many do not know the origin of lightning bolts nor their real strength," Patrick added.

I nodded my head and continued, "Next, the horse stopped, and the man got off. I heard him say, 'I am your Rainbow Warrior. I have raced from the heavens to spread the great wisdom of light, and I will protect you. My words are spoken with great truth, and clouds will roll and rumble with powerful messages to you. Just listen and hear my voice through the wind. I come only with the pureness of love.'"

"I opened my eyes and sat up thinking 'What a dream', and my dreams always come true. Following, I thought about what this man looked like, climbing off his horse. He was approximately 5'11", thick, dark brown hair and his eyes were different—hazel eyes, yet they looked like wolf eyes. I thought maybe it had something to do with meeting the Aborigines. The guy in my dream baffles me because you have the same description. I was shocked when I saw you at Gershwin's. It was a though I had met someone from my past, but I didn't know you."

Patrick smiled, "Tell me more!"

~~~

"Cyrus was eagerly waiting for me in the Sydney terminal. After gathering my luggage, we left for his house. Brigitte was working and would meet us later. I felt uneasy as Cyrus drove fast on the hilly streets of Sydney. He laughed when I told him I was uncomfortable; it was an odd feeling, driving on the opposite side of the street. He pulled into a parking place in front of their home, which was built on the side of a hill. We had to walk down to enter the front door. It was a small home but nice and appealing with a large patio in the back surrounded by beautiful lawn gardens.

"Cyrus had hired a computer tech to work on the right program for the floppy disks that I had brought to edit my book *Angel with Muddy Feet*. Since this allowed time before starting work, Cyrus decided to show me some of the Australian sights. The first weekend we went to Palm Beach.

"The coastline was brilliant in the morning sun with its boulders that stretched out to greet the coming waves. The foamy crests of the crashing waves were the only sound other than the cry of the gulls.

"Cyrus and Brigitte prepared for the picnic. I sat on the beach, my eyes moving from sand to stone, from rock pools to breaking waves. In the gentle spring sunshine, I felt as if I were swimming in the briny aroma as if the new rays of the day brought a frisson of energy to my fingertips. It was a day for letting my eyes stay open, as I was an old-fashioned camera, remaining still while the image developed. The gulls brought their high notes to the percussion of pebbles at the shoreline. It was a day for dreaming, for allowing time to move fast and slow.

"Cyrus dug a hole in the sand and started a small campfire, while Brigitte happily placed the food on a folding table. The wind causes the tablecloth to whip around as though it was dancing. The heat of the campfire struggled to penetrate the air. Cyrus said that in his mind, the best Billy Tea comes out of his old tin pot. The more it is used, the better. Once he had the campfire blazing good, he filled the old pot, which was dirty on the outside but clean on the inside, with cold water. When it started boiling, he dumped the tea grounds into the water. After steeping it for a while, I was handed a tin cup full of very black looking tea. It had a flavor I had never tasted before; it was smooth, not bitter, with a hint of smoky flavor.

"Sitting close by the glowing campfire, Brigitte explained for the extra 'bushy' flavor Cyrus had thrown in a hearty blend of Australian grown black tea, Peppermint Gum and Lemon Scented Gum with a hint of smoky Lapsang Souchong for that authentic campfire flavor and aroma. The Bush people like sitting by the nightly campfire, and in the comfort of the black sky comes the boldest star of the heavens, they look at the stars as if they were raised on Billy's tea. The term Billy tea refers to tea brewed in a Billy can, which is a small can, tin, or pot used by the bush people on a campfire for boiling tea. So, the term 'Billy up to the fire' basically means, 'put the kettle on' at the same time, it was a symbol of Bush hospitality, and it represented the independent, self-reliant Australian spirit.

"It felt good to be outside, get some exercise, walk, climb boulders, and have a picnic. Overhead there were sailboat clouds making good time with an ocean-blue sky, the wind was their companion and cheerleader. My hair was blowing, as the clouds raced by. It was not a day for loose hats or umbrellas, but a day to tuck my head to my chin and let my hair whip around my face. There is something about these windy days that blow the cobwebs right out of my head. I watched the waves come like a coiffured fifties hair do, over pronounced in the arch and impossible to avert the gaze from. They roll as the ocean does, bringing the music of the beach, the percussion section roaring from the stony bed below yet softened by the water.

"We left the beach for a ride in the beauty of Australia's sand dunes. The climb up a steep sand hill seemed to cause a struggle for the SUV. The sight of steep turfs up the sand dune appeared to go on forever. Upon this primrose sand, the hue as gentle on the eye as a vintage photograph was a steady warmth from the grains. This great day had come as the opening of a treasured book, the story ahead promised happiness.

~~~

"Back at the office, Cyrus said we needed to have a business meeting. He explained he was going to be filming the Reincarnation #2 video and needed my help. He wanted us to work together imputing Maggy's numerology material for computers, publish her books, and film movies. I was to keep my passport up to date because we would be traveling a lot internationally. Cyrus didn't like Maggy's book titled *An Angel with Muddy Feet*. He said it just wasn't the right title. I told him Maggy had named her book. I had already copyrighted it so I didn't want to make any changes.

"He answered with a sharp voice, 'No. You're being too negative.'"

"I felt my stomach hit the floor.

"I told Cyrus, 'Let's talk about this problem and then we can move forward into whatever business we are to do. We need to form a solid foundation of getting to know each other with future business. It can be challenging, yet possible. Being troubled is normal until we get to know each other. It's good to remain real and engaged in what is best; we don't want to mask our emotions in our work. I'm saying to you, I don't want to change the title of Maggy's book. Maggy received the title through automatic writings while writing her life stories.'

"He went on, 'I'm the director and know more about the business. Don't be so negative regarding this.'"

"I felt stonewalled. I hadn't expected problems with the title of Maggy's book. Emotionally, I felt devastated; my efforts for my dreams to come true were being squashed. I knew it was time to slow this fast-moving train as I squirmed in my chair. I felt that old control feeling I had with my ex-husband and wasn't going to allow myself to be in bondage again. I now understood my last dream. In the dream, I was back in Herrick riding in a blue and silver bus with Maggy driving. Maggy parked in front of a church. We walked in, and it was filled with people. Men were walking down the aisle carrying a small baby's wicker white casket. I realized this was a funeral and started crying. I heard Maggy say to me that every emotion is right, helpful in the right situation. Any dark emotions are like salt, just a pinch adds flavor, yet too much ruins the entire dish. The trick of it all is to remember what is salt and what is food; the food is love, empathy, kindness, joy, compassion, nurture, protection, and integrity. The salt is envy, hate, greed, anger, sloth. If you have vastly more food than salt, everything will be alright.

"Then Maggy stated, 'You trying to take a shortcut? You can't do that. You have more work to do.'

"I had just arrived, and the only people I knew were Cyrus and Brigitte. I did not know what to do.

"I heard Maggy whisper in my ear, 'Ask me for help; just ask. I promise when you do, it is a blessing on us both. To help is a gift; to be asked is trust and it is one way we love one another more deeply. Calm your thoughts and live in the present moment; be careful and have the courage to say, 'No' to this man and to a world of greed that exploits people in the same callous way it takes from Mother Nature. In a world such as this, radical self-care is part of not only surviving, but also learning how to succeed and make new and better choices. Your heart and soul are worth keeping and protecting."

~~~

"Kenny called asking if I was okay. After telling him the story, he advised me not to say anything. He reminded me that Cyrus had paid my expenses, so I would have to stay until the return date scheduled. This time, I knew I would have to burn a bridge to get myself out of the mess I was in.

"The next evening, Luke, Brigitte's dad, invited everyone including Brigitte's sister Anna and Rick her husband, over for his famous Barbie with Liquid Courage. It was soon explained, 'Barbie in USA is BBQ and in Australia, Liquid Courage is alcohol.' I thanked Luke for his hospitality and great food. Luke walking toward me, 'I appreciate that, Shirl. It's my belief to eat well is to love yourself; to share good food with others is to create the bonds of heaven. People you have just been bonded by 'The Australian Luke or the famous Bloke from Sydney. I answer both.' Then Cyrus started a conversation with Rick, which grew from nowhere into a tornado. Cyrus was taking his argument with heat in his voice, accusing Anna and Rick of taking advantage of her dad financially. As Luke came in from the kitchen, Cyrus voice changed and he stopped. Cyrus announced he and Brigitte were ready to go home; I wasn't, and it created a problem. Anna told me not to worry, Rick, would drive me home. Anna kept asking what I would like to do. She knew I was upset and repeatedly asked what was wrong. Not wanting to say anything about Cyrus's business offer, I talked about my dream, seeing this beautiful waterfall, and thought maybe I would find it on this trip.

"Anna turned, looking at her dad and said, 'That is by our family cabin at Blackheath.' She then turned to me and explained that Blackheath was a small town located near the highest point of the Blue Mountains. She suggested to her dad that they take me there.

"Luke decided he would drive us to Blackheath and let Cyrus and Brigitte drive by themselves. Luke was an attorney and an artist. He loved his family, and they respected and loved him. Luke was concerned for his children. The doctors didn't give Wanda much hope with her lung cancer. Luke asked if I would help them to accept her health issues. Wanda was a creative, talented woman, being a decorative/design artist, jeweler, in addition to being a loving mother.

I told Luke that I was friends with Dr. Elisabeth Kubler-Ross who had written several books about dying. One was *Questions and Answers on Death and Dying.* I told him that her books would better help him by understanding about the five stages of grief.

"Luke looked at me with hopeful eyes and mumbled, 'Yeah.'

"Luke explained how he felt his children would better understand if I talked to them. He felt people didn't understand and they have no way of knowing when their time is up. That is only between them and God.

"There is no Death. Wanda will make her transition from earth to the Other Side, a place of her choice. Death is only her earth vehicle, the physical body, but her Soul lives on,' I explained."

"Luke's tears came as if he realized what I said was true. 'I love Wanda, and I'm not ready for her to permanently leave me,' he said with a quivering voice.

I continued, 'The death of a loved one it is not easy to deal with because there are different emotional ups and downs that come with it. Grief is the reaction to those who are left behind and will affect your body, mind, emotions, and spirit. Your thoughts can be happy memories of Wanda when she dies, worries, or regrets, or thoughts of what life will be like without her. Death isn't kind; it snatches, taking people we love. It will not pretend to care or to distinguish; it just rips away a part of you, the part of you that is most loved.'

"Luke walked a step or two closer to me, 'When Wanda dies, she will be out of her pain and will be in a better place, but he and children would still want to feel and see her physically. There is a strong bondage with mothers.'

"I explained it was so because they carry their child for nine months. While they are connected, they are nurtured, having a strong sense of being loved. It is a heart-to-heart feeling.

"I then gently told Luke, to help his children, allow them to come to him, a hug and I'm sorry is something you must go through and this helps immensely. Hugs are especially important and allowing them to talk is a must. It is important for them to realize it is a time for acceptance. Mother is gone but Dad is still with them, and their sorrow of Mother's death is the proof of their love.

"I kindly told Luke, after their mother's death, he would have to help his children realize it is a time for accepting, understanding, and growing to help them have a greater sense of peace. Grief takes as long as it takes, and there is no right or wrong way to express it. It never truly ends; instead, we gradually take new shape around it. It truly is a spiritual practice.

"Luke nodded his head. 'We are a tight-knit family. We will stand together and strive not to be afraid of what is ahead. I don't like fear; it is anyone's worst enemy. We have faith, and that will carry us through this ordeal.'

"He stopped for a moment and stared off. Then he continued, "I want to show you one of Australia's famous artworks at the Norman Lindsay Gallery & Museum. Norman Lindsay was an artist, cartoonist, and writer, and this was his home place. For a treat, we'll visit their coffee shop and then walk through the gardens with a lily pond and many sculptures. You can feel the history as you walk through this magnificent specimen of a building that represents the Norman Lindsay era.'

"I certainly felt that I knew this dwelling the moment I stepped inside. It made me appreciate the works and life of one of Australia's leading artists. I then understood why Luke felt this urge for them to tour his home, gallery, and its surroundings. We walked through the historic home and then through the beautiful gardens. There were two studios with some of Norman's unfinished work. It was like looking into the past as one observed a famous artist that was not finished. It was an odd feeling. It made me want to step inside his room and complete the half-done canvass work. With the gorgeous view of the Blue Mountains, it was apparent why Norman Lindsay chose this location for his artwork.

"When we arrived at the cabin, Cyrus, Peter (Cyrus's son), Brigitte, and the rest of the family were waiting, except Rick and Anna. I was disappointed but was told that Anna or Rick didn't want to be near Cyrus. Family is family, and I wasn't going to ask why.

"Later that evening, Luke and I went for a walk. We watched the clouds roll in, forming an eagle, dolphin, and then a pair of eyes. It was as though someone was watching over us. Luke was a good-looking, 6-foot-tall man with dark hair. No one feature made Luke handsome, though his eyes come close. People often speak of the color of eyes, as if that were of importance, yet his eyes would be beautiful in any shade. From them comes an intensity, an honesty, a gentleness. Perhaps this is what is meant by a gentleman, not one of weakness or trite politeness, but one of great spirits and noble ways. What he is, what is beautiful about him, comes from deep within.

"We were attracted to each other, but I felt Luke's devotion to Wanda, and he did too. Luke and I continued our walk along the mountainous path happy as a leaf flowing upon a river.

"Early Sunday morning, after a good night sleep, I woke up at 5:00 a.m. I felt energized, and I thought anything was possible in this magnificent land of the down under. I quietly took a shower and then sat at the kitchen table. The window view calmed my soul; it was as if those mountains cradled me. The writings quickly started with words about a medicine man, drums, rainbows, and Hawaii.

"Luke was the first to rise and came rushing in with his white night shirt, showing his long hairy legs. I knew his smile was an inspiration when he saw I was writing. I could see how his smile came from deep inside lightening his eyes and spread into every part of him. He started a fire to rid the cabin chill. While cooking breakfast, the rest of the family came in. I was busy frying eggs, Cyrus yelled, 'You're not frying the eggs right; you're flipping them too soon.' I spun around and handed him the spatula, telling him to do it himself. Then tears burst forth like water from a dam, spilling down my face. I felt the muscles of my chin tremble like a small child. I rushed outside to gain control of my hurt feelings.

"Suddenly my crying turned into sobbing. It was my tears that kept my soul alive in the furnace of this pain. They cannot extinguish what has been, yet only carry a person forward until a time comes when that searing pain is distant enough to forget more than remembering, and one day erase itself from my brain.

"I went back inside thinking I had control and to find Luke had fried the eggs. I tried to stop this emotional outburst, but it was impossible. I went back outside crying. This time, I realized the tears were more than just being yelled at about how to fry eggs. My emotions were heavy, and I wanted to go home. Luke came out asking if I was okay. I knew life was too short of making such a big deal out of nothing, but my eyes dripped with tears. My walls, the walls that hold me up, make me strong just... collapse. Salty drops fell from my chin, drenching my blouse. I couldn't stop. Even as I pressed my hand against my face, it was raw, everything, raw tears, raw emotions. I thought I couldn't stop... I can't stop. Why can I not stop crying?

"Luke said, 'Come on, Shirl. Let's go for a walk.' We walked until I finally gained control. Luke handed me a handkerchief, I quickly wiped away my tears, blew my nose, and we went inside. Brigitte started telling jokes and everyone was laughing.

"The walk was the same as my dreams. The path was filled with colorful bushes, flowers, Blue Gum trees, and birds were singing as though to welcome us. The roaring of the waterfall was God's graceful poetry told at full roar. There was something about the violent cascade of water down the side of a mountain that was thrilling. The spray of the water, the slippery footholds, and the smell of the clean mountain air mixed with the scents of the trees, all combined with the adrenalin rush created by the voices I heard in my head. God had created such an incredible playground in the wilderness for people to explore. Every day brought a new adventure, a new sight, a unique experience. How much more of blessings in this life can one hope for?

From a distance, the waterfall had been like a silent white stream cascading over the rocky outcrops. As we were drawn closer, the noise had increased steadily until we were only a few hundred feet away. We could no longer even shout to one another over the deafening roar of the water. Closer still, we drew until we were in the plume of water vapor that hung over the plunge pool. In only minutes, I was as wet as I would have been in any rainstorm. My hair clung to my head and around my face, but no matter how wet I became, it could not dampen my spirits. We stood in awe.

"I felt like a kid at Disney World for the first time. I finally completed my waterfall dream. The water rapidly tumbled down the mountain to a bliss-pool at the bottom, and the trees next to it were nodding."

CHAPTER 10

At the Falls

Shirley felt like she had stepped out of the modern world and gained a lifetime of priceless spiritual wisdom.

Shirley—1990

"Luke and I stood under the falls watching the pounding water on the edge. There was a brilliance of power in the tranquility, a place of stillness even in the roar of the water. I could watch this streaming water even in my sleep. It was not the gentle sort of waterfall you might see in a garden; it was the kind where torrents of water are poured over rocks hard enough to crack your skull and mash your brains on the way down, and then swirl in a plunge pool below deep enough to drown you if you survived the fall. From the bottom, it was awe-inspiring. From the top, it was brutal and terrifying. It was an invigorating feeling filled with the desire for a new life. We laughed and acted like children who were doing something we weren't supposed to.

"Then this laugh came from Luke like a newly sprung leak—timid at first, stopping and starting. He wasn't done yet, though. I could tell from the way he rolled his brown eyes to the sky and half bit his lip. From deep inside his chest came a great shaking motion and his face muscles grew tight. I folded my arms, eyes wide open, waiting. In moments, Luke's laugh was more like a bust water main arching into the brilliant summer sky soaking everyone around him with unrestrained gales that debilitated him to a picture of glee. I wanted to stay straight-faced, flip my hair, and storm off—after all, he was laughing at me, not with me. But before I could stop myself, my poker-straight mouth twitched upwards, and I was giggling despite myself. 'You Americans,' Luke blurted out, 'are all the same. You love waterfalls but don't want to get wet and you want to touch the moss. Well, you're wet. Your mascara has blackened your eyes and your hair is a mess.'

"Cold water was seeping into my shoes, stealing the heat from my soles. My face soaked, the drops coming together to run into my eyes and drip from my chin. Cold water is the most efficient thief of heat, I know. It takes what it does not need. My skin was rough with goosebumps, pointless as they are.

"Holding my crystal, I held my hand under the rushing water, which caused my hand to sting while it sprayed, making me scream. I was cold and shivering, causing my teeth to chatter. I started laughing. As my laughter rose and Luke joined in; our laughter echoed through the mountains.

"Luke had brought a towel and to keep me warm he gave me his sweater. He didn't want his American friend to be cold. I knelt, touching the soft velvet moss that reminded me of Maggy. She taught me the health benefits of standing on moss. I loved it.

"Luke replied, 'The ending of life is expected; we all live in this mortal plane. What I resent is that death is longer and more painful than it needs to be. Wanda's body is self-destructing, day by day. The tumor is growing, spreading, consuming, and squashing the very organs that work to sustain it. She's had a fairly good life, better than most; I know she doesn't need to hang. An "exit" pill would be kinder than the hospice staff."

"We were hugging in consolation when the rest of the family walked around the bend of the falls. They weirdly looked at us but continued walking on, out of sight.

"Luke, you know what they are thinking?' I asked."

"He said, 'Shirl, I don't care. It's my time, and you make me feel good. I have to get this pain out of me.'

"Luke was considerate, a good artist, and we were friends. We just march to the beat of a different drummer.

We continued our walk until we came across a rock shaped like a chair, we stopped and sat down.

Luke asked, 'How do you recharge your crystals?'

"I told him some of my stories about the Indians and UFOs. Luke, reached over, took my hand, and said, 'Look, Shirl, where we are. This is why you are telling your stories. It's the energy from these hieroglyphics."

"I felt like I had stepped out of the modern world and gained a lifetime of priceless spiritual wisdom.

"Then he said, 'Shirl, Anna knows something is wrong. You are a good person who helps and gives to people. We are concerned about you. Are you okay?'

"I'm okay, Luke. Let's have fun. Life is to be happy," I replied.

"He agreed and said, he, Anna and Rick, wanted to take me for a picnic on the beach."

~~~

"I was sitting on the patio writing letters when Luke came to pick me up, for our picnic at Palm Beach. We met Rick and Anna, at a park, spread a blanket, and ate fish and chips. After Luke swam, we started walking towards the car. Luke invited me to visit his home art studio.

"The studio was a spacious room with large windows and a view of large trees and green bushes.

"Luke said, 'Green leaves protect the earth, earth that cherishes their lacy roots.'

"The brilliant greens banished every dark thought, and the sky lifted the eye in a way that brought me to admire the strands of drifting white clouds. The trees were deep with late spring foliage and the flowers rioted in the jubilant way that only the most divine of blooms can. The landscape was every vivid color, every one of them as fresh as a new painting straight from France.

"Luke pulled out a large drawing drawer filled with several big paintings. I didn't know much about art or an artist, so I asked Luke.

"'Art is part of our human soul,' he answered. 'It is dreams emerging from a part of me, a way to communicate with the deeper self of both the artist and others. The same piece evokes different emotions depending on the person, their mood, their time of life. Art is pictures; art is sculpture; art is the creative word; art is music. We are all artists in our various ways, all born to be creative. Now, Shirl, it's time for you to pick out two of my paintings to take home and remember me with.'

"I was excited to see his art studio, to see how he did his paintings and to think I would get to take them back home. I felt very touched that he wanted me to remember him by taking a painting home.

"One was titled *The Phoenix*, and the other was a woman's upper body, titled *A Woman*. He had made a sculpture piece for this painting, so I was given that, too. He carefully packed them for my trip back home. When I showed Cyrus and Brigitte my gifts, to my surprise, Cyrus became angry.

"He sharply asked, 'Do you realize how priceless those paintings are?'

"I felt a jab of hurt when Cyrus said that...like he thought I was a thief stealing them. I let him know I didn't ask, and that Luke voluntarily gifted them to me, and I was thankful.

"I thought to myself *I feel happy now and I'm not going to allow Cyrus or anyone to spoil it. Happiness is in everything, and it brings forth different emotions. I want to enjoy the moment, being present for that gift that is living while allowing it to become intense.*"

~~~

"Cyrus decided it would be nice to take a trip where he once had filmed on a friend's sheep station. I was excited to get out of the city and hopefully connect with the Aborigines.

"Before leaving, we visited Wanda at the hospital. We met Luke there and were informed Wanda's medical report was not good. Cyrus told Luke where we were going and gave him a phone number in case we needed to be contacted.

"We chose a small motel close to the 98,000-acre Kalyankia sheep station located near Wilcannia. The station was an enchanting place on the Darling River, with lots of trees along the riverbanks. The rest of the acreage was red dirt desert. The owners were gone on vacation, but their son Bart and wife Jackie were taking care of the station.

"After Bart and Jackie greeted us, Bart recommended we go for an afternoon drive. Gazing straight ahead, only half-aware of a world outside the claustrophobic comfort of the SUV, of Cyrus's hands stroking the wheel, the almost soundless changing of the gears. It was intriguing to watch the ostriches and kangaroos running along the side of Cyrus's four-wheeler! Suddenly, he drove up this embankment and we were looking down at a gigantic pond filled with black and white swans and different ducks. Their honking and quacking sounds noisily filled the air."

At this point, Patrick stood up and walked to the patio railing and said, "That would be a sight to see."

"Oh yes, and those birds would be moving through the water like they had some kind of outboard motor. They don't though."

"Oh yes, Patrick continued. "Underneath the surface their legs are working hard to move them along at that speed. The effort never shows on their faces, but then swans and ducks have the emotional range of a wet hanky. As a duck alights from air, it almost jumps. It lands with a splash making a long wake behind it, the ripples spreading out like those behind a speedboat, meeting the banks before rebounding and fading."

I continued, "On the surface of the pond a duck, white with the most orange bill was dipping his head in the water and shaking it. The drops flew outward landing in the almost ripple-free water to make tiny waves that moved outward in ever growing circles. The ducks quacked and swam toward us when suddenly they realized people were near and flew off."

The sunset looked like someone had poured a mixture of orange and red over the blue sky. As the sun set lower, the sky became like a canvas with a drawing of a big battleship. Gazing at this sky scene made me feel like my child self was set free, inviting me to join the infinite horizon of my soul, it was truly a lovely time.

~~~

"That early morning hour, it had rained. I thought honeyed rain before a golden sun promises new rainbows for the day, but not so good to drive in the desert. There was a loud noise. Thump, thump thump… And suddenly the vehicle came to a screeching halt, jerking us forward. The men got out, talking how great it was to have a wench with this four-wheeler. Cyrus said, 'Look, there is a tree. I'll use the tree to wench, and we will be out of here in no time.'

"Bart standing near the window explained, 'Shirl, our land is a honeycomb so when it rains it will cause big holes. That is what we are in.

We are stuck in an Australian mud hole. Now, no worries, Cyrus's winch has enough controlled power to pull this vehicle back onto its wheels.' The men quickly fastened the wench, but something snapped.

"Cyrus began yelling, 'Get out! Something damaged the motor, and we would have to walk back.'

"Brigitte easily got out standing by, but when I stepped out, I started sinking; it felt like the earth was sucking me inside, sinking fast and it made me feel the ground was going to swallow me up. My thoughts were, *I have stepped into quicksand and my whole body is going to sink. I will be buried alive.* Finally, I stopped at my shoulders, the thick red paste clung to my body, and it was as if the smell of earth had entered my blood and was not allowing me to get myself out. I felt panicky, and it seemed like forever; Brigitte realized I was in trouble. The men stood staring at me like they were frozen; Brigitte put out her hand and I grabbed it. Covered in this red mud clinging to my body made me want to cry. I was wet and muddy, and we had a long walk back.

"Bart warned us that we had a lengthy walk, and nightfall will soon be upon us. It would be extremely easy to lose our direction, and people have been known to be lost for days and even died. But don't worry, he'd told us. No worry, he was a Bushman and to follow him. Suddenly we heard Bart yelling, 'Don't follow your Bushman!' He had walked into a mud hole. Standing in this hole up to his chest as he is laughing yelled, 'Getting muddy was all part of the Bushman's experience.'

"The long walk was filled with stickers, and the earth felt like it was moving. Bart explained the land being honeycomb, and at night the kangaroos hopping, literally shakes the ground.

"I had a very uneasy feeling.

~~~

"What made you feel uneasy, Shirley? Were you scared?" Patrick asked in a friendly way.

"The eerie darkness of that night would never escape my memory. I clearly remember the pitch-black curtain draped over the sky, and the twisted, warped shapes that the stars made against the blackness. The milky speckles twirled and danced along the sky in various patterns. It was hard to shove aside the worries of animals attacking; my thoughts were corrupting my mind, but eventually, I stopped walking and just... stopped thinking. I wasn't alone. Not a single thing would harm me. I stared up at the sky and studied the silver glow of the moon. The moon under siege by stars seemed to lighten the night bringing forth stars that shone and hung in the blackness. Even the shadows were swallowed by the encroaching darkness. In the gathering gloom, the stars and the moon shone brighter in the sky, as if to remind us that even in the darkness there is light."

~~~

"I watched the way others walked, in one direction, weaving a little, chatting as they went. Brigitte walked with her head down and lost in thought. Bart and Cyrus walked differently; they were striving men protecting the women. Brigitte didn't have the proper shoes, causing her to struggle. After hours of what felt like endless walking, Bart yelled, 'We have made it to a road!' Cyrus yelled back, 'Now for a car to come and pick us up!'

"The dirt road stretched onward, hugging the land, making each turn an easy stride. It was a red dirt road that welcomed us. Soon, we saw the lights of a vehicle, and as it got closer, the sounds, letting us know it was a truck. Bart flagged it down. The cab was full of family members, but they offered Bart a ride in the back of their truck, to his home. We continued to walk until he returned. Happiness is what we all felt once Bart pulled up and laughingly asked if we needed a ride."

~~~

"We could hear the phone ringing as Cyrus struggled to unlock the door. Finally, it opened with a creaking noise, bringing in a chill, for it sounded like some dying animal, crying out its pain and sorrow with its last breath. We hoped it wasn't the news that all three of us were thinking; however, it was Luke. Wanda had passed away at 5:45 p.m. Cyrus had been told the vehicle part had to be ordered, and then bused to the sheep station from Broken Hill. It was important for Brigitte to get back to Sydney to be with her family. She started crying when Cyrus explained the vehicle part wouldn't be in for a week or so. Brigitte would have to go back by herself.

"Later that evening after Cyrus returned from taking Brigitte to the bus station, he took a shower and went straight to bed. I decided since it was a clear night it would be a good night for a view of the Southern Cross.

"I stepped outside and had a weird feeling. I noticed the darkness caused my senses to enlighten. There were only small sounds of rustling bushes and the howl of the wind. This night robbed me of one sense and heightened the others. This darkness was disorientating to be almost blinded but given the ears of a wolf and my sense of smell was sensitized to the loam in the earth. I didn't know what lay in the dark night. All I knew was it was going to be a peaceful journey.

"When I tilted my head skyward, I could clearly see millions of bright stars dotted on the black canvas of night. The chilly night air made me feel good about having a warm jacket. Looking up at the bright sky, the Southern Cross brightly stood out in the dark sky. It gave me chills. Mysteriously, the four stars that comprised the Crux constellation looked like a perfect small cross. It was a symbol of a cross from Mother Earth and Father Sky. I marveled that the nightly sky had guided travelers, inspired writers and astronomers who still enjoyed and cherished the time of seeing the Southern Cross. I heard a sound, and knew it was a didgeridoo. The music's rhythm created a peaceful and clamming energy flowing through my body. The stars were the only light. However, there was an orange glow flickering from afar.

CHAPTER 11

Dream Time

He didn't scare her, and there was no need to talk for Shirley as she heard clearly what this man was thinking.

Shirley—1990

"I slowly walked toward that direction when out of the darkness, a man slipped out from behind a tree and started walking beside me. He didn't scare me, and there was no need to talk because I heard clearly what this man was thinking. This was the same telepathic experience I had at the Hopi Reservation.

"We continued walking slowly, I heard him say, 'When your love becomes your protective inner lion who is the servant of self-love, bound in duty to obey the light, the darkness becomes the softest of black velvets illuminated by heaven-spun stars.'

"We were walkers of the velvet night, born to embrace each onward path and seek horizons others dare not gaze upon. We came upon the campfire where people were sitting in a circle around a glowing fire. The dim, lambent light cast by the flame showed several dark skins. No words were spoken, yet I felt safe with these people. I knew they were the Aborigines that Richard, my Shaman friend, said I would meet.

"The blazing fire formed into a golden ball, igniting a glow that highlighted a face. I could easily see that the map of wrinkles on his face told of the most incredible journey. His eye lines told of laughter, of warm smiles and affection. His forehead told of worries past and worries present. But mostly, they were so deeply engrained, they told of a man who had travelled through eight decades to that moment. They made room for me to sit by this dark-skinned, white-headed elderly man.

"Telepathically I heard him say, 'I am Grandfather.' Then he turned toward me and nodded as a jester to make sure I heard his thoughts. Letting him know, I nodded back.

"We know you are the Golden Mother. We knew you were coming. Our ancestors told us. Arriving here completes your full circle with our teachings. You understand when we say, 'We are on this planet, but we are not from this planet; we are from Orion. You already know through the Orion constellation there is a planet named Orion, our home. We still enjoy the sight of the Milky Way Galaxy directly above us. We have named the groups of constellations. The Southern Cross is known as Dream Land. The heaven is our blueprint so what people think and do here on Earth is printed in the sky for all to see. Every moment people breathe, move, express, connect, create sound, light, and frequencies are etched in the heavens. People are connected in all ways through holographic images. Every single movement you make affects another as it affects the whole. Every thought, word, and action, conscious or unconscious, changes the energy field and everything within and around them. It is through these energy sounds that heals everything.'

"It felt like a hot blue fire was flickering in my heart and soon started to grow. It was burning within me, all the dark unbalanced emotional energy in its path. I began to cry and crying felt good, especially when they were tears that I didn't want to push away. They weren't drops of sadness. NO. They were more like the feeling of joy, relief, happiness, and freedom streaming away from my eyes. They were temporary cleaners to wash away the old pain. I had never cried like this. It just wasn't like me. But that night, under the protection of millions of stars and around these wonderful people I felt so safe that I could let the floodgates open with a single snap of my fingers. I stared at the fire as I continued to allow my pain to run away forever. Everyone knew what was happening to me. I was giving birth to a new spiritual awakening. It is called a spiritual rebirth.

~~~

Patrick walked over to me and patted my shoulder. "I hate that you had to cry so much," he said.

"It was a release," I heard Grandfather say. "You know our DNA has been proven to be the oldest on Earth. We have great respect for this planet. People must understand the Earth is our Mother. Mother Nature and her beauty is a beautiful piece of art. People need not forget the sky is our father. Father Sky has great beauty and is all mighty. He changes our scenes from daytime to darkness, from sunshine to moonbeams. Mother Earth and Father Sky's energy fills the sky like a canvas for their symbol of love. Earth nurtures everything. Father Sky sends energy to assist Mother Earth in nurturing." Then, Grandfather was silent as I looked up to the sky. He knew I needed some time to think.

~~~

Shortly, Grandfather continued, "Mother Earth's harmony was in balance, and it has been taken out and must be put back. And that is why people must again learn to love one another. People must realize they are only visitors on this planet. People have lost their truth. They no longer trust themselves, so they look to others for their answers. In doing so, it has created many lies, fear, and greed to take over this beautiful planet. Words have strong powers, and they can shake a person to their roots and create a new concept of life. Embracing any challenge will take them away. People have become lazy, wanting someone else to take care of their life's unbalanced situations."

Again, he gave me a few minutes to savor his words.

"People are lost!" he sent out the thought. "They have lost themselves making it necessary to start all over again on this great planet Earth. They must start all over again to get back to the basics of life to know their power of Self. Earth has a vibratory field that connects everything on this planet. People have lost their connecting power of love. They must learn that their hearts will fix themselves. It's their minds that lock in memories of hurts and pains. People need to convince their minds to let go because the heart knows how to heal and move on with life. To love yourself is to understand the hidden secret connection to the power of love. Love is like a river. It flows and flows into the bigger sea."

My eyes watered with tears. I solely understood because I had experienced some of those things.

Grandfather began again. "People are lost in lies. The only thing they know to search for is betrayal. It slowly seeped in how many fools we have living in our own dream world when truthfully, we are living in a wasteland filled with lies and greed. It is as though the humans are in a horrible blizzard not allowing us to know which direction to go. The ancients had taken the landmarks with them. The usual spiritual landmarks are hidden. The true secret is inside our heart. This enormous flow of love flows into the higher consciousness connected with universal love energy. Nothing will stop the flow except FEAR. People have allowed their fear to disconnect everything and create everything to be out of harmony balance."

Fear is the source of any negative situation with life and our great planet earth. It's the polarity of love, positive energy that has been taken creating Earth's power to be out of polarity. A true balance of earth's energy, the polarity is vibrations of negative and positive energy. The power of love is the All of the All. All hearts know of love; it's the brain that sidetracks the great love.

"It is the people that have disconnected the Earth's energy field. People are Earth's living life cells. They have created disharmony, and it must be changed. This significant change will have occurred through the basic steps of learning to love and trusting themselves once again. It can be done with people through baby steps of learning self-love."

I thought this to be true. I understood people were afraid of their future and most didn't like their past. I believed that neither exists in any place but their imagination; even memory must be imagined. Fear will take people by the hand to the things they keep and guard as precious. For some reason, I had always faced fear with courage, understood it, and then let it go.

"Allow your fears to wake you up. Let them show you the path to your true self, to your brave soul whose love shines like a star," Grandfather confirmed. "This fear is useless once you realize it. For without fear, love is brighter, stronger."

The man who walked with me was stirring the fire with a long stick. He told me that we know that everyone exists eternally in Dream Time. Dream Time is known as the 'time before time' because it has the energy of beliefs and spirituality. Dream Time consists of many parts. It has the story of happenings connected with the Universe and how humans were created to function with the cosmos. The potency of Dream Time constitutes the sacredness of Earth. People must practice more to love and to learn the connection with the Universal Love power. Our legends of Dream Time have been handed down by word of mouth from generation to generation. We have secret rituals, rites, dancing, and colorful art, for they are forms we use to pass on great stories of Earth's creation.

The glowing fire whispered low with each flickering flame dispensing an indiscernible secret enhancing Grandfather's stories. To know love is to know a star has been born in the heavens. To express love is to have touched another for that heavenly moment. He went on telling me that one must take time to be still, with every great idea there is a silence of the soul, of the self, so welcome it and listen. It is through silence people will see the wonders of a new planet Earth created. The celestial objects in the sky show how we conduct ourselves. What we do on land will transpose into the sky.

Dream Time has shown the Pleiades; the seven sisters left Earth and flew into the sky. Before going, they went into the mountains and made springs of water to feed the rivers that flowed into the sea. The waters represent the creation and cultures here on Earth. The alignment in the heavens is like a blueprint upon which those on Earth can follow. The Pleiades is a major factor for they represent the Goddess Neith, the Divine Mother of Heaven. Anytime humans have calmness within, they have found peace, love, harmony, and balance for they are all within.

I felt the urge to lie back on the ground. As I did, I relished Grandfather's words.

"People must learn to align with the natural law. It has been said that wise people see the results of their actions. The slow learner of natural law doesn't seem to get the result of their actions. On one level, there is cosmic flow and cosmic ramifications. The other level must do with natural law. If you try to break the laws of nature, they will crush you. It's not a break-even situation. You will lose. People must learn it's not what they have materially outside; it's what they have inside. Integrity, love, and truth are the keys to success for any soul. Humanity has made their struggle through greed. They must learn to love and trust again."

I stretched my body, letting it soak into the earth sending out my thoughts to Grandfather. *My heart belongs to Mother Earth. I love her so. She is beautiful; she is wonder; she is heaven by divine design. She is ecology; she is genetics; her lifeforms evolve and our love for her is absolute. In this wide universe, there can be no finer planet for any species than their natural home. I say to people, 'Please, open your eyes and see this Planet Earth's gifts. What more do you want? What more do you need? Somewhere above this sky, born of the swirl galaxies of brilliant stars. We must not pollute Father Sky. We must allow the sky its energy freedom.'*

Grandfather continued, "Part of people's wisdom is to understand the laws of nature. Much of their work is to seek and know how they can align themselves with the laws of nature to optimize their function and their soul's expression on Earth. When they follow the natural laws, they can maximize the experience of that function."

This knowing is their sacred design of being able to express it. The minute that their mind takes control and not the cosmic awareness, they are no longer in the wisdom energy. When we talk about wisdom, there is a need to combine the understanding of the natural and cosmic laws in life to create the whole picture. Cosmic Law is the basic law of creation. The ever-changing creation of infinite variety that is grounded on stable plane of existence. Natural Law is knowing the difference from right and wrong. Those who lose their connection with the natural law will go into the energy of lies, fear, and greed. When people go into this negative energy, it is difficult to maintain, ultimately, an ongoing socially uplifting situation for life. It is a must to follow the natural ways allowing wisdom to align with the Divine.

People are unaware of how much thoughtfulness, heart-centered energy, the Great Spirit-centered energy, is needed. It keeps everyone on track in bringing forth their sacred design, as individuals and as the world, resonating with the highest wisdom consistently. Tell people, 'The treasure of life is knowledge. Knowledge is wisdom and wisdom is freedom.'"

The heat from the campfire seemed to suck into the air. A man added more wood, and sparks came, dancing embers of energetic flame. The heat felt good as the orange flames celebrated with their wild flickering dance. I thought that wisdom could be handed from one generation to another, but so can hate and intolerance. If people are wise, they learn to distinguish the positive from the negative and discard the latter. That way, they multiply what is wise and let go of the darkness that would lead them to the wrong thoughts.

Grandfather resumed, "People must learn that all answers to all questions are within. There is a saying, 'Show your love for all to see, for I am you and you are me—We are all One. One in consciousness.' Golden Mother, continue your path of light and others will see your rainbow colors. Your colors have an ultimate high, creating a sphere of energy that illuminates the sky. Your aura glows a rainbow color, and it flows through the air with great power to the Father Sky's connection out in the universe.

"The Rainbow Warriors call out while directing their love to you. They dance in the heavens on this great night as the drums do beat, spreading the news like the running feet of horses. Colors and light spread through the waves spreading peace and harmony along the way.

"Universal Love is kindness and truth so many search for, yet they do not understand. They call out to the wind; they look around to only find the search is their truth within. Humanity must learn to understand that love is the answer to the truth of all life. These words about Earth, Father Sky, and love must be told. Upon your return home, significant changes will happen. Even your lifestyle will be different."

"You have accomplished more than you realize. You have devoted friends, and they stand behind you. Bringing people together for this love project will not be an easy task, but you are devoted. It will be done. Changes are good. It is the energy created for you to teach Universal Love on this great planet Earth. Teach that we do live within our own hearts, within our own souls for the soul is what is before any consciousness.

People must learn without consciousness the body is dead material. When consciousness leaves the body, there is no individual, no world, and no God. Consciousness can only be conscious of itself when it has manifested in a physical form. We can only know who or what we are by personal experience, not others. We shall rejoice in our Dream Time."

I felt the power in his messages but began to tire. It felt like my brain was full. Then the man who walked me to this campfire, stood up, and I knew it was time to go. I felt sad and really didn't want to leave. It was a strange feeling as I knew this was my only time of having physical presences with my new friends. I continued to sit by the fire with my new friends thinking why I would want to leave now. I just found these loving friends, a place where fond memories grew as fast as the clover in the grass. I saved my memories so that I could live them again. I knew that the strands of love would keep us together in thoughts even when we were far apart. It is now time to depart so I could teach others what I had learned. My thoughts were going every direction, but all of them made sense.

Grandfather's telepathy sent me a message. "You have been with us longer than you realize. The night has slipped away. You can only absorb so much. However, we will always be with you in Dream Time. You connected with the Comanche medicine man, Hopi, and the Mayans, our brothers and sisters. Now you're related to us. You must go on and teach. People must learn that it's all about energy, love, and the importance of how to respect themselves and Earth. It is time for people to know every-thing is connected on Earth. It is time for the mystery of unknown truth to be solved. It is time to wake up and realize the higher truth of what is going on. It is time to see the good in every situation—to touch, taste, see and feel the essence of the greatness in every moment."

I stood up thinking that this mystery of unknown truth was so basic and natural that nobody could know or use it unless they were prepared by diligent self-purification. Then the mystery would be solved. I under-stood his words. It was time for the advancement of souls to know the transitional planetary energy awareness. All people are magnificent beings and creators living here on this wonderful planet Earth.

Self-love and universal love were something I had chosen to teach in my lifetime—words I heard for years from many sources. When everyone learns how to love themselves, then Earth would begin to mend her wounds. People needed to enjoy their life's circle, for their rewards would be an awareness of this great power of Earth's love connecting to Father Sky and then out to the universe. Their love would always be with me. Anytime I needed them, we would meet in Dream Time.

~~~

"You didn't want to leave, did you?" Patrick asked.

Nodding my head, I answered, "There is such sadness in leaving a place of strong love, a place where fond memories grow fast. I knew I would savor each memory so strongly that I could live them again and again. I knew that the strands of love will keep me and my friends together even when we were far apart. I only had to reach out with my mind and there they are, waiting to shower me with love. But right now, it is time to teach their messages of self-love to help Earth."

~~~

I felt as though it was a shorter walk back than it was going. I could feel the protective energy of this gentleman who was walking by my side. I stumbled over a branch, but before I fell, he grabbed me. He put his arms around me, and I laid my head on his broad, warm chest. I felt his heart beating, beating his enduring tender love and his arms felt so protective. It was different; it was like two hearts that become one on a different level of energy. It was a very magical time being held in the arms of this strange man under the Southern Cross.

He telecommunicated a message before we parted. "Love is like our breath. To live, we must have it. We sense it, but you really can't touch it. It's just there."

I walked unusually slow, robotically, as if my brain were struggling to tell each foot to take the next step. I honestly didn't want him to leave. I had a thought that love was the foundation of all humanity, and to build a solid foundation for self-love gives one the needed power to conquer all things. It was time to realize if I ever needed my new friends, I would meet them in Dream Time.

I was happy to get back at the Sydney airport and board my plane.

I loved Australia, especially its outback but like the saying, there is no place like home and three months is a long time away from home.

~~~

Patrick put his jacket on and said, "Your Australia story makes me feel content. So, with this content feeling I'm going to kiss you goodnight and leave. See you later, Shirley."

CHAPTER 12

Life Is Fun

With a firm voice Patrick gushed yes, but first, t
hey needed to talk.

Shirley—1990

The sunset was casting its brilliant colors as I walked into the Inn San Francisco, located near the Bay Area. It was a quaint place with an English garden capturing the spirit of the Victorian era.

I hurriedly unpacked knowing I was behind Patrick by two hours as his plane had already landed. I had just finished getting dressed when I heard a knock at the door. I quickly looked in the mirror before opening the door to a broad smiling Patrick, holding a bouquet of red roses in a crystal vase. We kissed, and I welcomed him in.

Stepping into the room, Patrick hugged me. His hugs could never be long enough for me. There is the hug of gentle arms that still gives the space to breathe; then there is the hug of strong arms that tells that their body, brain, and soul are with you. I loved both. In Patrick's arms, I felt safe, and my worries disappeared like rain on a summer day. In that embrace, I was cocooned more than any butterfly-to-be.

"I meditated and noticed that my ability to create colors has an amazing powerful energy. It created a laser beam that I could use to both send and receive information. I noted it's easy to be distracted because I familiarize myself to constantly change in the flow of the fast world, which I think dilutes the power of my energy. To me, an integral part of meditation is shutting down the distractible, my outer mind, so I can keep my attention upon what I desire with ease. Sometimes, meditation urges me to contemplate nothing or emptiness. While other times, the contemplation of something such as my breathing or the form of some object helps. What do you think? Which method works the best?"

I was re-arranging the roses. "The basic idea of meditation is to give the soul something to fix its attention upon while wrestling with and ultimately conquering the flow of impressions and thoughts. It is our lower minds normally that indulge in ceaselessly. When we succeed, and then our soul's consciousness—the real you—is awake but your body and mind are asleep.

I'm hungry. How about you?"

Patrick walked over to a love seat and sat down, "San Francisco is unfamiliar territory for me. Where do you recommend we have dinner?"

"Gold Dust Lounge at Fisherman's Wharf has a little bit of something for everyone. It has good food, a great bar, and music. Does that sound like a good idea to you, J. Patrick?" I replied playfully.

With a firm voice, Patrick gushed yes, but first, they needed to talk. He patted the cushion beside him. He told me that while we were apart, it gave him time to think. "It was difficult to concentrate on my business since my mind was with you."

Sitting on the love seat, he took my hand. "I have given you a new name, Shirley, and it's 'Favorite Person.' Do you like it?"

"Well, of course, I like it. My name for you will be 'My Love,'" I replied firmly.

"Oh yeah, right," Patrick said, making a face. "I'm a guy, and you don't call a guy My Love. Favorite Person. Do you really hear me when I tell you I've fallen for you? I need to know right now if you don't care. I need to know. I will walk out of your life and take the next flight back to Texas."

Instantly, I realized my problem. I was ruining my life with old memories. My first marriage was one of being controlled, and I swore never to marry again.

Nervously, I stared in Patrick's eyes. "I do care, and I love you too. This trip gave me the needed time apart to explore my new feelings too."

"Now, I'm ready to go eat," a smiling Patrick said.

After dinner, we both were tired and ready for our rooms. Tomorrow would be a day of helping Patrick better understand his warrior abilities in the Muir Woods Ancient Redwood Forest.

Lying in bed waiting for sleep, my mind wandered to the past few weeks.

When I'd first met Patrick, I hadn't paid that much attention since I was not going to marry again. Then when we started dating, I had to pay attention. I knew why I seldom dated men. I hadn't forgotten. I allowed the hurt from my first husband to affect my life.

Patrick had been calling and calling, wanting to know if we could have coffee or go for dinner. Patrick was always so charming and kind, but I wasn't entirely truthful with him because of my past. I thought those old emotions had been released and taken care of. Maggy had taught me, "Feelings are there to educate ourselves and others of the very real and necessary needs of the human soul." I thought, when I let one hand on my wheel be my feelings, and the other my intellect, I become my own GPS, always finding my way.

I knew it was time, "Know thyself, Shirley. If you are 'hung up' on yourself, then your life is hung up. Pick up that phone. Dial into your real self and figure out your true feelings. Figure out why you react and respond to situations the way you do. Will you have personal freedom with a good future for you and Patrick?"

In meditation, I visualized my memories in my head. The good, the bad, and the ugly. The positive. I reread the good ones more often; they reminded me of everyone's best traits. The bad or ugly ones I had reflected upon and come to a healthy form of acceptance, one that was protective of myself. The good memory and keep the bad and ugly in easy reach. The negative, I ignore. Thus, when I am in any combative frame of mind, I bring them up quickly and with force, creating negative emotions. By choosing my memories carefully, by learning how to process and let go of the bad and ugly memories, I can change and have a wide-open relationship with Patrick.

I visualized all my dark emotions into a golden balloon. As the balloon floated up, I could see a string attached to my heart. I visualized silver scissors, cut the cord, and watched the balloon disappear into the sky.

~~~

My mind ventured to one night while on a date, Patrick seemed in a strange mood. Finally, after dessert, he reached over the table and took both of my hand in his and said, "Shirley, do you honestly like me being in your life?"

"Patrick, until you came into my life, my love I protected with everything that I had, even my soul. I can only take down my barriers when there is safety and trust—something that only comes with a real sense of love. In my first marriage, I'd essentially lost my self-esteem. I had been climbing my way back when I met you. I didn't think I would ever meet a man who would respect me or even understand my career. My work is especially important to me, and my ex didn't approve. It was as though I was an embarrassment to him. I'm asking you to be patient, and I will drop my barriers. I'm not one who believes in fear. While training in law enforcement, my professor said since I had no fear, it worried them. Sometimes fear is good. It can be a warning device. When we first met, I was surprised. In Australia, I constantly dreamed about an Indian man who looked just like you."

I took a deep breath and continued, "To meet the person in your dreams is amazing yet a little unsettling. After meeting you, I asked myself if you would accept my spiritual beliefs, my goals to help others with this mighty Universal Love energy. Maggy left me trunks filled with information to teach about this Universal Love energy. I promised to get her books published and movies filmed. Will you expect me to live your life, or can you live in my life? I'm getting more comfortable with our relationship. I love your personality; you are kind and considerate, and your outgoingness is great. You appear to care about people and Earth. That is especially important to me. So, to answer your question: do I see myself with you? Yes, Patrick, I have fallen in love with you."

It felt good to me that Patrick was a straight, honest man who voiced his thoughts without fear. Had I finally met a man who was so secure in himself and in his own life that he was incapable of being jealous of mine? He praised my success, never envied it. He built me up. He never tore me down. His love felt like strong sunshine on a cold dreary day. And his love was a refuge to lean on, a safe place to land. Time had shown me his truth.

I woke up to a breathtaking sunshiny day and felt it would be a day filled with magic and wonder. Although sometimes one can feel intense sadness, profound happiness can be just around the corner. One step away. One thought away. One kiss away. Sources of joy are literally everywhere; one must overlook all the negative things in trying to cover them up. Life is always good. People must allow it to be.

CHAPTER 13

The Muir Woods

We. Are. Alone. Busy streets of cars, people, and noise are left behind, overthrown with tranquility.

Patrick—1990

I awakened realizing while reading the seminar manual that I had fallen asleep and had left the light on all night. I trotted off into the bathroom eager for my morning shower. There is nothing better than a good hot shower in the mornings to wake a man up. Invigorating, for sure.

I lifted my face to the warm water and started thinking about what this day might have to offer with Shirley's teachings. The Awakening Seminar manual was impressive, but I had questions. I was sure everyone did. I liked what she told me about the Muir Woods Ancient Redwood Forest. This forest was known as the Kingdom of the Giant because it has the tallest trees in the world. Shirley and I loved hugging trees. She had told me the park was magnificent yet unknown to most. It offers unforgettable experiences as a person walks along the quietest border by the stunning scenery of the ocean, meadows, rivers, wildlife, and redwoods.

After leaving our inn, we drove through the fog that had rolled in from the ocean as the rising sun heated the land.

"It's incredible how a little fog can turn an ordinary scene into something out of a dream," Shirley said.

"I've read your Universal Love Awakening workbook," I emphasized. "My first question is how and when was your first awakening?"

"My awakening started from the moment of giving birth to my second child. It was during an emergency cesarean I had a vision of Jesus. As the old saying goes 'When the pupil is ready the teacher appears.' Maggy Conn, a highly gifted intuitive woman, came into my life at this perfect time. That is exactly what happened for I found no one to answer my questions of what I was experiencing. To have someone give you the answers is nice. However, Maggy taught me all answers were within. Therefore, all she would do was to tell me stories. Through her stories and my experiences, my awakening was on a day-to-day basis. Often, I would say to Maggy, 'This is so simple. Why can't we just go and tell everybody?' The workbook has her stories and teachings."

I calmly asked, "What exactly do you have planned for me today, Shirley J. Smith, my awakening teacher? You better watch what you awaken in me, little girl."

"Now Patrick," she interrupted.

"Hey, I take this awakening stuff serious, Shirley. I want to learn about myself. Let's continue." I added.

"We will talk about the workbook, and I'll answer your questions. You never know in the Universal Love seminars what energy will surface to discuss. It carries the energy of releasing any old data that holds us back from a balanced life. We will walk the trails and have lunch at the Pelican Inn."

I asked, "Hmm, Pelican Inn. What kind of place is it?"

"It's a romantic escape over the hills to the beach. The Pelican Inn captures the spirit of sixteenth-century England's west country.

I interrupted: "My Grandpa was from England; he was a smart businessman. He died before my Granny."

Shirley continued, "The Inn rests at Muir Beach in the sea-blown fog, among the pines, alder trees, the honeysuckle, and jasmine. It's a lodging refuge between the ocean and Muir Woods. This place opens its doors for the fellowship of its Tudor bar, country cooking, overnight lodging, and a getaway of carefree feasting and relaxations. I think you will like their seafood."

Walking in Muir deep woods with its acoustic quality felt so inviting as though it held life's secret. After walking a mile or so, I asked Shirley in a quizzing way, what it was she wanted me to know/ I told her I sensed she had something to say, and that it would be special.

Shirley was taking each step slowly. "We are electric beings within the energy of nature and the universe. We are both receivers and transmitters of energy. We are constantly sending out signals that attract other vibrational beings. It's your decision what level you chose for your events of experiences. Earth's magical energy has the honor of having sunsets that are merely a prelude to the dawn, yet its majesty fills one's mind with the most beautiful dreams. As your eyes drift to rest, you are one with the stars, your skin cooled by the breeze, and when you awake the sky will radiate with the first kiss of the new day. Concentrate on what I just said, and you will start feeling an energy shift of new vibration. It's all done by our thoughts and emotions."

We came across a large log that was perfect for sitting on. I looked up at the large redwood trees and remarked that the forest impacts lives in so many ways, from the air a person breathes to the wood they use. These trees, this mighty feat of nature, have taken so many years to grow, all those tiny moments morphing imperceptibly into the present. Yet, that is the thing about growth. It is only when we compare with a sense of the months and years past that one can make such amazing changes.

"I'm glad you picked this place to teach. It's a perfect setting for us."

Shirley asked me, "Are you discontent with your life? If you are, then change it. Move elsewhere. Do something else. This world is not a single plane; it is vast and varied and waiting for you to experience it."

"Uh? I'm happy now. There are some things in my past I would like to change, but that's all," I replied.

Shirley stood up and looked at the sky. Then, she turned to me and said, "If today is not a good day, wake up and start a better day. Better yet, close your eyes for one minute and open them looking for the beauty, the complexity, the awesomeness that is this on earth. Forget the ugliness, the adversity, the vacuous nature that so many impose upon the world for those details are not worth paying attention to, nor remembering."

I patted the log for Shirley to sit back down and she did.

"What good does your negative thoughts and actions serve? They only hurt or suppress positivity. It is only with optimism, altruism, and compassion that we can cure this world of its ills. Judgment, hatred, egotism, bitterness, and despair only bring more negativity into a world already riddled with problems. Even an exceedingly small amount of good can exponentially spread because there are so many who prefer the bad on Earth."

"I have found," I said with interest, "it's best to surround yourself with people you can trust."

Shirley calmly said that when regarding the good, people are the ultimate source of it. Every single human being is entirely different from their own flaws, skills, experiences, secrets, and dreams. Every man and woman hold inside them a story so infinitely interesting that it could be never told completely in a book or conversation. People cannot be defined as ignorant, petty, or selfish. Every person is a unique being shaped by the infinite number of variables that our Earth-bound existences offer them.

"The Earth is a museum, and we all are the art within it. Study all the art regardless of its shape, color or texture, and you will gain a greater understanding of the museum."

A noisy woodpecker got our attention. It took a while to locate the bird, but I pointed it out and asked her what the meaning of this woodpecker visiting us was.

Shirley quickly responded, "A woodpecker totem is letting you know that it is time to pay attention because an opportunity has come knocking along with it. In other words, the woodpecker is signaling you that great changes are happening in your life. Therefore, it is up to you to seize the moment. Whether it is the renewal of an old project, the finishing of a new project or simply a serendipitous meeting with someone in your life. Furthermore, whatever way you perceive it, you must understand that the door is wide open for you right then and that success is yours for the taking."

"I like changes sometimes," I muttered.

Shirley just looked at me with a look, "Time to continue with the awakening teachings now. Life is what you make of it. Life is perception: sight, taste, smell, sound, and touch. Reality depends upon the intensity and angle with which light hits your eyes. Reality sounds are only because of the way your brains decipher the vibrations of the air around you."

I started running away, spun around and ran back giving her a hug that almost knocked her over. She started laughing but became serious again.

"A negative sensory input can be a source of anguish, or simply an inspiration to change everything and attract more positive inputs. It is up to you and you alone. No one thing or one person can decide or influence how you feel. That is entirely up to you. Decide to be happy about life, and you will remain that way. It is your perception, so why not make it a positive perception? We live in a beautiful world. It's time to see the beauty. It's ever pervading and impossible to miss unless your eyes are closed. So, open them."

"Yes, ma'am!" I said, as I opened my eyes as wide as I could and stared at her without blinking.

We stood up and started walking again. Shirley told me that Maggy had taught her that people create their own storms. "Do you have any old emotions that you need to talk about? Maybe some old emotions that are blocking you from flowing your energy. Do you understand or feel the powerful healing energy you have? It truly feels like a warrior's energy to me. Have you ever heard or know what a warrior is? I feel you are a warrior who has no idea about your warrior abilities or its power."

I was a little perplexed. I said, "That's what my Cherokee granny told me when I was about five or six years old. She would say 'J. Patrick, you are a warrior and a healer. Now don't throw your sexual energy to the swine. Instead of using it with women, you must use it to heal.' And I must admit I have thrown my sexual energy to the women—thousands of times. One time while in college, my roommate and I had a bet as to who could have sex with the most women in a year, and I won. Later in life, when I was married, I came home early from work and caught my wife in bed with one of the guys who worked for me. After knocking him around a few times, it didn't take me long to get a divorce. Granny also told me it wasn't necessary to fight. I always liked fighting and the more blood, the better in my mind. I didn't understand or appreciate what Granny was saying. I always thought a warrior was one who engaged aggressively or energetically in war. What is the meaning of a warrior?"

Shirley was surprised that I told her about my bet with my college roommate, but she tried not show it. She said in a nonplussed way, Sitting Bull said, "The warrior, is one who sacrifices himself for the good of others. His task is to take care of the elderly, the defenseless, those who cannot provide for themselves and above all, the children - the future of humanity." I was also told, "A warrior is a person who knows his power, and he challenges fear, lies, false beliefs, and judgments that create suffering and unhappiness on this planet Earth. Leon told me a spiritual warrior faces challenges with clarity and awareness. The only war within any spiritual warrior is fought within himself and truth, and unconditional love is on the other side of these battles. To win the war against fear requires awareness, courage, discipline, and commitment to transform the emotional body. The first and most vital tool of a warrior is awareness. One may think they are aware, but pure awareness has no thinking involved. It has no thought because it has no interpretation. Awareness is to perceive with clarity the truth of what is happening without interpretation or opinion. In a moment of awareness, the dialogue in the mind stops. You are 'seeing' from a point or view separate from the reasoning part of your mind. Warriors live in awareness at every moment."

I pointed my finger in the air, "Whoa, every day I am aware. It must be with my type of work and really with my life. The oil and gas business, working with machinery and earth can cause catastrophic incidents making me responsible for men's lives."

Shirley smiled and continued. "Spiritual awareness is essential because it is the state of consciousness that allows you to discern between the facts and the truth, and between the story and what lies in your mind. The realm of your mind is filled with false perceptions and false beliefs. While the mind can be very clever with stories and lies, it is the consciousness of awareness that is the discerning intelligence. You may use highly intelligent reasoning to make a decision that is not good for you; only to look at it in hindsight and realize that you discounted indicators that told you otherwise. The mind is clever, but it is also full of assumptions and limited paradigms of perception. Conscious awareness allows us to see clearly instead of being blinded by these false belief paradigms."

"Now that we have met, it will be different, Favorite Person. I honestly want to learn about my warrior abilities and energy and what I have chosen to do. I have promised you I'll not fight anymore, and I have no interest in other women. I'll make my life suitable for my warrior energy to flow for healing and assisting Earth. I like working in my business, but I've never met anyone to help me understand my spiritual or warrior abilities. Although Granny tried. Most of the time I follow my gut hunch and sometimes it would get loud if I didn't. But it's always served its purpose, and I do trust it," I said.

Shirley stopped and touched a tree. I listened. The forest was filled with the deafening sound of nothing. Just us in the whispering redwood trees filled with awakening wonder drawing us inside in awe. We weren't in control of our bodies, as the forest brought us in with a force stronger than any gravitational pull could compel. As we stepped, one foot in front of the other, we listened to the trees.

"What are they telling us? What do they say? We. Are. Alone. Busy streets of cars, people, and noises are left behind, overthrown with tranquility."

The damp smell of the pungent scent of the tree underneath our feet was strong. Our noses tingled with the scent of mystery.

Shirley asked, "Patrick, have you never experienced such a rush of power, connection, and peace before that you are too overwhelmed to continue? Do you feel you have been put on pause by the remote of life? Do you feel at any time that nothing could touch you but the slight wind? Step by step you remembered how to walk and continued slowly, taking in your surroundings?"

I yelled, "I'll have to say my senses are full of joy."

"Have you been meditating?" Shirley calmly asked.

"Yes, every night. I have trouble sleeping. If someone or something touches me or makes a noise, it causes my body to jerk and come up swinging. It's been that way since I returned from Vietnam."

"What do you think happened to create this emotional action? You must release it."

I stood stone still. "A good soldier never talks about the war. What meditation do I need for releasing it?"

Shirley knew I was ready for what she was going to say. "Through automatic writings, I was given a subconscious clearing meditation. A Dallas psychologist and her patients tried it with success. I will teach you. This meditation with your energy will release and calm your emotional body."

We found a mossy area for me to lie on the ground for my meditation.

~~~

After my meditation, we continued our walk. I appeared to be lighter and more relaxed.

It was a short drive to the Pelican Inn. The surrounding had colorful flowers and their aroma created a peaceful place.

"Our everyday rush of life creates a fast pace of energy rushing us through each day. It affects us to only look at the outside world. Turning the dial to news be radio, television, or reading the newspaper you will see the negative actions throughout the world."

She took a bite of her salmon, watched me eat my crab cakes and continued. "This is an example of humanly creative negative energy within the human mind projecting itself into the individual's conscious mind. Once you acknowledge your energy within, you will connect with your higher self. It is the higher self-vibration that connects with God or a Higher Power allowing you to receive guidance from that source."

I put my fork down and asked, "What if I question myself?"

Shirley took a sip of her water and continued, "You may often question yourself about who you are, what you need to know, what you need to do, and what your lesson is. By doing so, you will then create a force of energy allowing yourself to realize your special talents on the physical, emotional, mental, and spiritual levels. Having harmony for your human needs allows the reality of your master self to come forth. When you look within you, then you can turn to your mind relating and know your power thinking. It is through this power thinking you can tap into the spiritual realm of self's hidden mysteries."

I told her I attended a Catholic School, and sometimes the nuns answered my questions. However, most of the time I found my own answers. Any time I questioned their belief, the nun would hit my knuckles with a ruler. "I got sent to the principal office many times," I told her.

Shirley laughed, "I bet you did! Let me go on. The history of our disconnection is in the book of Mark written in circa 55, which was many years after the crucifixion. Someone had to have an excellent memory to write about him, word for word."

"Just like mine," I retorted.

Shirley smiled and moved closer to me. "Man did have good memories in those days for all the myths started when Mark's teachings reached Rome. The religion there was pure Mithraism, what is called the Christians pagan teaching, and from century to century watered down and added to by leaders in different areas to become at last the King James Version in the Bible.

"I always thought King James had the Bible written to hedge his bets as to whether there was one God or more than one."

"Now, where did you get that idea?"

"Well, not from the church."

"It was in A.D. 180 Irenaeus, Bishop of Lyons, attached independent thinking and all teachings relating to the oneness of God and man believing that spiritual consciousness and a personal union with God would undermine the authority of the priests. He directed his wrath upon Gnosticism. First, he issued his five books against Heresies, followed by a list of acceptable writings choosing only those words, which supported his demand for a fixed dogma. The shift in mind from within to without had begun and the innate power of the individual was gradually given to another structure and lower authority."

"Hmmm…sounds kind of like a political system, doesn't it?"

Shirley nodded her head. "The Encyclopedia of Religions talks about religions from Taoism to Babism; the alpha and omega of the religious world, the histories of religions, which people pay little attention to. If they did, it would be an eye-opener to those who believe so wholeheartedly what is written between Genesis and John's Revelation. That book ended 1900 years ago, but religion has gone on, and more Biblical history has been written since 100 A.D. than ever before. For the last twenty centuries, emotions have ruled the world, not reason".

"You got that right! The first time we met, my emotions took over for no apparent reason."

"So, did mine," Shirley came back.

We looked into each other's eyes and were quiet for a moment. I kissed her, and she sighed.

"In 300 A.D., all Roman countries were Mithraism; Octavius was their leader. Now, the people who called themselves Christians had infiltrated the Seven Hills of Rome to such an extent that Octavius said, in words of today, 'If we can't beat them, let's join them.' All early Christians believed in rebirth. Octavius did not. He was a pagan, so he abolished that tenant of the faith. So much was taken out."

I was excited. "I can see how one man with power can change things."

"One universal law, rebirth, is coming into its own. As the Christians say, it's God's law. The Muslims say it is the law of Allah and the

Hebrews say, it's Jehovah's law. The Hindus say it is the law of Krishna and so on. It is Universal law, love and mind goes beyond all tribal gods," Shirley explained.

"What a story! Did that come from automatic writings?"

"Not really. It's history about religion that most churches choose not to teach. Maggy used to tell me churches are an excellent for children; it gives them a solid religious foundation. A few years ago, living in Illinois, I gave a lecture at Millikin University. I told my story about how my spiritual abilities were started. I told my story about how my spiritual abilities got started. Then at the end, I always closed by allowing question and answer time. There was a young man in the front row, who stood up and said, 'Lady, if you would say in Jesus's name you would have it all. It would be more real.'"

Shirley told me what she replied. "I have gone to church and said in Jesus's name. I believe in Jesus. Now let's talk about a church. First, you are a Baptist. Is that right?"

He answered, "Yes, Ma'am. I go to church every Sunday and praise the Lord in Jesus's name."

"That's great! Now let's take the time to build a church. First, men must decide there is a need for a gathering place for their church. No woman can help because that is a man's job."

He replied, "That's right."

I looked at him with a pretend made smile. "Next, we file as a non-profit organization, so we don't have to pay taxes. It's a gathering place for people to worship paid for by donations."

He said, "Oh no! That's not right. We have many office buildings we rent out in Chicago. We are not a not-for-profit organization. We are a business, and I'm sure we pay taxes."

I reached in my pocket as if to take out some money. My hand was empty. "See, all gone to taxes," I teased.

"Go talk to your preacher."

"I will."

"Let's continue building this church. Next, we must get donations to buy the land and get the building material. We will get volunteers to help build the church. It's time now the women can help because they need to cook for the working men and help decorate the inside the church.

"Well, they got that right," I joked. "Favorite Person, you know I don't believe that. Who does all the cooking when we're together?"

Shirley interjected, "But we both clean up together."

Then she went on. "The young man agreed it was time to bring in the women. Now we have gotten the church built, a preacher is hired, and everyone is ready to have services. The young man agreed, yes that the bell would be rung, looked at the cross hanging above the altar and praised the Lord in Jesus's name. "Oh, what a fine church we have!"

Shirley got up and looked directly at me. She was not in a serious manner, but quiet. "I'm teaching tone but rather in a kind one and went on. "The church would be as good as the people's hearts. That is what a church gathering is all about—love, supporting others, being happy and recharging their energy for another week's work." Two weeks later while walking down the street, this young man came running up, gave me a hug and thanked me for educating him about his church. The preacher told him I was right. His church was non-for-profit. They pay no taxes."

"How can I make my business non-profit?" I paused. "Well, I thought I had a good life by having a successful business and plenty of women but meeting you made me realize I have lost out on other avenues. I got too busy studying the outside world that I have forgotten to study my inside world."

Before leaving Muir Woods, we found a fabulous view overlooking Muir Beach. It was a nice small beach in a cove—a perfect place to watch the whales swim in and out of the stunning sea while hearing the loud splashing sound from their bodies hitting the water.

I said, "Your teachings with all nature surrounding makes me feel refreshed and newly alive. I did feel this calming, restorative effect on my mind and body."

"While we may intuitively appreciate a walk in the woods, the benefits may seem somewhat intangible and undefined," Shirley spoke. "But the silence of the still forest has a calming effect, a chirp from a nearby bird could lure one into quietness, and the air rich with earthy smells had a soporific effect on any stressed person. The benefits are a gift from the forest."

Patrick continued, "On a fine day such as this, I felt earth's energy from the trees, the birdsong and the very soil upon which I stand. My summary of your, Awakening Universal Love Seminar, the definition of Universal Love is a harmony energy connection with everyone and everything as we are a part of it all. We all relate to earth, with one another and the Universe. Thank you for the personal seminar."

We looked ahead and spied a pod of barnacle encrusted humpback whales breaching in the daylight. In their exuberant display each whale jumped many times in series. About ninety percent of their forty-five-foot length cleared the water each time and then they turned to land on their side or back. White spray erupted around them as about forty tons of warm-blooded mammal hit the surface.

Patrick announced, "It's now time to take my new energy back to the outside world and my business and yes, pay those taxes."

CHAPTER 14

Hawaii

"Favorite Person, when I look into your eyes, it's as though I can see mysterious secrets in your heart. Life is all about how we respond, and you respond in a magical positive way."

Shirley—1990

Traveling to different cities and meeting new people was always exciting, but for me being home was more invigorating. My home was filled with the essence of silence that I loved. Silence was precious. When my mind was silenced, my heart could experience a state of acceptance for me to love others. I thought this was true for all humanity. I was grateful to be nestled in my home relaxing and having not to rush with a busy schedule.

Patrick and I hadn't seen each other since we'd returned. His business was occupying his time nowadays. We did talk nightly. Patrick told me that the meditation worked; he was sleeping well and getting more rest. He invited me for dinner at Gershwin's on Saturday evening. Patrick had some exciting news and thought it was appropriate since we first met there.

Gershwin's was always busy, yet it had quietness about it tonight. There was the absence of loud chitter-chatter allowing a more relaxed atmosphere. Or maybe it just felt that way because I was feeling relaxed being with Patrick.

"Favorite Person, I have something important to tell you," Patrick said. "I hope you like my idea. I have thought about it and even meditated. I have the opportunity for my working buddy, Mitchem, to buy my business. I feel a need to help you with your mission and have this feeling to protect you. Let's get married and fly to Hawaii for our honeymoon. Upon our return, we will write Maggy's book for a start. How about that?" His broad smile showed me it came from deep inside and his eyes lit up.

My eyes widened, "I am surprised, to say the least." I shook my head. "Patrick, I swore never to marry again. My work has me flying more than I am home. I love you and want to be with you, but to get married is something I don't know."

"Favorite Person, when I look into your eyes, it's as though I can see mysterious secrets in your heart. Life is all about how we respond, and you respond in a magical, positive way. It makes me want to dance in the rain because you bring sunshine into my life. I've had many women in my time, but you are different. You are the only woman that has held my interest. I am committing to you, and I need you in my life."

Patrick looked directly at me very seriously, "I have it figured out. Let's see if you like this plan. We can have a ceremony without a marriage license. Neither of us wants our commitment soiled by any mean-eyed lawyer and rules. I know we are different, so our pledge will be to each other, our hearts, and the stars in the sky. We are free-spirited people who do not need a piece of paper to bind us. Only our hearts and love will do the binding, like the Indian ways.

I told Patrick that I agreed wholeheartedly with the Indian way.

"While you travel teaching seminars, I can work more with my spiritual evolvement. This warrior needs some awakening time. Also, there are physical exercises I need to strengthen my body. My back and knees are weak. I would have time for that, too," he added.

I started laughing, "It's like a runaway car of its own with you, Patrick. But I do like your idea. What other plans do you have?"

Patrick had a big grin like a kid who just got his first bike. "I've been busy. If you agree, I will arrange for a ceremony at the Botanical Gardens in Ft. Worth. I know how you love that place. I will arrange for a preacher, and then afterward a limo to drive us to DFW airport and fly out to Maui. I need to meet Leon, your medicine man. I feel Leon can teach me… you know, in a man-to-man sort of a way."

Patrick, though never unsure of himself, appeared to be now. He wasn't used to letting others take the lead. He took a drink of wine and said, "I've been told a small, intimate ceremony at the Fort Worth Botanical Gardens has a spot that will help to fulfill any woman's dream. Their perennial garden has a frothy waterfall framed with sparkling floral colors to a soothing brook-laden with ferns offering a whimsical setting to tie our nuptial knot."

I nodded my head in complete agreement. My heart was on an elevator going up.

Patrick confirmed earnestly, "Consider it done!"

This day was one of those baby-blue skies; the clouds were as puffs of radiant joy, ready to disperse into the wind, to travel our Earth. It was a Robin Hood sort of a wedding in a natural woodland setting. We wanted our love to honor what God has given rather than the world of money and bling.

For my wedding attire, I chose a Todd Oldham teal blue suit with gold buttons. I held a fresh and vibrant bouquet with hand arranged red roses and lilies. Patrick looked handsome in his black suit with a white shirt, and a burgundy tie. He wore a stunning boutonniere of red and white rose on his lapel.

We stood alone, facing each other while listening to the words of a Preacher from Unity Church of Arlington. "Marriage isn't a ring worn or a signed paper. It is the union of two hearts beating as one, each that would sacrifice for the other's happiness and wellbeing. Marriage is the blessing Patrick is giving to Shirley, and Shirley is giving to Patrick, for an eternal bond of soul-mates."

After the short ceremony, Patrick scooped me up in his arms and spun me around, singing in my ear, "Oh come with me, little girl, for your magic carpet ride."

It was apparent while making the accommodations Patrick had spread the word his Favorite Person had chosen to fly on their plane to Maui on a honeymoon. The flight attendants upgraded us to first class.

Patrick jumped up from his seat and quickly grabbed the intercom. One of the flight attendants started toward him. But Patrick didn't let that bother him. "Hey, everyone, me and my Favorite Person just tied the knot and are headed to Maui for a honeymoon. I am buying champagne for everyone who wants to celebrate with us."

Loud applause filled the plane, and people called out for the newly-wed's to stand up. Everyone was having a fun while our plane rode through the sky as if it were on sleek and perfect tracks.

Picking up our luggage, we went to the rental car counter and were told they only had a small green Toyota Corolla. Patrick was not happy, but no matter how much he talked it was their last rental car. Getting into the small car was a tight squeeze with Patrick's body size and five pieces of luggage, Patrick learned that I never packed light. The car was not clean inside nor out, another disappointment but we were not going to allow this to ruin our honeymoon.

"This old rent-a-wreck is slowing us down, and it won't go any faster. Hope this old thing will get us around okay," Patrick grunted.

"Must think positive, Patrick," I teasingly replied.

~~~

We arrived in the wee hours of the morning, at the Grand Wailea Beach Resort-Marriott in Maui. A patio breakfast was filled with the sounds of the sea creating its symphony, and every so often a seagull called out, making a start for a wonderful day.

After eating my breakfast, I started writing in my journal.

Patrick finishing eating his bacon and eggs and asked me if I was getting an automatic writing.

"No, it's a dream I had last night," I told Patrick. "Dream.... Let me tell you about it. I was sitting by a campfire when a man walked out from behind a teepee. He walked over and sat beside me. When I turned to look at him, I realized it was you, Patrick. You said, 'An eagle flies high as it goes on its way. It cries out to the land, "Let's all be brave." The higher he flies, the happier he is for he knows how to get away from where mankind exists. The freedom he feels can be felt within creating a truly blissful feeling right to the end. The love you seek is truly in solving any mysteries, stopping all whims. Mother Nature and her beauty are a wonderful piece of art. You must never forget her co-worker, the great Father Sky. The beauty is mighty while he changes his scene from daytime to darkness, from sunshine to moonbeams. Their loving energy fills the sky, and their symbol of love creates a masterpiece of art! They have the answers. You need to look no more. For I am your warrior,' this man in my dream said. 'Somewhere above this sky, born of the swirling galaxies of brilliant stars, I promise you comfort. I have plenty of love to kindle your soul and bring the sorts of smiles you thought only belonged to the stars. I am your warrior who carries the love torch.'

Patrick became incredibly quiet as if trying to understand, "What does that dream mean?" It seemed all had stopped around him as he focused on just me.

I told him that the dream was showing one of our past life stories. "It's showing our working together with the Universal Love seminars. Maggy once told me when science and spiritually come together they will create a strong power of love. You have three degrees in engineering, so you are the science, and I have spiritual knowledge. So how about that, J. Patrick... are you in?"

"Count me in, Favorite Person. I'm willing and ready." Patrick jumped up pretending to leave to get this part of their new life started.

I stood up and pulled him to me. "You're not going anywhere without me!"

Mid-day, we went to visit Leon and Mary. My last visit with them had been in Portland, Oregon, right before they moved to Maui. It had been a few years, and I was looking forward to introducing Patrick to them.

The narrow and winding two-lane road with a slow-moving car played havoc with our patience, but Patrick and I barely noticed. Leon and Mary lived on a Japanese plantation with a fantastic view at the top of a mountain. They were waiting for us in their driveway with open arms. I jumped out of the car and went running to hug Leon, and then Mary. Patrick slowly walked up sticking his hand out, but Leon gave him a big manly hug with a loud pat on his back, saying "Welcome, my warrior Brother." Next, Mary welcomed him with a hug.

After the introductions, Leon invited us in for his meatloaf dinner. Mary said he had a particular recipe and everyone they had served it to thought it was the best.

Patrick looked at Leon begging for his recipe. "If I cook it for Shirley, she'll follow me anywhere."

Leon took my hand while Mary took Patrick's hand as we walked into the house. Standing in the dining room, actually calling it a dining-room was somewhat misleading. The huge mahogany table with a red and white checkered tablecloth took up most of the vast space the large room offered. A Lazy-Susan with a napkin holder commanded attention from the center of the table. On the other end of the room was a big full kitchen. It was a grand space, to say the least. Sitting at the dining room table, Leon spoke, to eat my meatloaf in a good way to love thy self, to share good food with others is to create the bonds of heaven. Patrick took a bite, nodded his head yes, and replied, "Wow! This is so good. I'm impressed."

Turning toward Patrick, Leon said, "I knew in my vision it was time for a Shirley visit. We are happy you two lovebirds chose to visit us on your honeymoon. I think every love story is beautiful, but yours is one of my favorites. It was no coincidence you two met at that bar looking at one of my paintings. I call it fate for you are the master of your destiny and I believe the stars control our destinies. My visions show, Shirley, you are seeking my approval and wondering what your spiritual daddy thinks of Patrick."

"Of course, I would like your approval," I replied instantly.

Leon turned and directly faced Patrick. "Patrick, you are a spiritual warrior." He stopped for a minute, waiting for Patrick to say something.

Patrick said, "I can say inside me, I feel your heated words of spiritual warrior, but I'm not sure what you mean. My question is how can I help Shirley with her mission?"

Leon's deep voice had a way of igniting one's internal engine. He continued, "A spiritual warrior upholds the truth and the right action of their society. You have the ability and power to spiritually stay focused while working in the business world. Daily you must ask yourself if you are exploiting the population or uplifting them, especially in relation to the young. For what is psychological maturity other than learning how to make wise choices to protect others? The business world has the glorification of greed as a golden tricycle being pedaled in circles at the end of a cul-de-sac... yet believing itself a fancy car shooting into the far horizon. We need more changes in the business world and it will take spiritual warriors like you."

Patrick listened as if Leon's words were golden, perhaps some elixir he'd been waiting all his days to hear.

Leon resumed, "Also, Patrick, within you is the energy of a healer from another lifetime. Your body's DNA carries this healing energy."

Patrick leaned toward Leon, and spoke, "My mother was a nurse, and she felt I would be a good doctor. I went to Medical College in Dallas for two years. I quit; I didn't like their politics."

"People need to stop relying on doctors and take control of their own body. Our planet has everything we need, and all we must do is learn. Most have no idea the brain can heal. It's past time humans connect their brain with their heart, and emotions is the energy to do just that," Leon gruffly replied.

He continued, "Two years of college, then you know the body; now it's time to learn the body's energy. When you send healing energy towards someone, they might be across the globe, they might be in a group, or it might be one-on-one. But know when you send the energy—to their hearts, to their shoulder, to their brain, to wherever-when you send that energy, know it has reached there. See it clean, clear, and healed. It will slowly get better and gradually come to perfect healing. This healing energy is already inside you so it will be easy to get you started. When I do my healing work, I add color; it will enhance while creating a more powerful energy. I am asking you to study the spirituality of colors and learn their true power."

Patrick nodding his head, "Yes, perfect. I do believe. Talking about it I feel a heated energy especially in my hands; my heartbeat is faster, but my mind is clear."

Leon replied, "You will release and experience powerful healing directly from your brain, heart, and out your hands or mind. Allow your brain and heart to be your director of where to put your heated energy. You are carrying a strong healing power from another lifetime, and It is ready to be released. "

Leon continued, "We, Indians are deeply spiritual people, and communicate our history by our thoughts, ideas, and dreams from generation to generation.. The way of a spiritual warrior carries the responsibility to live by a code of ethics that serves to help reach a higher standard of living. We have this built-in code in our DNA with all its information. Examples like our past lives, past experiences, etc. Our DNA vibrates very important data. Once we learn its coding, then it is easier to awaken your body with more information. I say you're a sleepy spiritual warrior working to awakening. It must be done naturally. Key words will help you. You must do what you feel to help yourself. Shirley or I can only be a door opener through our words. Words are powerful with the element of fire. Our duty to ourselves is to reach inside and interpret this code when we are faced with tough decisions about what to do in difficult situations."

Leon looked at both of us. "Patrick, I see and feel the love you have for Shirley. It runs deep in your soul through numerous lifetimes. You want to protect and help her spread the spiritual word out to the world. Shirley is extremely special to me and this planet. I have been her protector. Her heart is big; she speaks the truth, and she can see the past, present, and future. It's a unique gift she was born with."

Patrick stared at me. "I will always protect her. I know it sounds trite, but I would give my life for her."

Leon, facing him, said, "Patrick, you are a spiritual warrior." He stopped for a minute, waiting for Patrick to react. It was obvious; Leon was waiting for guidance of a direction to move in.

"That's a tall order to follow," Patrick said without realizing what he said. I looked at him, and my face expressing respectful, awe-struck curiosity.

"Today, we have a tough time finding this code in the face of so many contradictions in society. However, the way of the warrior is as valid today as it has always been. Think about your warrior-ship before you exit your home into the alien world where evil waits to distract. Truth is lived by every Indian who has been raised in the traditions of our elders since time began on this continent. It is indeed strange how these rules of a creator can be felt even in the remotest depths of every land where honor lives. May you, Patrick, always walk in the highest path that has been set by the masters that came before you!" Leon added.

Leon got up and walked around the room. Mary started to clear the table and make coffee. "That's another tall order to follow," Patrick said, realizing the importance of what Leon was saying.

I looked at Patrick, moving my chair closer to him. I took his hand and squeezed it. "Leon, Patrick wants to learn from you. He is Cherokee but doesn't know yet is eager to learn about his warrior abilities. Many times, he has told me he has strong desires to learn from you."

"You have been a warrior in many lives, and you were Looking Glass in one of those lifetimes, so you carry this DNA. Looking Glass was a prophet for Chief Joseph who was killed trying to help his people move to Canada rather than live on the government Indian reservation." Then looking serious, Leon added, "You must overcome the strong current you have swimming inside you and remind yourself that you have the freedom to move in any direction you choose. There is no need to push or struggle when you allow your energy to flow."

Patrick gulped the rest of his iced tea and said, "I don't think I'm pushing anything in my life. I'm learning to be a more laid-back kind of guy nowadays."

Leon, with tight fists, stopped his pacing and stood in front of Patrick. "Stand up, Patrick. Stand up like a man."

Patrick stood up. Leon pushed Patrick's shoulder and brought his fist up to Patrick's face. "Go ahead hit me. I'll fight you. I'm an older man, but I still have fight in me," Leon gruffly said. "I'm not afraid of you. I know Shirley, but I just met you. I don't want Shirley hurt. Are you going to hurt her, Patrick? Don't you want to fight?"

Patrick put his hands beside his body and told Leon, "I don't want to fight. You're my brother. I want to learn from you. I want to learn how to help Shirley with her mission."

They both sat down. Leon looked at Patrick as if he were the only person in the room.

"You must not allow the karma of fighting to cage you in. Many a battle you have encountered, and countless women will hold you back. You are a warrior with healing energy manpower running deep within you. Now, it is time for you to allow your healing energy to surface. You want to come aboard and help us with our mission. Then learn to love and touch the Earth. Rest your spirit in her plains, her valleys, her flowers, and her seas. Love Earth, and she will reward you with freedom. To love and have freedom is a great honor!"

Patrick sat down and was very still, obviously in thought. "I do understand my fighting and women. I have promised never to swing my fist again, and I have lost the desire for other women. I have drilled into Mother Earth many times for money, but my desires are now to help clean her. It is now all in the past. This is true, but I can't change my past. I know meeting Shirley is my present and with her; I look forward to a non-confrontation future. She is the only woman who holds my interest, and I am committed to her and her spiritual work." He leaned over and kissed me.

Leon smiled and continued, "Your power is your brain. Emotions are your action, and your heart increases the energy for completion. My advice for you two is to understand that love and marriage is like a staircase, you have your ups and downs, but you take each step together." Patrick and I became very still. We were allowing Leon words to reach our hearts.

"Shirley was annoyed with religion, its rules, and found spirituality to be more personal. Her mentor Maggy and I taught her world religion. The Bible is written in code, and she understands its coding. We have named Shirley 'Golden Mother' because of her heart and the love it projects. You are an educated man, and with your abilities you must not allow your brain to get in the way of your heart. You will be of great assistance to her and this planet. I will be looking over your shoulder so be careful." Leon's eyes twinkled as he said this, but he was very serious.

Mary, who had been listening all this time, quietly got up and softly said, "We have a surprise for you. It's a video we thought you would appreciate. Shirley, remember during our visit to Texas you sent us home with a big notebook filled with copies of your automatic writings? At that time, we were researching color and sound with crystals to teach people. Your writings explained how some crystals are transmitters while others are receivers. Your information was exactly what we needed to finish our work."

"What work?" Patrick was mesmerized and asked quickly, knowing he would want to be a part of anything with me, no matter if it were only a spec in the universe. He wanted to be there, right by me. Mary could see he was serious and was thrilled.

"The film actually shows the energy working from crystal to crystal, and we titled it *Genetar*. We have shown it on large screens at our Tetr X11 seminars, even in Honolulu. It's amazing, and we made you a copy." She got up and picked up the gift from the side table. Giving it to us Mary said, "So, happy wedding gift!"

Leon stood up, asking us to follow him. Upon entering the room, I felt a serenity yet elusive energy with a strong presence of peacefulness. I sat down next to Patrick on a couch.

The large room was filled with a polished black baby grand piano, drums, guitar, crystals, video equipment, and cameras. The numerous crystals had a way of mesmerizing the room, to take what was good and make somewhere beyond amazing. There was an aura about them, a calmness that inspired a steady creativity that felt the same as a playful dance.

Patrick commented, "I told Shirley her writings have information for future technology and with any luck your video proves it." I touched his knee trying to calm his energy.

The room became silent as Leon prepared to play the video. As we watched, I got excited and scooted to the edge of my seat. "Oh, my God, Leon! That is what I saw when Grenada took me aboard his ship."

Leon answered, "I know; this technology creates a high-powered frequency…nothing like I have ever seen. I have worked with a lot of crystals, and I do know about all types of energy, but putting this together was a rather simple task as long as I followed your writings""

Patrick stood up and said, "Can't say it surprises me but will say it's incredible. That video is proof her writings are correct."

Leon was serious and said to Patrick, "Once again, Brother Patrick, you are Shirley's protector, and I will watch over you through my visions." Patrick took my hand and kissed it.

Patrick took my hand and kissed it.

We watched the video showing how successfully the crystal energy worked. They looked like lightning bolts spreading quickly from one crystal to another.

Leon stopped the film and said, "this energy will supply a city with electricity for ever and its free. I'm already talking with Japanese officials about it."

Patrick was looking at his watch as we all stood up.

Leon related, "Mary and I never say goodbye. Instead, we use the phrase 'see you later.' We will see you after this parting, maybe later in this life or the afterlife. We will meet again."

Patrick responded, "I've always liked 'see you after later.'" And we all laughed.

Driving out of Leon's driveway, we heard Leon yell, "Go in peace; we love you both."

Patrick and I didn't want to wake up at 4:30 in the morning, but we also didn't want to miss a view from Haleakala's First Light of a new day. There was just something so raw and untouched about the early morning hours of the day when the world around was so still and silent with a sunrise.

Without awareness of the road, the car chugging along the narrow road, lights on full beam, calmness filled the car as we drove up the Haleakala Mountain. It was a narrow one-lane road, each way with lots of cars, so quiet was necessary for Patrick to focus on driving.

At the entrance, a park staff man directed us where to park. Getting out of the car, we could sense the mountain air was cool and fresh and as I breathed it in, something inside me awakened the magic of being alive. We noticed people had already arrived walking quietly, carrying flashlights and cameras.

"I feel this special place vibrates with stories of an ancient culture here," Patrick whispered.

I noticed others were whispering too, and asked, "Why is everyone whispering?"

Patrick explained, "Guess, they are respecting the connecting link with this famous sunrise to unite between the universe and themselves. Leon did say the sunrise at this location is a spiritual experience. Must whisper to respect and not to disturb anything. What a wonderful experience for us to view the sunrise over the crater," Patrick continued. "I know watching the sun rise above the clouds here at Haleakala will be unique and memorable. What energizes me about this place is the high elevation, lack of light and environmental pollution. Dynamic weather patterns make it an ideal sky watching location—no telling what we might see. I'm glad we dragged ourselves out of bed for this experience."

Patrick turned looking at me realized I was shivering. I was cold. He quickly got a blanket out of the trunk and placed it over my shoulders just as the sun started to peak over the summit.

As the sun rises, mountains exposed to the direct sunlight under-goes an optical phenomenon and assume a wheel of colors, creating an illusion of the air being tangible enough to reach out and grab a handful of it.

We first witnessed a silver arc before a beautiful display of colors illuminated the sky. It looked like one could walk on a road off the ledge 10,023 feet over sea level into the clouds. Local legend has it that Maui, a demigod, was imprisoned in the sun at Haleakala to make the day longer.

On this gorgeous, but chilly morning, it felt good when Patrick snuggled in the blanket with me. I whispered, "It's like night gave birth to the light. Maggy and my Indian friends taught me while the sun is rising, always say your desired thoughts of what you need to bring into your life. And at sunset, you say what you no longer need in life."

"Haleakala means House of the Sun. It's time for us to put our thoughts out for the Universal Love teachings to successfully be known worldwide," Patrick proclaimed, still whispering.

As we began to drive down the Haleakala Mountain, the world's largest dormant volcano, the bi-coastal views of Maui's central valley carried a great beauty with a strong floral fragrance. The road was exhaust-ing, and many times narrowing, numerous hairpin curves and several unforgiving one-lane bridges, not to mention an incredible number of blind spots along the way. Patrick was a good driver and drove slowly.

"This old rent-a-wreck is better than I thought. It makes us sit closer together," Patrick said.

I moved even closer to him. Almost immediately, there were these puffy white clouds, floating and dancing around the car. It was a strange sight, and something neither of us had witnessed before.

I shouted, "Patrick, STOP! Stop this car now!"

Patrick was frantically looking for a place to pull over along this narrow road. I felt a strong need to get out of the car and touch the dancing clouds.

A strong wind blew, pushing me back as I stepped out of the car. The wind gave off soft howling sounds of drums and Indian chants. They sounded way off in the great distance. I thought, *These sounds were the creation of the loving universe, and it is fine-tuning our souls.* The sheer force of these clouds' manifestations was mesmerizing.

Patrick said, "Look at that. Some of those clouds are shaped like angels. They have wings while others look like a man wearing a robe. There is this Indian man carrying a peace pipe. What is going on here? I am experiencing this, but there is no logical explanation. Are they ghosts?"

I told him that some call them ghosts but they are only non-physical realities because the soul carries the conscious data and life continues after this dimension making its energy manifest into reality. "They are called Guides."

"Why do you think this is happening? Did Leon cause this?"

I answered, "Leon doesn't have the power to create something like this. It's the Guides'! They appear when they think we are ready and willing for them to teach us. But we have our God-given free will so that we can accept or reject their appearance and their teachings."

Patrick waved his arms and yelled, "I accept you. This hairy legged fellow is ready for your teachings!"

It was late when Patrick and I arrived at our hotel room. We decided to meditate since we felt the need to calm our energy. What we had experienced with our Guides had caused an unsettling feeling.

After meditation, I had fallen asleep only to wake up to Patrick shaking me and whispering. "Favorite Person, do you see the Guides at the foot of the bed?"

I rose up and saw the Guides. I told Patrick he was being visited by three masters from the Brotherhood of The White Light.

"Oh, yea, right! What and who is this Brotherhood of the White Light?"

"Some people call them the Great White Brotherhood. They are supernatural beings of great power, which spread spiritual teachings through selected people. The Ascended Masters are a part of the Great White Brotherhood, spoken of in the Bible book of Revelations Chapter 7. As the great multitude of saints, clothed with white robes, stand before the throne of God. The Brotherhood work with earnest seekers of every race, religion, and walks of life to assist humanity in their forward evolution. It's a Spiritual hierarchy."

"Really? A hierarchy? Are you sure?" Patrick was not testing me. He craved my knowledge.

I explained that the word hierarchy, as commonly used in English, might seem an inappropriate choice, but the Great Ones have a consciousness that is so far advanced beyond human's intellect that it's not easy to comprehend. The dense physicality that we experience on planet Earth is working on the Third Density Reality.

I stopped. Patrick grabbed me and gave me a good kiss.

"Wait, I want to continue," I insisted though I didn't want to. "When we meditate, we can be enlightened to the Fifth Reality where it is easier for the Masters to communicate with us. These Masters are teachers of mankind. They teach the path of overcoming victory where the soul can reunite with your higher self, walk on Earth with self-mastery. They reveal to you the next step of your spiritual evolution."

"Are they asking me to do something?" Patrick quizzed me.

"You are being visited by Master Koot Hoomi, Master Mayra, and Master Serapis. Their purpose is to help you understand your warrior's spiritual power. You are a man who knows your physical, emotional, and mental body. Now you are learning about your spiritual body. It's a powerful energy."

Patrick could hardly absorb it all but wanted to know more. "What do they want to teach me?"

I gently touched him. "They have come to visit and teach you, Patrick, not me, so you need to talk with them."

CHAPTER 15

Electrifying Changes

"I am your Master living within you."

Patrick—1990

Early the next morning, Shirley and I woke up to a tapping on the window and then it became a pitter-patter. Shirley sat up in bed, stretching said, "The watery alphabet of the clouds comes to sing upon our roof. I'm not ready to rise and shine yet." She glanced out the hotel window at an overcast sky with dark moving clouds hiding the sun. Me being sleepy walked unsteadily to the bathroom and muttered, "I hope it clears out soon. We must get back to Texas and start making plans to write your books."

It was my choice to have breakfast at the Café Ole' in the beautiful Dunes Golf Course. I loved to play golf. I didn't have time during this trip but wanted to visit the course. After the rain, everything looked and smelled refreshing, making us want to have a picnic on the patio. A waiter rushed to our table opening an umbrella, and a waitress started pouring our glasses of water.

Placing a napkin on my lap, I looked in the distance and said, "I love it here. We can watch the golfers play while eating."

"I don't know anything about golf. It looks like a game that isn't easy to win. Why do people want to chase after a little white ball?" Shirley asked.

"It's a mind game," I answered. "When the going gets tough, I get going. Winning isn't the only thing, but it sure feels good when pride is on the line."

"Is it a partner game or play by yourself?" Shirley asked.

I smiled. "The only reason to play golf alone is if you want to practice. Otherwise, it's best to play with others. Years ago, one of my fun tournaments was in California at the Santiago Golf Course in Orange County. I was with Roy, my bank buddy, and Ed, my CEO buddy. I insisted Anne, a pro-golfer, join our group to play. I had watched her at the Irvine golf course and thought she would be a great asset for us guys. She was good. I called her a week ahead of time trying to prepare her. She didn't get the seriousness of winning. It was the day of the tournament when she realized how important it was to not go into battle unprepared or you would get slaughtered. I told her, 'You've got to get inside their heads to know their strengths and weaknesses.' We lost that day, but if we had won, I wouldn't have taken the prize anyway. Old Roy cheated by moving his ball closer to the hole. The judge didn't catch him, but I did. Nonetheless, we had fun. That's what games are all about, having fun."

I told Shirley, "I had learned a hard lesson about this great game of golf while playing in a Dallas tournament. I lost my temper and the game. I got so mad that I pushed my caddy and threw my golf clubs and bag in a creek. It was later I realized how stupid it was in allowing my temper to take control. I remembered having a good talk with myself about it and vowed never again to act that way on a golf course. I knew it was a gentleman's game and needed to be respected even if it meant chasing a little ball all over."

Sipping on a glass of pineapple juice, Shirley asked, "Okay, Patrick, what did your Guides tell you last night? I'm sure you learned a lot from those three appearing."

"Before it was all over, the room was filled with twelve Guides, ready to teach. I began to count.

I am your Master living within you.

When your brain is blank, an imprint from your heart will be reached, and you will retain it.

You must live your life from the beginning to end. No one else can do it for you.

Know the teachings always come from within instead of without."

I had to throw in a little humor, "And to think I went to college when all I only needed was to learn from you. But let me go on."

Happiness is an attribute of love. You cannot be apart from it.

Take care when you speak. Words are powerful weapons.

Happiness is the experience of living every moment with love.

Love is the answer to all.

We are only visitors on Earth. It is a place we are just passing through.

Our Earth's purpose is to observe, to learn, to grow, and to love. Then, we return home.

Every human being has its own uniqueness. Every person or incident is a universal teacher.

Energy works with colors and will connect to the Universal Light Energy.

"I won't forget their teachings. To me, they are the most influential and precise lessons I have ever had. They don't teach you this in college, and that is where you are supposed to gain some wisdom. College didn't do that for me, but I did learn a lot about oil."

"This is a lot of information for anyone to comprehend in one night," Shirley added.

"The Guides told me I needed to process this before moving on. I plan to write it down. Could be good seminar information. But for now, we must start thinking about writing Maggy's biography. It does take time. What information have you collected?"

Shirley looked at me remembering, "I have Maggy's scrapbooks when she was a young Vaudeville singer. I have her diary, newspaper clippings, cassettes, and videos. I have written 1,500 pages filled with her life stories. I have the story organized, and now it needs editing. *An Angel with Muddy Feet* is the title Maggy named it."

"1,500 pages? I would say it's editing time."

Shirley wondered, "I say, why not move to a more secluded place? Dallas and Ft. Worth are big cities still growing. We need more quietness and nature around us, a place with lots of trees so when we walk, the twigs will crunch under our feet. The forest comforts our hearts. Let's go somewhere where we can see the animals in the daytime and the stars at night. I would rather be among the forest, animals, and the sound of nature than among city traffic and its noise. Fresh air and sunshine are the best for us, and it will help our creative juices to flow."

I quickly responded. "Dallas is my home. I have never thought about moving. I've always been happy there. I do understand what you're saying. The city is a human zoo. I know nature will never fail me. Do you have a place in mind?"

"I have clients who have offered their cabins when I'm ready to write my books. We only need to pick and choose the place. Jim and Jane have a cabin that is located on Gillespie Road near Jackson, Mississippi. It's Jane's family cabin and her Uncle George built a lake. Also, I have Roger and Darcy, law enforcement buddies. We worked together. They have a second home in Thermopolis, Wyoming. Clinnon Alexander is hosting the next seminar in Jackson, and then on to Lafayette and New Orleans. It would be a good idea for you to come. After the seminars, we could take our time driving and check out what place we would like the best," Shirley was excitedly telling me this.

I looked around. "It's time to leave this island and get busy with the Universal Love mission. Here we go, Maggy. We will get your book published."

I looked at my watch, aware we had to pack. Shirley wasn't a messy person. She just brought a lot of stuff that had to all go in a suitcase, so I helped her. She sure had lots of shoes. As we were stuffing her things in suitcases, Shirley thought that at least I didn't say no to the idea of moving.

Mike had told her not to expect me to move out of Dallas. It would never be done. I am a Dallas man. With those thoughts whirling in her head, she rushed to packing.

The passengers were boarding when we arrived at the small airport in Maui. It was in Honolulu where we had the long wait.

Quietly, we sat in the Honolulu International Airport waiting for our layover to pass by. I started writing my messages from the Masters. Shirley felt the energy of a message coming in, so she started writing. The electrifying energy was powerful with each dynamic word she wrote.

Love is a flow that warms your heart. It never stops beating to the essences of your needs. Flow it out to others, and your rewards will return from the higher vibration of Universal Love. Love is balance, and in the big picture in the Universe, you are a part of it with love in your heart. With love, there is no need to fight darkness. Negativism feeds negativism. Therefore, love and positivity feed love, and positive thoughts cause happiness to grow. Negative and positive energy is a harmonious balance and sets forth a stronger love feeling. Flowing with your love creates a form of atoms from your body. These atoms continue creating a love light from you forever.

She showed me what she wrote, and then started writing again. I was glad she brought a notebook. *You are all living life cells. The atoms you generate enhance each of your love cells many times. This energy that comes back from God is both positive and negative polarity. This polarity gives you an equal balance. How you chose to use this balance is your polarity. It can create the energy of love and light or fear and darkness. All darkness is the lack of not knowing the light.*

"This is the start for your next seminar titled Mastering Self-love." I knew I understood completely. "Let me continue for you to see if I understand. 'When anyone opens their love within, they will open new doors. Behind each door is a newer and lighter energy source and it sends its beautiful messages of pureness to your heart. People will learn from this boundless love teachings.'"

Shirley was thrilled I knew. I would be a perfect co-presenter.

The intercom came on, and a flight attendant announced it was time to board. We put our journals away and started toward the gate. A man rapidly rushed up to Shirley and grabbed her arm.

I quickly got between them. I was mad but restrained myself from punching this guy in the face when I saw a security guy headed our way.

"Hey, Mac? Who are you and what do you think you are doing grabbing my wife's arm?" I sharply asked.

The man answered, 'I just had to touch her. I just had to touch her. Besides, I've seen her before, I know about her teachings."

I then realized how important it was to protect her, how vital it was. Besides, I didn't want Leon coming after me. I had promised never to fight again even though the man had come out of nowhere and the incident happened so fast.

Sitting in our plane seats, I asked her if this had ever happened before.

Shirley answered, "Not where someone had to touch me. People have approached me to talk about what they see over or around me, you know my Angels or Guides, but it didn't scare me. I am filled with these exciting ideas about moving to a secluded area, and it created anticipated energy within me. When I get excited, my energy grows."

I firmly added, "Then tone it down, Shirley. We don't need this packed plane with people to come rushing over to us. Do whatever you have to do and cool it now." I threatened lovingly. I was protecting her and always would.

Pushing back her seat with closed eyes, Shirley started meditating. It always calmed her energy. The airplane felt like home to Shirley. She'd flown in them so often. She curled up and slept as easily as dozing on the couch. The engines roared and the wind buffeted. It was her sky-born cradle, rocking by the winds far above the ground. Even as the engines turned, her brain relaxed into dreaming mode. There were thousands of miles to go, and all she had to do was let this technological bird fly them there.

I was feeling good about no one paying any attention to Shirley and I started to relax. I pushed back my seat thinking about the move she had talked about. My thoughts were strong on what my friends would think. When I sold my business would they like a new boss? Could they be long-distance friends, especially Mike Rogers? Mike and I were long-time buddies working together ever since our return home from Vietnam. We were close buddies.

I felt Shirley placing her hand on my arm. Still, the feel of her warm hand was reassuring. I realized how lucky I was to have true friends, but this love Shirley and I had was a top priority. True friends would want me to be happy, and I was sure that would be their wish with this moving situation.

I leaned over and whispered in Shirley's ear, "Favorite Person, I know what needs to be done about our relocating. You will have to give me some time to prepare this major step. It never entered my mind to leave Dallas, let alone sell my business. It will take time, and then my friends will want to say goodbye. Being in the oil and gas business, I do know a lot of people, especially in Texas."

Shirley leaned over and kissed me.

CHAPTER 16

A Texas Wonder

"We are to care for Earth and not abuse the sky."

Shirley—1990

My mind was whirling about what furniture to take or what goes in storage. Our next home was partially furnished so there wasn't much we needed to take.

A hot and sweaty Patrick came in from helping men take some items to our storage unit. "What's next, Favorite Person?" Patrick asked while getting a drink of water.

I sat at the dining room table, looking at my list. "I'm not for sure yet. Everything is happening so fast. I need time to get better organized. We must take some of my office furniture, books, cases and my five trunks."

Wiping his brow, Patrick said, "Mitchem called, and our move will have to be put on hold a few weeks. He needs my help on a well site near Paint Rock. Wanna go?"

"Why do you feel I need to go?"

Patrick grabbed a chair and sat down beside me at the table. "It was while I was reading your automatic writings I had this feeling that it's important to show you Paint Rock, Texas. There is a bluff along the banks of the Concho River in west-central Texas where there is the most outstanding rock art site of over 1,500 pictographs. Besides, Kenny lives close by, and I want you to meet him. Kenny is a good buddy and has been my pumper for years. I respect him and love his family. I also want to show you Big Bend before we leave Texas. We can get it all done in a week."

While packing, I thought Patrick had never pushed any ideas before. This must be something special.

Driving on I-20 out of Ft. Worth, Patrick turned off the radio and started my Texas history lesson.

"The Paint Rock pictographs were first documented by a guy named Jackson, one of the earliest Texas archeologists. Then this rock-art illustrator, Kirkland, visited the site to document his paintings. After his visit, he estimated that vandals and the forces of nature had destroyed at least a quarter of the pictographs. Fortunately, the family owners of Campbell Ranch, where the site is, have been watchful in protecting the site from further vandalizing. It has drawings a lot like your space friend Gurnada."

Looking at Patrick, I responded, "Really?"

"Yep, some of the paintings look to be of human scalps figures and have been interpreted as abductions of the Anglo settlers. Though there is no lack of interpretations of these Paint Rock pictographs and there is no way to know their true meaning. I'd say you and Gurnada have the answers."

"So, you have seen them?" I was excited about the possible connection.

"No; I know the history and always wanted to go. It's best I go with you anyway. Kirkland's images are watercolor copies of the pictographs recorded by him. As he put it, 'Here was a veritable gallery of primitive art at the mercy of the elements and handful of destructive people.' His watercolors of those rock arts did preserve them. Otherwise, they would have been lost forever."

Patrick looked down at the gas gauge and saw we needed gas. He pulled into a roadside gas station and asked me if I wanted anything to drink. I told him to get me whatever he wanted for himself...that I would probably steal from him anyway. After he got back from paying for the gas and bringing two identical bottles of water, we continued on our way.

"First, we are exiting here at Cross Plains, where Kenny lives," Patrick gestured toward an exit. "Kenny and I have worked these oil fields for a while."

The barren countryside filled with its pump jacks nodding up and down made me uncomfortable, and Patrick sensed my uneasiness. "The oils fields are estimated to have a good reserve in this area."

"Pumping oil looks painful. Earth is a living planet, you know."

Patrick explained to me that oil gets refined into gasoline, kerosene, heating oil and other products. It helps people to live a more comfortable life.

Parking in front of Kenny's home, Patrick turned towards me and said, "Looks like we'll have to finish this conversation at another time. Here comes the family."

Kenny came rushing out shaking Patrick's hand, followed by his wife, daughter, and son. After introductions, hugs, and smiles, their ten-year-old son, Adam, showed his pet snake. I jumped back with a squeal. "I don't like snakes! I don't care if it is your pet! I'm sorry I don't like them!"

Adam protested, "But he's not poisonous. He's a king snake, and he likes people." The tiny greenish blackish snake started crawling around Adam's arm while sticking out his tongue now and then. "I let him move freely around the house, and he doesn't harm anything," Adam proudly announced.

I was moving beside the14-year-old daughter. "Lola, do you like snakes?"

"Yes, ma'am. His name is James. James is a good snake, and we like him."

Kenny apologized adding, "Adam is studying dinosaurs and reptiles, and that is why he's allowed to have James." Laughing, he continued, "A snake is better than an alligator."

His wife, Evelyn, welcomed everyone to a glass of her fresh home-made lemonade. I knew I couldn't say no to an invitation like that.

We were seated at a large, round kitchen table with a blue and white checkered tablecloth. I was twice as happy as normal because Adam didn't allow James around while we drank our tasty ice-cold lemonade. The men gulped down their lemonade and walked to the dining room table that had maps spread out.

The guys were bent over looking at the maps. The rest of us could hear Patrick telling Kenny the solution to his problem. Adam and Lola had left the room, leaving Evelyn and I sitting alone.

"We are going to miss Patrick," Evelyn said. "He comes a lot, always paying special attention to our kids. Adam likes to show his pets and Lola liked him to commenting on her dance. We can tell Patrick loves children and he constantly reminds us we are raising the future. He is a kind-hearted man, and we hold a family affection towards him. Plus, Kenny thinks he's one of the smartest men on this planet."

"Thanks, Evelyn; it makes me happy there is a family connection with Patrick."

Stepping outside to leave, Patrick slapped Kenny on the back playfully and turned to open the door for me.

Kenny yelled, "Nice to meet you, Shirley. You're going to be missed, Patrick, but I see why you are leaving. Mitchem and I will work well together. Our buddy Mike Rogers will see to that. Have fun and let's keep in touch."

"Next stop is Paint Rock," Patrick said as he started the car.

~~~

Patrick turned off the highway, drove through a wooden gateway onto a dirt lane. Stopping in front of a house, we got out and knocked on the door. Patrick looked at his watch, wondering if they would be allowed to tour this late in the afternoon.

A smiling woman opened the door welcoming us in. Her name was Kay, and she introduced her husband, Fred Campbell. Patrick explained we were interested in touring the rock art. He apologized for not calling ahead of time, but we were in the area and had failed to get their phone number.

Fred, looking up from a newspaper, said, "It's okay. It's not too late. You will have to follow us though; it's a short drive back in the field."

Patrick and I stepped out on the porch just as the sun burst forth from behind a cloud. It was shining, with rays still half broken by the clouds. Driving behind Fred's rustic red truck, was an ominous roll of dust rising from the dirt road making it difficult to see. We were glad when Kay finally stopped the truck, on this road not travelled by many.

Before Patrick could open my door, I grabbed a legal pad and pen and bolted out of the car. I saw the bright, colorful pictographs and was excited. Walking along a bluff, observing the drawings, Kay, a former art teacher, started her lively narration weaving the history of the area with that of the Plains natives. She handed Patrick and I a pamphlet she and Fred had written about the possible meanings of the paintings.

"The image of a canoe, for example, could represent an actual boat, or a burial practice," she said. "A shaded circle may portray a solar eclipse. A turtle within a circle is probably a solstice symbol."

I immediately started copying the drawing images with Patrick standing close by. Fred asked, "What do you think these drawings represent?"

"There is more than what meets the eyes here," I answered nodding my head. "These sketches have some Indian etchings and then some show UFO information. They are coded."

Kay turned toward Fred in a challenging way with a frown on her face. "Fred, we already know what they mean. I don't know why you ask. Our preacher and various universities told us the meanings. Now, leave Shirley alone so we can get out of here."

I stopped drawing and turned towards Fred. "The Indians have similar drawings to the UFO coded drawings. They go hand in hand and work together. Some people say the UFO is the work of the devil; however, I say, the Bible has its stories. There are numerous accounts in the Bible of strange happenings and other worldly occurrences. The story of Ezekiel is one of the more fascinating ones, especially when looked at through our existing technology. When biblical texts are interpreted through this perspective, an interesting picture appears showing that our ancient ancestors were visited by an advanced race, rather than gods. This idea, known as the ancient theory, sees Ezekiel's vision of the Merkabah, or wheeled chariot, as more likely to be a spaceship or space shuttle used by an advanced species to reach out to humans. The J. J. Hurtak's book, *Keys of Enoch*, explains several of the codes and their meaning. The main purpose of all this is to help planet Earth and its people. If you are afraid, then fear will not allow you to be open-minded for learning new and different information."

Kay took Fred by the hand, and they walked away. Smiling, Patrick moved closer to me and whispered, "I say old Fred is afraid and it's not just with the coding. Kay doesn't like what you're saying."

During the rest of our time at the bluff, Kay made sure Fred didn't talk with me. If he started to walk near me, she would get in front of him. It was an awkward feeling, so Patrick and I left with a big thank you.

Settling in the car, Patrick said, "It's time for the next journey—a place in West Texas where the night sky is dark as coal and rivers carve temple-like canyons in ancient limestone. I'm taking you to Fossil Knob Ridge Motel, and it's located on a hillside from the Terlingua Ghost Town. That is our next stop."

"Ghost town?" I asked. "This could be fun!"

Patrick told me the motel wasn't another Hilton. It was in a primitive and isolated area, but this motel has a patio with an open fire pit. "I've been there, and the rooms have spectacular views of endless mountain and desert vistas from the ghost town ruins, rustic adobes, and ranch home. People say that at Fossil Knob Ridge the sun sets in the east. All I can say is tonight the view will give you some happy memories."

"I like happy memories! Don't need any downers."

Patrick nonchalantly continued, "If I can throw out a few rotten apples I can throw out a few lousy memories. I've kept my good memories safe and sound."

I smiled. "Guess I need to go see it and then I will believe it." I playfully punched him in the arm. Patrick laughed.

CHAPTER 17

Science v. Spiritual

Without that fire, you're just another person
with another idea.
With that fire, you are a force to reckon with,
a wind of change,
a person on a mission.

Patrick—1990

Walking to the patio, I noticed there was an assorted beauty so much like the rest of the mountainous view. The patio stones made a mosaic of sorts. I'm sure the stones collected were leftovers from renovations. They were sitting together as fallen autumn leaves from different trees. It had an artistry to it, a fluidity Shirley loved. Shirley and I stood holding hands looking at the Big Ben, Chicos Mountains. There was a limitless sunset view. I spoke, "We'll see every shade of red imaginable and I will serve you a glass of wine to make your day."

Shirley laughed and said, "Bring it on, I'm ready."

As the sun went down, the fire became bright and vivid, as though someone had shown a spotlight on it. The intensity and excitement of the flame colors were brilliant reds, oranges, and faint yellows.

The night brought such a silence that the crackle of the fire was all that could be heard. The flames flicked in the air as the red sparks danced in the cool breeze. We sat close on a bench, our faces toasted warm and our backs cold, mesmerized. It was like the fire was charming any worries from us and sending out to the heaven's bound along with the dark smoke. Clouds drifted away from a full moon, drenching the patio with a soft lunar light.

Shirley stared into the fire, thinking it was a fairy like night.

"Fire reminds me of my granny. She would call my name, 'J. Patrick, keep that fire inside you, burning bright. It's what keeps you up all night or rising first thing in the morning. Without that fire, you're just another person with another idea. With that fire, you are a force to reckon with, a wind of change, and a person on a mission. Therefore, you must keep that fire lit, at all costs. Granny spent many a day gently rocking to and forth on her oak framed rocker, with her can of snuff nearby. She didn't smoke it. She didn't swallow it. All she did was slosh it around her mouth and spit out the brown juices every few seconds.

Her rocking chair was nothing special. It was that unattractive mid-brown colored wood with knicks and scrapes from decades of abuse from children and grandchildren. But to my granny, it was the bastion of all her favorite memories. It was in that creaking wood that she had nursed her newborns–read story books to her toddlers. Just to sit and rock would transport her to these memories as effectively as a time machine and she would tell us vivid stories of the past Cherokee days. Without it her recollections would feel distant, as if the memories were really borrowed from someone else, or perhaps she had read them in a book.

Her period piece had seen better days, and no amount of polishing could conceal the circular stain on each arm, the chips on the curved gliders, or the scratch marks on the seat. Even her back-cushion upholstery had a small rectangular tear, and a tobacco stain or two.

After she was gone, it was an eerie sight to see her rocking chair still rocking and her empty slippers close by. I felt a little sad. "My Granny, with her Cherokee blood, loved and taught me to have integrity. I miss her."

"You don't need to miss her; she's right behind you. She is with you. All you must do is accept her being on another plane where she doesn't have a physical body. But she's with you," Shirley said.

"True. I feel her patting my back. I love you, Granny!" As soon as the words left my lips, the fire soared higher with a loud crackling wood fire sound.

"Now that is strong! Favorite Person. My Granny loves us. I say she and Maggy arranged our meeting. When I was a little tyke, my Granny loved me. Well, she loved me even when I wasn't a little tyke. We had a gardener working in the flower bed under her window and from time to time she would laugh because when she spit the tobacco juice her aim was good, and her chew got him. He would yell, and she would tell me, "Good one, I got him."

I didn't realize what she was trying to teach me until now, but tonight is a good time to accept her wisdom. Many a time, she sat me on her lap and told me Cherokee stories about our family. She would try not to chew but from time to time she had to spit. The more she rocked the louder the rocker squeaked and the more she had to spit.

No one dared to sit in her chair, it was for only her, I still can hear her say, President Andrew Jackson, the old bastard, ignored the Supreme Court decision, enforced his Indian Removal Act of 1830, and pushed through the Treaty of New

Echota. And then she stopped rocking and spit out the window." We sat motionless for several minutes just tightly holding each other.

"I never moved," I said, "I liked hearing her stories. 'Your ancestors were a part of that movement J Patrick. You are my grandson and it's my duty to teach you about the Cherokee story to educate you, to never be forgotten. You must help our heritage; you must love the land and you must be a strong man with a kind heart.'

The legend of her family stories has resonated within me. I still feel it to the core of my soul. My grandad Charles E. Cox was from England. He belonged to the Royal Aeronautical Society established in the United Kingdom and originating out of London, but today it is a British Aerospace engineer organization, not in the United States. His family moved to Oklahoma where he married Granny in 1920. They later moved to Colleyville, Texas and had six children, nineteen grandchildren and nineteen great grandchildren."

I stood up, looked at the flames, then sat back down.

Shirley scooted closer to me and said, "She was teaching you the threads of the divine, constantly woven to the legend of family. It's one of our blessings."

Shirley hugged me even tighter and was incredibly quiet—almost with tears in her eyes she said, "She was a spunky lady!"

I smiled, "My Granny was tiny but robust—like you. She liked walking in the forest and was never still. I was convinced that Granny's opinion was one of the greatest importance. She possessed that indescribable kind of manner which places you under the conviction that you are continually doing, saying, or thinking something wrong; and which makes you humbly obliged to such a person for coinciding in any of your opinions."

"I remember clearly to this day," I said, "Granny told me our family didn't like Stand Watie. 'Now remember this J. Patrick, Stand Watie, at that time was our Cherokee Chief and a Brigadier General. He was a back stabber. He signed the treaty forcing our people removal of their territory out of Georgia all for the sake of gold.' Granny called him a big fat traitor!"

"Oh, wow! What a statement," Shirley murmured and wide eyed at the same time.

"I chose the most perfect memory of my granny and clung to it. I chose it because she was the person who held something so golden and sacred. I wanted to keep it forever, like an old movie reel, I can play it at will. The finest detail is her face, creased with love and wisdom. I'm saddened that I didn't understand her until now. She always told the truth no matter if it hurt you. She was filled with truth," I answered.

"Numerous times, she called out, 'J. Patrick, you are a healer and do not throw your pearls to the swine. Have respect for what your ancestors did. Your great-great grandmother walked and survived the Trail of Tears. You must follow your heart, your intuition, and don't allow your brain to control you.'"

"Sexual energy is the most powerful healing energy there is," Shirley said. "According to ancient teachings, when sexuality is aimed at our spiritual paths, it can either be an obstacle in your way, blocking you from enlightenment, or it can open your heart to love and grant you the ability to enjoy enlightenment. To understand the difference between the two and place yourself on the path to enlightenment is the best; otherwise, you prevent yourself from evolving. First and foremost, you need to understand that the person you choose to have sexual encounters with can either make or break the energetic field necessary to become empowered through sex. This energy is powerful for a healer."

"Uh oh!" I sighed. "Many a time I threw my pearls to the swine. It was easy to pick up women in the grocery store. I enjoyed cooking so while getting my groceries, I would pick up a woman, take her home with me, cook, feed her then we had sex and I sent her home with leftover food. I didn't make her clean the kitchen though. That wouldn't have been gentlemanly."

We both started laughing hysterically. Shirley almost couldn't breathe.

"Since we met, I now understand what she meant—don't take your energy and give it away sexually, instead I was to save it for myself and help others. I've always had a strong feeling to help people but held back. I'm learning the other side of me. I know about the scientific world but not the spiritual world and that is strong in me, just as stout as this fire's flames working to reach up to the sky," I chatted.

Shirley got serious again. "I understand, Patrick. I had that same fire in me until I met Maggy. Her mentoring was the frosting of my life. It was real, true and I felt it all through my time with her."

I scooted closer. "Your fire is hot and steamy, Favorite Person! It always quickly excites me, and I like that."

"Warrior man, come into my blanket," Shirley said, wrapping her blanket around me. We sat aimlessly looking at the fire as though it held our past, present, and future.

"Big Ben is one of the most beautiful places on this planet," Shirley said with awe.

"The Chihuahuan desert area is recognized as one of the best places for dark-sky stargazing. Look up at all those stars, bright planets, and the clear outline of the Milky Way band. Oh, what a night, looking out at that starry sky! I could write a song about this adventure," I laughed.

"Can you do better than the one we sang to the tree?" Shirley laughed and then became curious. "I wonder if Indians lived around here. I'm sure they did."

I told Shirley the history shows Comanche and Apache many times crossed the Rio Grande River. "But that's about all I know. Best to ask Leon since he's Comanche. Let's finish our conversation about how drilling oil hurts Earth. I'm not sure about that?" I was somewhat despondent about how I might have harmed the Earth.

Shirley took my hand and rubbed it lightly. "Leon taught me Earth is a living planet. I believe humans are a unique combination of earthly, natural material and life-giving power of God. We are alive and so is Earth. Inside, Earth has bowels just like inside our bodies, so drilling inside Earth tapping into oil is like tapping into her veins."

"I'm full of questions about Leon's theory."

"Okay, here goes. Leon told me that centuries ago even scientists were comfortable with the notion of a living planet Earth," Shirley said. "According to Leon, James Hutton, often known as the father of geology..."

"Stop for a sec. I didn't get a degree in engineering not to know who James Hutton was. Heck, he was even a question on one of the tests I took in college. I remember, I'm amazed, that the Earth of a living superorganism and that its proper study would be by physiology. Hutton went on to make the analogy between the circulation of the blood, the circulation of the nutrient elements of Earth and of the way that sunlight distills water from the oceans so that it may later fall as rain and refresh Earth."

"I'm never amazed with what you remember, J. Patrick. Anyway, back in those days, Leon said science developed rapidly and soon fragmented into a collection of independent thinking. It became the province of the expert, and there was little good to be said about interdisciplinary thinking. To understand the world was a task as difficult as assembling a planet-size jigsaw puzzle. It was all too easy to lose sight of the picture in the searching and sorting of the pieces."

With a twinkle in my eyes, I remarked, "Well, I didn't learn that in college. Leon is starting to make sense. So, you believe Earth actually goes through pain and moods?"

Shirley firmly stated, "I believe Earth is our mother and sky is our father. With their energy we have it all. We are to care for Earth and not abuse her or the sky. I believe we are Earth's living life cells and what we think is what Earth becomes. I'm not one to tell people what to do; everyone has their God given free will. What I can do is point out what we are doing to ourselves and our planet in hopes others will see the bigger picture. We are all ONE. This planet is all one and time has caused us to drift apart. It's time for unity! We need to protect the Earth and stop polluting father sky. Until we learn to love ourselves, we will continue to battle against ourselves. We must learn that the first step is to love ourselves."

I had a serious look on my face. "Years ago, the first pictures of Earth from space gave us a glimpse of what it was we were trying to model. That vision of stunning beauty; that dappled white and blue sphere stirred us all."

"Earth's view from space, confirmed James Hutton's vision of a living planet. When seen in infrared light, the Earth is a strange and wonderful anomaly among the planets of the solar system." Shirley went on lecturing. "Oh, Patrick, do I sound like a teacher now?"

"Sure do, but I don't mind. I wish my teachers looked like you when I was in school."

"Patrick, stop! You were probably in trouble so much that you couldn't go out to recess for weeks!"

I threw back my head and roared. "How did you know that? You weren't in my class. You weren't even in my school! But I'll be a good kid and listen some more. I was just using this as an excuse to kiss you." And I did.

My kisses were not always the same, but to Shirley this one steeped in a passion that ignites. It was the promise of realness, of the primal desire that lives in us all. It told Shirley I was awake, connected within as I embraced life.

Shirley pulled away after the long kiss, "Our atmosphere, the air we breathe, was revealed to be outrageously out of equilibrium in a chemical sense."

I couldn't help myself. "I know what it's like to be outrageously out of equilibrium. That's when you get a hangover."

"I don't have any idea what you're talking about, Patrick. I was a good kid in school. I was so shy I didn't think my teachers even knew I was on their class roll. Okay, let me go on. It is like the mixture of gases that enters the intake manifold of an internal combustion engine. You know—hydrocarbons and oxygen mixed, whereas our dead partners Mars and Venus have atmospheres like gases exhausted by combustion."

"Oh," I inserted, "you did listen in class." I jumped up, stirred the fire, and then got back in the blanket pulling Shirley close to me.

"Correct! I was always a good girl. The sense of reality comes from matching our personal mental image of the world. With that we perceive by our senses. That is why the astronaut's view of the Earth was so disturbing. It showed us just how far from reality we had strayed."

"I'm beginning to see the bigger picture now," I said.

Sitting by the slow burning fire, wrapped in our blanket, looking like two peas in a pod, watching the gorgeous starry sky made us happy.

A wolf howling in the distance altered my curiosity, "What does wolf totem mean?"

"It represents the teacher, pathfinder, and its howling is called singing," Shirley quickly answered.

I laughed, "Maybe he wants to help me with my song *Oh what a starry night*?"

We both giggled. "Favorite Person, how did you know what the messages at Paint Rock drawings were?"

Shirley hugged my shoulder and kissed me. "It was in Mexico. Abbot, my Mayan teacher, taught me pictographs, hieroglyphics, and their meanings. He taught me through stories. He had me use my abilities of what I felt while looking at the hieroglyphics and I gave him my interruptions. They were accurate, so Abbot said my subconscious mind was releasing the right information."

"Wait a minute." I said, "Everyone has a subconscious, but for most of us, our knowledge of it ends there. I believe my subconscious mind is a second brain, a hidden mind that exists within my brain. But my brain doesn't interrupt pictographs or hieroglyphics. What you're saying just doesn't make sense."

Shirley laughed affectionately. "Abbot knew Gurnada had taken me aboard his ship and given me information beyond Earth's knowledge; the knowledge is stored in my subconscious."

"That makes sense," I said.

With a sigh, Shirley leaned her head on my shoulder. My warm hands slid under the blanket, caressing her back through her shirt.

The evening slipped seamlessly into the night leading us to call it a good night.

CHAPTER 18

Enchanting Times

*"We must raise our vibrations and heal ourselves through
the love energy of our heartbeat musical flow."*

Shirley—1990

There is nothing cozier than arriving home where a person feels secure with everything that is going on. It truly buffs outside world events.

Early one morning, Patrick gave me a good morning and then a goodbye kiss before leaving for his office. I too, had a full day answering my clients' phone messages. I always put my heart and soul in my work and aspired to the highest efficiency in the achievement of results for each client. And it made me happy that they patiently waited until I was available to schedule their appointment.

Late in the afternoon while unpacking, my thoughts drifted off to us relocating to a quieter place. The idea of moving took root in my heart and became an earnest desire, which compelled me to smile. My heart was pounding hard, and warmth invaded my neck with the idea of having my promise fulfilled by getting Maggy's book published. I hoped Patrick wouldn't eventually be sorry for making his decisions. Getting married, selling his company and then moving was a significant shift for anyone. The front door opened, and there stood a smiling Patrick. He had come home early and happy.

Putting his briefcase down he said, "My employees are hosting a farewell party to wish us good luck for our journey ahead."

"I'm not surprised. I know how highly respected you are with friends and employees.

When?"

"It's scheduled for Saturday evening at Gershwin's. They said it all started there where we met…might as well say goodbye there. Mike says there will be at least a hundred friends and staff wanting to shake our hands." Taking off his tie Patrick said, "They say I'm going to be missed."

Saturday arrived fast, and I had carefully chosen my clothes wanting to look extra good for Patrick. I wore a long black, low-cut dress, highlighted with a swing pearl rope necklace grazing my chest. My accessories were dangling black pearl earrings, black leather heels and I carried a golden handbag. Patrick wore a black suit with a white shirt and a dark blue tie.

The evening was beautiful with its borderless flow of clarity. The stars winked like sequins on a dark velvet gown. The night chill made us walk fast. Patrick stuck out his elbow and I grabbed it. All dazzled up we walked the same cement parking lot where we first met, and it still looked the same. It had markings as though an elephant with stilettos had tottered down it is causing a great cobweb of cracks.

"This parking lot is where we had our first kiss," I said giggling. "Remember my car didn't want to start until you turned around, like you demanded, and it started."

"Think we had some help from above with that Favorite Person. It was a magical night for us." Patrick muttered.

Patrick opened Gershwin's door to people's laughter and loud music with a Doobie Brothers song playing "Takin It to The Streets," one of our favorite songs. Entering the large dimly lit room, Patrick whispered, "Are you prepared for this, Favorite Person? There are a lot of people here."

I nodded my head yes. The DJ stopped the music, and to our surprise, a spotlight moved across the room illuminating us.

I knew Patrick's friends were there to bid him farewell, but they were also anxious to see who he'd be riding off in the sunset with. I gulped.

The tables were arranged in banquet style seating, beautifully decorated white tablecloths, black napkins, china, crystal glasses, sparkly silverware, candles, and assorted colorful flowers. The room was sparkling physically and emotionally, and the energy was high. Men and women came rushing to shake Patrick's hand. Immediately, Patrick introduced me, directing all the attention to me. I soon learned Patrick was good at doing that.

A lady in a stunning red dress started walking towards Patrick and me. The dress traced her movements in a way that made eyes follow her body. She walked like a model, very tall and attractive with short black hair.

She stuck out her hand and said, "Hi, Shirley, my name is Barb. I want to invite you to our Ft. Worth Petroleum Club…hope you have time before leaving."

I turned to Patrick. Barb continued, "Patrick, for the sake of God. I have no idea why you would want to move out of Texas? Shirley, you would love our club's food and our dining room. We, women in the oil business, meet there once a month. What type of work do you do? My husband owns and operates his own oil company, and I own and manage a coffee and courier company. It keeps me busy helping young adults, who work for me."

Ron, her husband, walked over and stood beside her. She looked at me, "He says he's proud of me." She poked him. "Aren't you?"

Ron was not really paying any attention to her but agreed with a nod of his head and walked away.

I thanked her and said, "I'm a psychic."

Barb said, touching her extra-large diamond ring on her left hand, "Oh! You tell people's fortune?"

I shifted the way I was standing. "I don't know what you mean by telling people's fortune. I'm a psychic who helps people better understand themselves—you know, their strength, potential, and weakness. I also teach seminars for those who want to develop their psychic abilities. Everyone is psychic. Some people are just not aware of it."

Barb looked over her shoulder. "I told my husband I'm psychic, but he just laughed at me. I could help him find oil and make a large amount money if he would let me. I'm surprised Patrick doesn't laugh at you."

With a lovely smile, I looked at Barb and said, "Oh no, Patrick has never laughed. He respects my abilities."

Barb batted her eyes. I closely watched her eye movement knowing that eyes broadcast emotions. A person might be able to hide a smirk, but the micro-movement of her eyes, eyelids, and brows reveals the truth behind a face. I realized this lady wasn't truthful as I stepped aside.

"Congratulations, Shirley. Keep up the excellent work. The world needs more people like you. Please join us some time at our club. I want to talk more with you. Patrick, good to see you again. Hope you have a great life out of the oil business. Although Ron and I can't imagine you would. You must think it's a good idea or you wouldn't be doing it." Barb said as she walked away.

The next lady standing in front of me said, "Hi, I'm Jan, I couldn't help but hear what you told my Aunt Barb. The family calls her Miss. Hoity-Toity. She's so full of herself. Uncle Ron spoils her with money, and he gives her everything she can think of. Her wishes are always answered. She is spoiled and loved by her rich husband. I have been looking for someone like you to help me. Do you have a card? When can I schedule an appointment?"

She turned towards Patrick, "We'll miss you, Patrick. You're a good oil businessman. Wish you the best of luck. Shirley, it was my pleasure meeting you. I have never met a psychic. Maybe someday we can sit down and talk about it."

I turned to Patrick trying to shift the conversation. He instantly started telling everyone the reason he was getting out of the oil and gas business. He was going to help me with my important projects. The first on my list was to finish writing Maggy Conn, my mentor's book. He would still be working with the Earth just in a different way. Instead of drilling holes in the Earth, he would be preserving Earth any way he could.

The DJ announced that it was time to sit at our tables, so everyone started looking for their name cards. I took a sip of champagne and realized Patrick had more friends and business acquaintances than I realized. It made me feel proud.

The DJ announced, "Patrick, it's time for a toast."

As Patrick slowly stood up, raised his wine glass to eye level and started thanking everyone for attending. He gave a strong short speech to his business friends. He knew his audience and met their needs with his stories. He delivered by adding honor and personality into the entire time. Afterward, everyone stood up and applauded.

All good times must come to an end. Everyone was full, content and all talked out. They started saying their goodbyes with hugs and handshakes. Mike Rogers was the last to give Patrick a manly hug while shaking his hand. It was obvious their firm handshake showed a sign they had an eternal bond of real friendship. "Now buddy, I want to hear from you. Don't go off and leave me wondering what you're doing. You know I have always covered your back."

Patrick, still holding Mike's hand said, "Buddy, you have got to come and visit once we get settled. We'll go fishing and do the things you like to do. I'll be sure and keep in touch. I won't forget you. Love you. buddy."

I had never heard two men express their love for each other. Where I was from if they did, they were called sissies. These two were strong men, and they had no problem with it. I knew this was true friendship.

A hush filled the car while driving home. Patrick and I were in our thoughts.

~~~

Patrick sipped on a brandy and felt cozy while sitting in front of the fireplace with me by his side. "Favorite Person, I have no regrets in retiring from the oil and gas business. I want to be your business manager. I don't have any mixed feelings about it. I feel it's necessary to get on with it and I have started the paperwork to sell my business to Mitchem."

He took my hand in his and gave it a warm, gentle squeeze.

My eyes teared up. "I'm very appreciative, Patrick. After Maggy made her transition, I've been trying to do all this work by myself. I need help. I had a strong feeling to move out of the big city, and my goal is to continue private sessions and seminars while you edit Maggy's book."

Patrick stood up, sat his brandy glass on the fireplace mantel and then loudly affirmed, "Then consider it done! We're starting our mission!"

~~~

A week later, I was busy cleaning out my closet when Patrick rushed in, looking like the cat that ate the canary. "Favorite Person, come with me. Come with me now!"

I threw a dress on the bed. "Now, what's the big hurry, Patrick? I'm busy getting ready for our trip."

Patrick insisted and wouldn't stop until I agreed.

"It's important. Now don't open your eyes until I tell you."

Patrick put his hands over my eyes and led me outside. "Now stand here; don't move." Patrick removed his hands and yelled "Surprise!"

I stood, staring at a brand-new dark grey Lincoln Continental with burgundy leather interior. "Where did you get this? It's beautiful!" Is it actually yours?"

Patrick teasingly looked at me. No, Favorite Person. It's yours. I bought it for you. Happy Birthday ahead of time. I want you to travel in a luxury car to rest and be comfortable in a spacious cabin with easily adjustable seats."

I turned and gave Patrick a big hug. "Aw, you're spoiling me."

He quickly replied, "That's my job, Shirley."

The car was well-packed for our two-week trip. Exiting on the freeway, heading towards Jackson, Mississippi, locking the car on auto drive, Patrick started singing *I'm a Traveling Man*.

I chimed in, and Patrick quickly said, "You can't carry a tune. Let me finish the song without my ears hurting."

I laughed. "Maggy told me the same thing. She said I have a lot of talent, but it wasn't in singing." Patrick nodded his head, jokingly agreeing.

CHAPTER 19

Learning A New Way

"Without me reconnecting with myself, I wouldn't have my
freedom and fulfillment I seek."

Shirley—1990

Clinnon Alexander, the seminar host in Jackson, Mississippi, welcomed us with open arms. I had known Clinnon for a few years and knew she was raised to believe that southern hospitality isn't a choice. It's more of an institution. In her household, you abide by southern rituals and customs beyond swinging on the front porch, sipping on sweet tea, and gathering on Sunday for a sit-down potluck supper. While most would define southern hospitality as being neighborly and welcoming family, friends, and, yes, even strangers into their homes, Patrick and I felt fortunate Clinnon had invited us to stay in her roomy southern home. Her home was warm and cozy.

After the three-day Universal Love Seminar titled 'Freedom', I asked the group if they would like to discuss what they learned. A handsome middle-aged man with deep red curls, hazel blue eyes, stood up and introduced himself.

"I'm Jim, a CEO from New Jersey. I learned a valuable exercise in information exchange with this seminar. When you asked if we loved ourselves, I became all a tingle. My body was reacting like there was a gorilla about to beat the crap out of me instead of being faced with the truth of the question you asked. In the calmness of this room, if asked how to fix any business problem I can ace that stuff. I know I can. I drink it in, horror though it is for the most part. Who can conquer who? Who could rise to power and abuse it? Fascinating stuff. But my body is preparing for a marathon instead of sitting still for a couple of hours and pondering do I really love myself. That's heavy."

The group laughed.

Jim continued, "After you directed us through that color meditations I sat for a long time while my brain fought the urge to walk, no, run like hell out the door. I didn't though. I sat and thought about this. I can make policies ten miles long, attend meetings, and dress professionally. But when I'm asked if I love myself, my mind is full of pain. I saw myself as a young boy crying because my dad spanked me, and what hurt the most was I saw why I needed that spanking. I had lied to him. It wasn't about what my dad was doing that hurt. It was to see what I had done. I saw pictures of my life up to today of troubled experiences I had created. Busy thinking all this then figured, I couldn't take any more in. So, I told my brain unless you're gonna fix this, unless you're gonna care, shut up. Please, for the love of God, shut up. It was then I felt a shift in my body, like my body jerked, my brain stopped thinking, and my heart started pumping fast. I got hot. I could feel this heated energy pumping through my body. My shirt began to cling to my back in places, my hair was saturated, and salty drops ran into my mouth, so I knew what was going on. I used to sweat so gross. It was the dark stain under the pits of my dad that grossed me out. To a teenager that's right up there with puss and puke. I've become obsessed, part of being an insecure person."

I asked, "Did you have a good relationship with your parents?

Jim's body movement shifted. "Dad never said 'I love you.' He wasn't one of those fun parents who spun you around by your arms until you were dizzy. He didn't build me a go-cart or dance with me to rock 'n' roll. He watched his money and took care of the car. He didn't gush over me or inflate my ego in any way. He spent years filling a college fund so that I could have an education at any university I chose, but he never told me what to study. That was my choice. He never advised me unless I asked for it. He never really spoke unless someone else did first. Now every time I visit, he checks my tire treads and air pressure before he lets me go. My mother was one who showered me with love and affection. I'm the kind of guy who doesn't want others to see. I didn't want to be called a sissy, but it did feel good. I sense I have overcome this now I can say, I love you, Jim.

Debbie was an IT lady from the group, casual, but smartly dressed in jeans, a hipster jacket, and a neck scarf. Her face was made up, but not overdone, and her long black hair was pulled back into a ponytail. She cleared her throat and asked, "Jim, are you okay? I sat beside you and knew you were changing something in you. My dad never paid any attention to me. My mother was too bossy. But I don't allow emotions to interfere with my IT work."

"I love myself, Jim affirmed while frowning. "It is as if all my life I've been isolated, in a windowless room, in a doorless room. Then suddenly I felt my heart had awakened and walked in as if strolling over a summer meadow. 'How is that I am so much more than sunshine?' I asked myself. How is it I breathe life and love myself more than anything else? ME? So, my love knows while I breathe, my mind, body, and soul feels freedom."

I eagerly said, "While meditating, you made some energy connection with your brain and heart."

"I'm not for sure what I did; however, I like the freedom feeling. I feel so light and carefree for the first time in my life," Jim replied.

I smiled and continued, "Actually, through meditation you connected your brain to your heart by the flow of your emotional energy. That is the reason you got hot. It's a heated energy. Eons ago we humans disconnect our energy of the brain to our heart creating a battle within. It is written that fear is our worst enemy and the biggest weapons used against us. Worry, anxiety, fear, can overwhelm us with a thick shadow of darkness, controlling every move or decision we make.

The brain has control, but the heart has your soul's wisdom. Once connected you will get to better life decisions. Love is the answer for human's are the creator of all world problems. Love reduces cortisol, the stress hormone, which alters your brain architecture, the energy comprised of billions of connections between individual neurons enabling a lightning-fast communication among neurons that specialize in different kinds of brain functions.

A lady raised her hand and asked, "Does that connection really help, if so, then how?"

Directing my full attention to the group, I responded, "It will lower stress and eliminates fear. Fear is our worst enemy; I call it a sin to our soul. We counter act fear with love. Love is the answer because it heals the brain to enhance the ability for more love and nurture. Creating conditions for the healing of the brain is the answer to world problems. The brain and heart connections feed the brain to heal. It's all about loving yourself."

It was obvious the way Jim looked. He needed to talk more. Jim stated, "It was scary but most helpful opening myself to my love's infinite possibility. A spiritual key to finding myself. I was one that viewed my true self as I grew up and became fascinated by the cultural beliefs about worth, value, and success. I began to compare myself to everyone else until I had all but lost my awareness of what I inherited, which was innocence and perfection. The seminar helped me to stop seeing myself through the eyes of others but to see myself through my eyes. I learned I have a divine within. The presence eternally holds me in its arms and knows the truth of my perfection. I feel a new connection within me. I feel and know my love and freedom I was seeking. I put myself on a never-ending treadmill trying to fix life. I'm tired of my treadmill so today I stepped off it. Thank you, Shirley!"

I quickly thanked Jim. "Your testimony touches our hearts."

Everyone stood up nodding their head yes while applauding.

The group sat down except Joan, a Dallas bank president. She had the air of one used to punctual service, her face poised to give her order and her manicured hand flying while she spoke. Her eyes flickered, and her head tilted to one side just a smidge before she delivered an articulate answer. "You helped us to understand we weren't meant to be compliant; we have strong hearts and strong wills. We aren't supposed to follow and be told what to think blindly. You support us in using our strong hearts to love and our curious minds to drive us to learn, to seek new answers, to explore boldly. We are nobody's trained monkeys. Your classroom is a place of love, of learning, and compassion. You enable us to thrive and have self-confidence. You teach respect and to always question. I didn't have an experience like Jim did but wish I had. I think we all are here today and need to learn more about ourselves."

Linda, Austin CPA, charming brunette with a broad smile, spar-kly eyes and when she spoke her Texas accent was obvious. Giggling she told her story. "I first met Shirley during my car crash a few years back. The moment this car crashed into my car, I assumed I was dead. Then I felt myself flying out the window with my typewriter and books going with me. It was while flying in the air I saw Shirley's face. I didn't know her at that time, but I saw her face and heard her voice. I thought, when I land, this is going to hurt, and I hoped my typewriter did not fall on top of me. That would hurt. Once I hit the ground, I liked being unconscious rather than awake. Because when I was awake, I could taste the coppery blood pooling in my mouth. I could feel it grazing my teeth and soaking my tongue. I felt the aching and cracks in my bones. Each crack felt like rocks were burrowing into my skin. I saw the spots in the corners of my vision, making my head feel like the only thing inside of it was static. I heard a buzzing noise, filling my ears. I felt like I was there for hours, fading in and out. A few years later I met Shirley at a chiropractor's office in Arlington Texas. I knew then she was to be my teacher."

A big "AHH" was heard from the group.

Linda continued, "Shirley's seminars are always a mind and heart opening experience. I have attended several of her seminars. When we all came together as a group, she would work with us both individually and collectively, showing us how to draw in "our colors." This work allowed us to attune to and gather the energy of Universal Love, for healing, creativity, and protection."

Linda went on, "Depending on what kind of challenge or opportunity showed up, she would guide us toward the next step to take, never insisting but rather offering up the choice that was before us. I especially liked when Shirley always reminded us, Gee, You Are You." and that is a true GURU!"

I stated, "Thank you. And thank you with lots of love to all. Enjoy the new you in the outside world."

CHAPTER 20

The Self's Evolution

"Well, I won't forget that one, for sure. I don't want to lose my tail. I've already lost another part of my body too many times to count," he guffawed.

Shirley—1990

As the car engine sung to the road, I relished the roaring winds that twirled in my blond hair and whistled in my ears. Patrick was driving out of Jackson, hopefully to look at a new home, a cabin owned by Jim and Jane, located on Gillespie Road near Jackson. It was a quaint homey cabin with Early American furniture. Patrick quickly showed me where a desk would fit for the necessary editing. It needed to be in a quiet place so he wouldn't be disturbed. Walking from room to room we noticed lizards running around, climbing the walls and window curtains. I opened a closet door and to my surprise I had lizards running around my feet. I carefully stepped backward, watching them run every which way. Then the scream like a mountain lion came rolling out of my mouth.

"Those tiny things won't hurt you. What does the Lizard totem represent?" Patrick laughingly asked.

Catching my breath, I gasped. "I'm not afraid of them. I just don't want them to climb on me. The lizard totem is a reliable messenger from the spiritual realm. They are flexible and highly adaptive to their surroundings, capable of overcoming an excess of adverse circumstances and personal attacks. Their ability to thrive in such conditions earns them the symbolism of being able to go with the flow and the inherent value of amalgamating in the wild."

Patrick interrupted, "Okay, anything else? Don't see any big messages for us here." He hugged and held me in comfort.

I started to talk into his shoulder and then pulled away. "One of the most interesting traits of the lizard is the ability to break off their tails to escape predators. The tail is left behind hoping to take the predators attention off them, to flee.

Patrick interrupted, "I don't have a tail so I can't flee."

"Stop!" I laughed. "You're making me laugh too hard. Even if you had one, lizards are only able to perform this feat once. The new tail grows to replace the old one."

"Well yeah, their tails consist of cartilage instead of vertebrae," Patrick reassured.

"The main meaning," I murmured, "is that Lizard's power lies in the quality of being able to rescue himself from danger by leaving a part of himself behind. As a lizard, it can lose his tail once. We must make our choices wisely as the consequences may be experienced for a long-time hereafter!"

"Well, I won't forget that one, for sure. I don't want to lose my tail. I've already lost another part of my body too many times to count," he guffawed.

"Did you know lizards are very sensitive to vibrations from the ground?" I quizzed Patrick. "They are adept at subtle perception. They have an amazing hearing capacity. With their sharp eyes they can sense the minutest of movements. The psychic characteristics found in the lizard teach us how to awaken our abilities by choosing one path over another that honors every part of our lives."

"I just don't sense a message about our move here through lizard totem," Patrick voiced.

"Lizards also represent rain. Maybe it's just simply a message that it's going to."

Wee hours of the morning, it was no surprise being awakened by the sharp, loud crack to a long low rumble thunder caused by lightning. The rain pounded on the roof and the wind caused a hollowing sound through the windows.

I cuddled closer to Patrick and muttered, "I love you."

Patrick whispered, "I love you too, Favorite Person. We know what those lizards were trying to tell us. Now go back to sleep."

~~~

Driving gave Patrick and I time to discuss the automatic writings for seminar material. Patrick said, "First of all I like the title The Self's Evolution. The writing says self-evolution and the evolution of Mother Earth is musical. It is based on the rhythm of our heartbeat. Being the engineer that I am, how does my heartbeat make a rhythm of music with Earth?"

"Oh, that's easy. You took geometry in the 10th grade. The mystical Pythagoras was excited by his discovery of the heartbeat and believed humans could understand the physical universe energy through numbers, tones, and colors. The Universe is in perfect harmony. All is in common with the spiritual love energy vibrating in the Universe. Once you understand, apply, and align yourself with the Universal Love, you will experience transformation in every area of your life beyond that which you have ever dared to imagine. It can be transcended or at least, "better used" to create your ideal reality. When we are happy, our heartbeat is happy, and that vibration enters earth's energy. Universal Love truly is our aim to master."

"So, Pythagoras found souls heartbeat in the Universe?" Patrick asked.

Maggy told me, "He became convinced the whole universe was based on numbers, and the planets and stars moved according to mathematical equations, which corresponded to musical notes, and thus produced a kind of symphony, the 'Musical Universalis.'"

"I know scientists say listening to music is good for your health. Crank up the tunes and blast those beats because the results are in! Music is good for you. There is a healing power of music." Patrick went on, "There are some serious scientific benefits for our health and overall well-being by music. So, the writings are saying our heartbeat is like a drumbeat. It has its own music tone, and it needs to be in a rhythm tune to vibrate with the Earth's heartbeat."

"You got it!" I exclaimed. "Each person's heartbeat rhythm is the music that sends out and what we receive is the love from others. This rhythm vibration is your key to the tones and colors through the vibrations of universal love that you chose to send and receive. The atoms sent by these tones and colors are the crystal frequency unique to each one. Everyone has the intellectual capacity to accept this knowledge and logic to create a masterpiece of their own frequency to this new light coding, so each can reach more and more."

Patrick said pensively, "Now I get it. Everyone marches to the beat of a different drum. Each person's heartbeat vibrates a frequency of a love tone that will spread to others and over the Earth. Each flower, tree, ocean, animals, etc. has their own vibrations of tones to help Earth's vibration and it can create a peaceful planet. It's us humans that get in the way of a harmonic planet. And speaking of harmonic planets, I'm thirsty. What do you want to drink?"

"Now, Patrick, you said you were thirsty and asked me what I want. What am I missing here?" I asked with chuckles.

"Can't get one past you, can I? You know, you are not just another pretty blonde. Oh, but I already know that. Yes, I'm thirsty. Let's stop this lesson and get something to drink."

Patrick turned the car around.

"Where are you going?" I asked.

"If my Favorite Person wants some iced tea and she doesn't have any, I'm going to go get her some."

"Silly, I can live without it. Remember, you're the one who wanted something to drink in the first place."

~~~

There was a magical silence and then I began again. "I just can't help it. I love this life so much and I just want to do a brain-dump and give you everything I know all at once."

"Okay, go for it. I don't mean to literally dump your brain, which would be messy to clean up, but tell me more."

I took a deep breath. "It's so important to teach and help people understand to raise the human vibrations on Earth. People must learn how to get out of the lower vibrations to know that fear vibrates greed, hate, judgment and creates diseases. We must raise our vibrations and heal ourselves through the love energy of our heartbeat musical flow."

"Okay I clearly understand now." Driving onto the exit ramp Patrick jokingly said, "Think we need a pit stop before compassion fatigue kicks in."

"Oh, and don't forget, you want something to drink," I laughed.

CHAPTER 21

Earth's Beauty

"Yes, we are Earth-loving people. We like to walk, swim, hug trees and really, do about all outside activities."

Patrick—1991

At the same instant, the sun popped out from behind the clouds, a welcoming sign to the city of Cheyenne, Wyoming appeared. I felt the warmth in the sunshine, its brilliance, reflecting a shimmer from the ends of my eyelashes, deep brown though they are. It invites my eyes to rest, so that I may see the strong rays even when I appear to be sleeping. It's the kind of sunshine that comes at any time of year, illuminating summer meadows and alpine slopes all the same. I wish there was a word for the feeling it brings, for now I'm calling it "sunjoy."

It didn't take long before we parked out front of Roger and Darcy's home. As we were walking towards the house, Darcy, a petite, short haired platinum blond with boundless and bubbly energy threw open the door and rushed out welcoming us with a big hug.

Roger, sitting in an overstuffed recliner, laid his Western Hunting magazine down and took off his glasses. Morgan, their daughter, a cute little brown haired, brown eye, six-year-old, wearing a buckskin dress playing Indians, ran around in the living room with her little friend. Dancing past us I couldn't help but notice Morgan's few freckles across her nose, a sign of her individuality. Roger told the girls to play outside with Morgan's rabbit. Both girls squealed and the door slammed as they ran out outside.

After a short visit I informed everyone that dinner was my treat.

It was the first time Shirley had eaten Chinese food in a western atmosphere. There were big round tables with red and white checkered tablecloths that filled the room. The walls had a couple of moose heads and western paintings. The restaurant smelled of Chinese food and Shirley felt as if she had entered a dreamland. The restaurant was filled with happy chatter. The sight and aroma of the food floated by in the hands of waitresses gently massaged to our senses.

We were invited to spend the night with Roger and Darcy and drive to Thermopolis the next morning. Roger was a police officer. His work wouldn't allow him to leave before the weekend. Since Roger wanted to swim at the Thermopolis hot mineral pools, it was a good idea for him to come along for the weekend. That way Darcy could ride home with him.

Shirley overheard Roger telling me that the two of them met while he and Darcy worked at the Police Department. Shirley was the County probation officer. They met and instantly became friends.

"It's hard for me to visualize Shirley being a probation officer," I hesitantly said.

Roger laughed and continued, "Well, Patrick, when my chief told me the probation officer needed to talk about a drug bust I had made,

I told him, 'No way was I going to her office and there was nothing he could say to change my mind.' I was sure she was going to try and talk me into dropping the charges. Chief Prosser had to go with me to prove how wrong I was. He had already met her. To my surprise, she agreed with me and only needed to hear my side of the story for her pre-sentence report necessary for the judge. The State's Attorney, police officers and state troopers soon learned to respect her. We learned fast; she believed laws were not to be broken. Shirley's concern was for justice, peace, and genuine respect for those who followed the rules. And she wasn't bashful in letting people know it."

~~~

The next morning, driving out of Cheyenne, the car breathed and took energy as if it were part of the flora of the land. The driving became as natural as running free and the warm blacktop leading onward into the horizon, gave a sweet sense of freedom.

~~~

Darcy and Shirley hadn't seen each other after a long time, and Darcy couldn't hide her excitement that we may be moving to Thermopolis. She told the story how the house had gotten its Humpty Back name. Roger and his boss had a weekend trip to Thermopolis therapeutic pools. Roger gave him a tour of the house and while in the basement, he said that it looked like Humpty Back Trolls lived there. Darcy told us it had three bedrooms with two baths and two kitchens. The house was divided for renting purposes. It had a glassed-in front and back porch with a small outback barn.

Darcy turned her full attention to Shirley and said, "It has a clothesline too, Shirley. Just think, the wind can dry your laundry and it has a pleasant garden area."

"What about this clothesline? You want me to take it down?" I asked.

"No, lingerie tends to last longer with air drying so my intimates will dry out on a clothesline," Shirley replied.

"You're joking right?"

Laughing, Shirley said, "Haven't you seen pictures of bras that would hold their shape on a clothesline in a hurricane.

The three of us started laughing. We all needed that laugh so we kept on laughing. It was the best medicine for us.

Driving on US 20, through the windows of the car came a breathtaking view, it was a scene that could expand one's heart.

"What condition is the house? Is everything working properly, the furnace, air conditioner, plumbing, and sewerage?" I asked.

"We bought the house to have a place to stay when we went to the pools. Roger was in a motorcycle accident. The hot water therapy helped him tremendously. The house was a mess, but we cleaned, painted, and repaired everything. It should be in decent shape," Darcy answered. "There is no air conditioner, not necessary with the cooler climate. All you have to do is raise the windows, and you'll be plenty cool."

"Hard to convince a Texan you don't need air conditioning. Let's not do this, Shirley." I pretended to convince her this was not the place.

Shirley looked around. "The size of the place should be good, but we will have to see it first."

Darcy continued, "Sure, Thermopolis is a small community with laid back people, a lot like your hometown Shirley, Herrick, just bigger. You'll love the hot water pools. We go there every time work allows. It's a very peaceful place." The silence in the car captured the best of Darcy. She blurted "Okay, what do you think, are you interested? I hope so we can visit more."

Before we could answer, Darcy quietly said, "Roger told me not to ask. He said I needed to be patient and let you make your decision without a push."

It was obvious with no comment from either of us, Darcy facial expression showed, she sat quietly wondering what we thought.

Traveling north from Shoshoni, we come upon a view of Owl Creek Mountains, they were reaching high, as though to touch the blue skies. The only item more prominent than the range of granite peaks was the sky, dotted with the golden sunshine and as vast as any eye could wander. There was solitude here in the mountains where the lands were of a greater degree than mankind.

Darcy, looking out the window, commented, "The mountains have kept the soul of this land for time unmeasured and tell of it in words unspoken."

"Mountains talk and they have wisdom, their spiritual sounds are magical. They are one of God's messengers" Shirley stated.

Darcy replied, "Wind River Canyon is a scenic Wyoming canyon made from tectonic plate shifting, not carved by the Wind River."

"Ah ha!" I interrupted, "You don't have to explain what a tectonic plate shift is to this retired oilman."

Darcy commented, "I had forgotten that. But what I bet you don't know is that it is located between the cities of Shoshoni and Thermopolis. People say it's where you come face to face with the windswept west."

Shirley said, "Okay, I give up. What's tectonic?

I grinned. "Now it's my turn to teach, finally! Tectonic is a geology theory. The lithosphere of the Earth is divided into a small number of plates which float on and travel independently over the mantle. Much of the Earth's seismic activity occurs at the boundaries of these plates."

Shirley smiled, "Oh, its geometry."

"No," I immediately said, "It's geology, not geometry. There is a difference. The tectonic plate also called lithospheric plate."

"Hold on, Patrick. It's called a what?"

"Lithospheric—it's a massive, irregularly shaped slab of solid rock, generally composed of both continental and oceanic lithosphere. Geometry is the branch of math that deals with the measurement, properties, and relationships of points, lines, angles, surfaces."

Darcy busted out laughing, "Well, Shirley, you got that wrong, now, didn't you? Good, you have Patrick to help you with Earth's tectonic and geometry knowledge."

"I knew he wasn't speaking English," Shirley laughed.

It was the drive through Wind River Canyon that won our hearts. The mountains soared up like they wished to challenge the sky itself. They dominated the horizon in every which way they looked except back.

The winding stretch of highway was picturesque beyond belief–high cliffs and deep canyons with the turquoise blue river flowing below–just one amazing stretch of beauty watching the river run uphill. Shirley had never seen that before. Rivers always flow downhill. Occasionally Shirley would 'ohhh' or 'ahhh' and look at me while the water was running uphill.

I continued to drive steadily, "I'm driving, Shirley. Not wise for me to look around, don't you think?"

"Yikes, that's true! I'll just do the oohing and ahhing," Shirley muttered.

Darcy excitedly said, "Many locals know a trip up the Wind River Canyon has a surprising twist. While the scenery itself is spectacular, a mixture of optical and sensory illusions often causes people to think that water is traveling uphill going south from Thermopolis to Shoshoni. Just before going into the canyon, the river changes from being called the Bighorn River to the Wind River, a place known as the Wedding of the Waters. This is a unique place. The Indians say it is special. Wedding of the Waters is just four miles south of Thermopolis. It's where two rivers meet and become one. This river flows to a certain point, then changes its name and becomes an entirely different river. It isn't that the river was given a nickname, but rather its name was changed like a wife does after she marries."

When you travel south, the canyon walls get higher, so you feel like you are going deeper into the canyon, but if you look at the river, you can see you are going upstream."

I added, "Water typically flows with gravity, downhill Earth's gravity is strong, but water can naturally go against it and flow uphill if the parameters are right. There you go. Another geology lesson from this retired, now assistant to Shirley J. Smith. I'm a smart man."

Shirley sat quietly, and soon Darcy and I followed. The car was filled with quietness.

Finally, breaking the silence, Darcy pointed and said, "Look, a two-lane highway running along the side of blue turquoise waters, Wind River Canyon. The mountains are showing bare yellow. The rock stretched off to forever as the deep blue water ran uphill. With fallen rocks and boulders jutting from the riverbed, the unique water hydraulics make for some spectacular water views."

"The Indians call this area Mother Earth's womb."

Still riding through the canyon, Darcy scooted from her back seat, laying her arms on the back of Shirley's seat, and started talking. "The Arapaho and Shoshone Indian reservation, well their tribes still live here. It is located within the Wind River Basin surrounded by Wind River Mountain Range. All around Thermopolis are hieroglyphics, fossils, and rock petroglyphs. They are amazing. Do you like that sort of Earth art?"

"Of course. You know I have visited with the Hopi, Aborigines and other people whose belief is to protect the Earth." Shirley said.

I answered, "Yes, we are Earth's loving people. We like to walk, swim, hug trees and really about all outside activities."

"We are almost there," said Darcy as she sat back in her seat. Looking out the window, driving out of Wind River Canyon the view of a red, round topped mountain was capturing. Entering the city, Darcy suggested we look at some sites before going to the house.

Darcy began, "Thermopolis is home of the world's largest mineral hot springs in the Hot Springs State Park. Clouds of wet steam, the warmth of the waters, the allure of healing powers, the hidden source of the water, the smell of sulfur, and the scenic beauty make up the atmosphere of Thermopolis."

Darcy bragged as she continued her Thermopolis sales pitch, "I like visiting the Tea Pot area. It's a small pool of boiling water. Can't swim because it's too hot, but the water is hot enough to brew a cup of tea. It's surprising how it boils all the time."

Darcy excitingly continued, "This area was a notorious stop on the outlaw trail during the romanticized lawlessness of the American West. One of the most famous hideouts was Butch Cassidy's Wild Bunch and Jesse James's. The remote spot near Thermopolis is known as the Hole-In-The-Wall. This part of Wyoming, the real-life outlaws, has inspired books and movies.

Shirley took a deep breath. "I think we have seen enough for today. I need time to let this amount of beauty sink in. Let's go see the house."

With everyone in agreement, we drove to the house. Darcy happily gave us the house tour. She used the excuse of looking for something in the barn, allowing Shirley and I time to be by ourselves.

"Well, Favorite Person, what do you think? Is this our next place we call home?" I asked.

Shirley turned and looked at me. "I think you know the answer after that beautiful drive, learning about Indian history, the beauty, and the hot waters. What do you think?"

"I agree. This is our place."

We were hugging when we heard a squeak from the backdoor opening. Darcy was back. Her big eyes looked at me, then Shirley. It made us realize she was trying to figure out what our decision was.

I broke the silence and told Darcy we would be renting the house. "We noticed a desk and a computer in one of the bedrooms. We have an IBM typewriter, no computer."

Darcy said, "That was our surprise for you. It's an old Apple that Roger bought from work. We felt it would help you. Don't know how long it will last but it's yours to do as you please."

CHAPTER 22

Here They Go

"I had a dream showing our quest will revolve around historical mysteries."

Shirley-1991

The early morning was a ride like no other. It was a day, not a cloud in the sky and no chance of rain. Driving down the Texas interstate the car was packed to the hilt. Indeed, it was the perfect day for a drive to our new home in Thermopolis, Wyoming.

"I suppose I should warn you about this trip," I said. "I dreamed our trip would revolve around historical mysteries."

Patrick thought that any traveling they did was always full of mysteries, but historical, he wasn't so sure about.

Gazing straight ahead, only half aware of the world outside the comfort of their car, Patrick turned on the radio to one of our favorite songs, 'The Chain' by the Fleetwood Mac. The catchy sing-along chorus came, the drums kicked up into double-time, and suddenly my feet were tapping. The sound of my feet rang out a taping like Morse code, a code spelling out

h-a-p-p-y f-e-e-t.

"Behind the relationship between musical sound and body movement," Patrick said, "I have a theory for you. I have observed that people tend to perceive affinities between sound and body motion when experiencing music. My perception claims these similar relationships are deeply rooted in human perception."

Adjusting in my seat, I answered, "But of course. Music, tone, and color are one in the same. Pythagoras believed that the universe was filled with tones and colors. His teachings were overflowing with numbers and how they associate with musical tones and colors. Our soul chooses our parents. We chose our names. Therefore, through numerology, our name shows our strength, weakness, and our potentials. It's amazing," cheerily I answered.

Steadying his hand on the wheel, Patrick replied, "I know about the Pythagorean Theorem. Are you talking about that?"

"Remember, we talked about Pythagoras before. He was a famous mathematician and a philosopher. Pythagoras founded the Pythagorean School of Mathematics in Cortona, a Greek seaport in Italy. The main idea of religion that Pythagoras was known for had to do with the transmigration of souls. The Pythagoreans believed that the soul was a divine and immortal being, imprisoned in the physical body. He believed humans could understand the physical universe's energy through numbers, tones, and colors. The mystical Pythagoras was excited by his discovery and became convinced that the whole universe was based on his theory. The planets and stars moved according to mathematical equations, which paralleled musical notes, and thus produced a kind of symphony, he named musical universalis."

"Where did you get that information and what is musical universalis?"

"From Maggy. According to her studies, musical universalis is the musical harmony of the spheres. It's an ancient philosophical idea that regards proportions in the movements of celestial bodies, the sun, moon, and planets, as a form of music. It was Pythagoras' idea, and it continued to appeal to thinkers about music."

"I remember from being in school that in the 15th Century the scientists were able to determine the relative distances between planets in our solar system, mainly as a result of the work astronomers accomplished," Patrick calmly said. "Since Pythagoras lived years before that time, it appears reasonable to accept that he had no knowledge of interplanetary distances and yet he clearly believed there had to be a relationship between music and the distances between celestial bodies. You know, music does influence people and situations."

"Maggy taught me numerology. It helps me to understand people especially when doing their sessions. I can tune into their past, present and future with that tool," I replied.

"Whoa, there, Favorite Person! You're trying to tell me you get peoples' answers through numbers? I can learn numerology." Patrick chimed.

"That's true. I'm just saying it's a tool to assist anyone. That's all," I quickly answered.

While the warm sun drenched us, I studied the mountain ranges intently as we crossed the Colorado state line. The summits of the mountain covered with fresh snow.

"I love mountains," I excitedly said.

"Driving in the Colorado mountains can be tricky, maybe even a bit nerve-wracking," Patrick said. "But there is no reason to avoid its beauty. The main thing for me to do is not allow the breathtaking scenery cause me to drift out of my lane." Laughingly Patrick continued, "Next exit is ours, refill for the car and something to eat for our empty bodies. Bathrooms are calling our names."

~~~

Back on the interstate we cracked the windows a bit. The wind gushed into the car due only to the speed, pleading to break in from the minuscule cracks of the windows. There was a presence that lingered, the presence of "let's talk again."

Patrick broke the silence asking, "What do you think the meanings were for the Paint Rock drawings?"

"The pictographs at Paint Rock tell the story there was a battle with Indians and it was a bloody mess." I nervously said. "The drawings showed this battle had been tricky and one-sided. The sketches of UFOs show their belief of life on other planets. At the battle, the Indians knew they weren't going to survive but gave all they had to give. They knew, even if they died, their soul would move on to another life, known as an afterlife. It is seen as being like this life is based on a person's actions. Those pictographs told a very touching, emotional and spiritual story."

"You told me your story definition. Now, I will tell you the history," Patrick quickly responded. "It was during the time of this Texas Ranger, Jack Hays. He was meeting with General Taylor when they were supposed to have received word about a large, Comanche war party torching settlements throughout southwest Texas. The story goes, he knew he could never catch the elusive Comanches by following their trail. Hays quickly gathered up around forty Rangers, a few Tonkawa, and Lipan Apache scouts. They all rode hard in hopes to intercept the war party before it could escape. Hays and his Rangers arrived early the following morning to the banks of Concho River, only to find they had missed the Comanches. A severe drought had long plagued the area, and the scouts were sure that a small lake formed by the nearly dry Concho River would serve as the only watering hole in that direction for miles around. The lake stood at the base of Paint Rock. As expected, the Comanches approached the lake at dawn. I'm sure they were thirsty and tired. Hays let the warriors get close before giving the command to open fire. Smoke and fire billowed out of the willows with the roar of the Rangers' guns making the Comanches fall back, carrying off as many of their dead as they could. The Comanches found tracks showing there were no more than thirty or forty riders. They thought they could easily overwhelm them in the full light of a new day."

"Finally," Patrick said with a sigh, glancing at me, "by mid-morning all was ready. The chief rode to the front of his warriors, raising his lance high and ranting the Comanches into making one final supreme effort. Screaming his fury, the Comanche chief heeled his horse to a gallop and led what was to be the final charge. The Rangers calmly picked out targets, waiting patiently for Hays to open fire allowing the fear that churned their bellies as the painted warriors drew closer."

It wasn't easy for me to sit still while listening to his story. Squirming in my seat, Patrick lowered his voice. "The untimely death of the Comanche chief shattered the drive of the charge, and a terrible wail of agony arose from the Comanche throats as the warriors pounded around the battlefield. The Battle of Paint Rock was a victory for the Texas Rangers. Many dead Comanche lay scattered across the prairie in front of the willow thicket. Unbelievably, only one Ranger had been wounded in the fighting, and one unfortunate horse killed by an arrow. Paint Rock was to be Hays's final major engagement with the Comanches. He dedicated the remainder of his Texas Ranger career serving as a volunteer with the United States Army, riding for many generals."

Sitting straight up in my seat I firmly said, "The pictographs tell another story. The reason for this ferocious battle that you say history tells is not true. According to the pictographs, the Comanches were not on a warpath. Hays wanted to win over the generals and falsified the truth about the Comanches. The drawings shown in the early morning of a violent battle started. The Comanches were taken by surprise and shocked by the furious attack. The Indians rallied quickly under the leadership of their chief, who carried a vividly painted shield and sported a buffalo-horn headdress with a hide visor that concealed his face. The Comanches' persistence stemmed from the fact they were on high, holy ground and believed their ancestries' medicine would be enough to defeat their enemy. The shamans worked their energy for the Great Spirit to help in their struggle with Devil Jack, a name the tribesmen had given to Jack Hays. It's all in those pictographs. They are coded. And that's the truth. To me, it's very basic and simple to read, the UFO pictographs. I'm sure UFOs have been seen or reported around Paint Rock because it's a special spiritual area. Sadly, there is more untruth about the Indians than there is truth. Indians are always made out to be wicked, fighters or killers. Just because they have a different spiritual belief, they are lied about." I announced. "In the absence of official records, many question the truth of the Rangers' victory at Paint Rock."

Patrick quietly added, "Some have even suggested that Paint Rock was an attempt to revise history for the sake of glorifying the Rangers."

Clenching my hands, I said, "Indians are not a colossal body with one set of beliefs and practices. Indians celebrate like their ancestors before them, who practice the traditional ways. I prefer to learn Indian history from the Indians. After all, who can tell their stories better?"

Starting to calm down I continued from my passion, "Storytelling preserves Indian culture. Elders endlessly repeated stories and tested their children to ensure accuracy for future generations. It was through storytelling that I learned from Maggy, Leon, and my other Indian teachers. I learned the strength of their enduring culture. Some misguided historians and ethnologists think their stories are mostly myth, fairy tales told by primitive, simple-minded people, discounting their authenticity and validity. Their stories are filled with spirit because it gives them meaning and purpose. I believe one must see a man's heart to know him. It's seldom we read versions of our history that touch the hearts and inspire our children. Very few public and private schools teach real Indian history. Less than a handful teach it from the Indian perspective, and I wonder why? The telling of stories is the essence of our culture. We must respect our ancestors and learn their stories to keep our ways alive for the sake of their children's children. I believe it's important to encourage schools to emphasize Indian history. I want to ask them to teach more than just colonial and Indian wars. Why not order books and other things that teach written stories from the Indian's perspective?"

"Wonder why they are called American Indians," Patrick demanded.

My frowning face was pallid. I sighed, "The name American-Indian derives from the colonizers' world-view and is therefore not the real name of anyone. My Indian friends get upset when referred to as American Indians. The reason is because of its association with Columbus. There is an equally serious dilemma with the use of Native-American, which came into trend as part of a concern for political correctness. The word 'native' has a generic meaning, referring to anyone or anything that is at home in its place of origin. Native also has a judgmental meaning in English colonization, as in "The natives are restless tonight." From an English viewpoint we are talking about English words. Native carries the implication of primitive, which itself has both a generic definition, meaning first or primary and a scornful use, meaning backward or ignorant."

Patrick chimed in, "I've always said I'm Indian when Indians weren't cool. My Dad told me; Indians were treated badly after the turn of the century. When he was young, Indians or Blacks were not allowed in town except on weekends, all restrooms were labeled Black and White, and drinking fountains. Also, they had to walk miles into town." Sad. Indians and Blacks were disliked through his childhood in Oklahoma.

"Remember my great-great grandmother walked the Trail of Tears. My Granny passed down Cherokee family stories to anyone who would listen. I just wished I had been older and maybe that would have helped me to realize the importance of her wisdom." Patrick continued.

"You need to listen to her now and remember what she told you. She will communicate with you, just in a different technique," I said.

Patrick agreed and said, "Looks like the Wyoming road sign coming up. Glad we made good time."

"Welcome to Wyoming, Forever West." Underneath was a sign reading "Turn Around, State's Full."

"Those welcoming signs add a sense of mystery. Don't be surprised if we must be incognito. We're not turning back." Patrick said laughingly.

With each bend of the Wyoming highway, we found breathtaking views.

"I've noticed you talk about your granny but not much about the rest of your family. Did your parents tell Cherokee stories?" I asked.

"My mother lived in Oklahoma, but she was not Cherokee," Patrick answered.

"I was raised in a time when children were not to be heard, and I was heard a lot," Patrick affirmed. "Many times, my daddy disciplined me.

"We choose our parents, you know?" I reminded him of a prior conversation.

Patrick responded, "I say, don't use your parents as a whipping post. Be brave, look at yourself and take responsibility for your actions. I know psychologists or psychiatrists wouldn't like me, but that's what I have learned. It's not wise to give people excuses for their misbehavior. Too many people point their fingers at others accusing them of their problems. That's what's wrong with the world today. Everybody thinks someone else has their answers."

"What I have found is that science and spirituality connection within has ways for people to understand their life's experiences. It is a frequency of negative and positive energy on earth with support from the energy of the universe," I proclaimed.

"Aha," Patrick said, "science deals principally with the physical and biological dimensions. However, science's dualist approach encourages, even enforces, people to take sides and ignore, or flat reject, spirituality. We must learn to interweave science and spirituality to save ourselves and the planet. Earth's energy has been divided by the people. We must reconnect."

I glanced out the window, smiling. "I find it helpful to think in terms of dimension with human experience. The spiritual dimension is one. The others are physical-, biological-life, psychological minds, and social community. The spiritual dimension involves universal experiences of love, wonder, mystery, purpose. It is more significant that we all belong to something whole and indivisible; a divine and holy unity, in other words, God."

"I'm learning with love and joy, sharing with your playful heart and the innocence with which you teach is great. It is not merely knowledge applied to a circumstance. It's a skill of seeing beyond the thin surface of how things appear, Patrick declared. A wise person reaches to grasp what is the driving force beyond how things appear."

"Yes," I replied, "and the principle of wisdom begins with truth!"

CHAPTER 23

Wyoming Power

*"Your power is your brain. Emotions are your actions, and
your love will increase all your energy for completion."*

Shirley-1991

The Wyoming scenic drive through the Wind River Canyon to Thermopolis, was extra unique. The mountains have kept safe the soul of this
land for time unmeasured and tells of it in words unspoken. The splen-
dor displays the riches, dignity, and good look at the mountainous area
made my heart happy. It's acknowledged to be the gateway to Yellowstone
Park. This picturesque drive would calm anyone's nerves. Its energy gener-
ates a feeling of vastness and a wonderful sense of freedom.

Patrick and I drove into the driveway of our new home, a little
white house trimmed in yellow with a sunroom on the front that added
immense appeal and aesthetic fun value with a white picket fence around
the yard. It was an ideal place where we could concentrate, watch the

sunset over a mountain top and animals that frequent the place. This sunroom was where Patrick and I felt the utmost comfort, where we could relax, eat meals, visit with friends, hold business meetings, and write.

Our sunroom was furnished with an antique early American Oak round dining room table and chairs. There were also two white wicker rocking chairs with dark green cushions and an antique side table placed in the middle of them. Antiques are my favorite, they are gems of times past, the expressions of the human soul that echo my own. Adding to its comfort, every evening we watched the deer and antelope run up and down the street. We loved this room.

Looking out the window Patrick said, "A house is just four walls and a roof, but home is our sanctuary, a refuge from the world. On a little corner of God's green earth to call our own. This house is our genuine bit of paradise."

"Our new home has great energy," I affirmed. "Now visualize our souls as energy, bound to their matter which is energy. It's a discrete packet of energy in its own space and time but are still separate entities called souls. We know this energy cannot be created or destroyed. Thus, souls are eternal. But they are right here at this time, safe and sound in this house. The universe and our new home are saying 'Hello, be nice, share kindly, and take care of your planet. Yes, we will be happy here."

In the early morning, a ray of light escaped through the blinds and attacked my eyelids. My ears caught extra loud caws; caws coming from outside. I turned my body, breaking the seal of my warm imprint on the bed while moving closer to Patrick's warm body. A looming glow invaded the room; darkness turned to soft shadows. A low-level crisis began. The day was about to break free.

Patrick grumbled and flipped on his back. "What is that noise?" he gruffly asked.

I jumped out of bed. Looking out the window, "Its crows! Oh my God, there are hundreds of them."

Patrick scrambled taking hold of the majestic blanket that enveloped him like a warm hug. A leg escaped from under the covers, hoping to find the perfect balance of warmth and coolness.

Patrick yawned, "I think the mornings are beautiful sensuality. The feeling is not right or wrong. It's just a feeling. Those crows are still cawing, they are beginning to bug me."

Their cawing was becoming a mixture of grating caws and arranged in a sequence that was several minutes long. "Damn crows! What's their problem?"

"Leon told me crows aren't known for their songs," I reassured him.

"They're associated with the great mysteries of life. When you keep seeing or hearing crows, it is important to pay closer attention, they are messengers. Crows know the secrets of balance within your heart. Deep in a crow eye you will find the gateway to the supernatural, they know the mysteries of creation and keepers of the Universal Law. I feel they are welcoming us."

Patrick continued to lay in bed, his head against the pillow, running his fingers through his hair and muttered, "I ought to get up and check on everything and maybe start unpacking."

Excited, I said, "Let's get going and explore some of Thermopolis and its history."

It was a place I felt Patrick would love living with the hot spring's pools, the Hot Springs State Park where the buffalo roamed, the Legend Rock Petroglyph site with at least 283 different petroglyphs with some of the ancient rock art that dated back 10,000 years when Indians were living in the area. I was full of morning energy and ready to go.

"Come on Patrick. Let's go visit our new town," I babbled.

Patrick slowly crawled out of bed mumbling, "Don't be in a hurry."

"But I want to visit the Plaza Hotel," I yelled from the kitchen. "It was built in 1918. It is a two-story yellow brick building that overlooks the Big Horn River and originally had seventy rooms with a common bathroom at the end of each hall. The bathrooms were all with mineral water, good for soaking. Now, that is exciting."

Filling the tea kettle with water, I continued, "A spa area was divided into men's and women's areas with soaking tubs and a steam sauna, using 127-degree water from the big spring." I continued, "The hot water was piped in a loop under the Big Horn River to temper for bathing. How exciting is that? Plus, I'm sure Indians still live around here too."

Patrick, tying his robe belt, walked into the kitchen where I was brewing tea.

"What's so big about this Plaza Hotel?" he asked.

"I don't know yet, but there is something awesome waiting for us at that place. You will love it," I teasingly said to get Patrick's approval.

Driving to the plaza, I felt the road was leading us onward into a new horizon. It gave me a sweet sense of warmth in my heart. I started rubbing my chest,

"Are you okay," Patrick asked.

Stepping out of the car, I answered, "I just feel a lot of love and excitement here at this place."

Upon entering the historic Plaza Hotel lobby, we felt overwhelmed by its size. It was extra-large with tall ceilings, hardwood floors and surrounded by floor to ceiling windows with no curtains, only blinds. The least little noise echoed throughout the place. In the center of the room was a couch with a handmade wool Afghan thrown across it, multi-color area rug and coffee table with magazines strewed across it. Along the southeast wall was a bookshelf filled with books and magazines scattered around, unorganized. We heard noises from what sounded like a kitchen with pots and pans rattling and people talking loudly. From the west side of the lobby, we could hear water running.

We walked over to the books, and I started organizing some of them when a tall dark-headed man, wearing Levi's and a red and black plaid flannel shirt came in from the noisy room.

"Hi, my name is Melvin. How may I help you? You folks need a room?"

Patrick stuck out his hand and said, "My name is Patrick Cox, and this is my wife, Shirley Smith-Cox. We just moved here from Texas. Shirley wanted to visit your hotel, she feels it is somewhat special, actually she has a strong feeling there something sacred about this place."

Melvin's eyes lit up. "Really? You're THE Patrick and Shirley from Texas?"

Still shaking Patrick's hand, Melvin exclaimed, "Sandy, my wife and I, bought the Plaza. We have big plans for this historic place. We moved here from Billings, Montana, thought it would be a better school and place to raise our kids. We have four you know. Two boys are old enough to play high school football. The whole town shows up for these games. We like to show our support, you know, the players like it. We've even been winning a few, may even go to State this year, one just never knows."

Letting go of Patrick's hand, Melvin continued, "We plan to renovate this place back to its originality. Yes, sir, we got big plans. Besides renting rooms, I am a certified massage therapist. People here in Thermopolis are happy we moved here, and we're going to clean this place up. It sure has made the Indians around here happy."

For unknown reasons, Patrick and I didn't understand why Melvin was excitedly walking around in circles.

"Are you okay, Melvin?" I asked.

"I have a message for you two from my Indian friends, *Snaggle Tooth, Paintbrush* and *Princess Crow*." Melvin was making elaborate hand gestures while talking. "My Indian friends predicted Patrick Cox and Shirley Smith would move here from Texas. They said you were moving here about three months ago and when you arrived at the Plaza to be sure and welcome you. I'll have to say; I'm a little surprised but thrilled. So, welcome to our fair city."

Melvin then opened his arms and gave Patrick a big manly hug with a slap on his back. He turned to me, "*Snaggle Tooth*, said you two nice people were working big time to help our great planet Earth. We know it's in need to be restored just like this hotel."

Melvin turned and hugged me. "We are to open our arms to you and Patrick. *Snaggle Tooth* wants Patrick to know that in a past life he was '*Looking Glass*,' Now with Earth name "*Wolf Eyes*" and Shirley, *Princess Crow* says you were given the name '*Golden Mother*.' We welcome you with open arms and hearts."

Patrick turned towards me, the look on his face was real, making me realize with hearing the words, *Looking Glass* did something to awaken him emotionally. It took a second or two for Melvin's words to sink in, then he blinked his eyes and said, "I've been told about *Looking Glass* before, but this time I feel him. I feel different yet with a powerful energy. I hear the words, *The emotion of your reunion sealed as a perfect photograph in your soul. Your ancestors survived because of their deep feelings and their ability to read emotions in others. They knew the meaning of love and unity.*"

Melvin looking stunned, "I agree our ancestors were a lot smarter than we are now days. They knew how to live off the land."

Patrick asks, "When can we meet your friends?"

Melvin smiled and said, "Oh no, it's not necessary. They said you would ask, but they keep track of you through the realms." In fact, '*Princess Crow*' left you a gift Shirley."

"Really, for me?" I surprisingly replied!"

Melvin left the room for a few minutes and returned holding a brown bottle covered with lime and a heart shaped on the side.

Here he said, "This is a bottle of water from a sacred cave where only *'Princes Crow'* knows of. *Princes Cow* told me to put this bottle in my spa room and see what the Great Spirit would show us through steam. Something about the power of stream creation. Shirley it's a heart and that is why you were named *Golden Mother*. Here is a special gift just for you."

I thanked him as I took the bottle.

I asked, "Do I drink the water?"

Melvin answered, "Let your heart be your guide."

"Thank you."

Melvin turned to Patrick, "Our gift to you Patrick, we will communicate through the realms. The Rainbow Warriors know what to do and will help if needed. We will keep in touch.

Patrick smiled and said, "There will be people throughout the world visiting Thermopolis. Shirley is a psychic and teaches self-help seminars for personal and spiritual growth with her Universal Love seminars."

Melvin anxiously asked, "Explain a little more about self-help seminars? Is there anything I can do to help?"

I replied, "Self-help seminars teaches people about their own abilities, their own strength and potential and to trust their intuition. In doing so they will overcome fear and be more independent."

Melvin with a puzzled look, "Huh?'

Patrick quickly answered, "All answers to all questions are within. "

Melvin waved his finger in the air, and said, "Oh! Got It."

"People will need lodging so we will add your brochure, they can make their own arrangements." Patrick added. "We must check the outside activity around here; the seminars are designed for outdoors more than inside. Must have Mother Earth's energy to help out."

Melvin asked, "So do you help Shirley teach?'

"Na, I'm more of a tote and fetch guy." Patrick said nonchalantly.

"Now Patrick you know better than that," I quickly interrupted. "Yes, Melvin, Patrick helps teach."

"I can't picture Patrick just toting and fetching his life away," Melvin said laughing. Then the three of us started laughing, our laughter vigorously echoed around the lobby. A good laugh is a signal of feeling safe and comfortable.

It was time for us to leave, but not to say a forever goodbye. We would return to Melvin's hotel.

I continued private session work along with the seminars. I love helping people and this fulfilled my desire. We soon learned Thermopolis was a perfect area for our work, so I scheduled four-day seminars throughout the summer. The seminar material included booklets with awakening self-help teachings along with activities of Hot Springs swimming, whitewater rafting, hikes, petroglyphs, and a night star gazing and hopefully UFOs would give us a show.

It didn't take long for friends to learn we lived in a special place. The attraction of history, nature and mineral baths created our home to became more like a cozy B&B but included all meals as well as visitors having days stretched ahead with great possibilities. Instead of a quiet home, it was incredibly busy with noisy interruptions. The visitors' noises became a sort of fabric that weave into the matter of our home and was getting to our soul along with becoming part of us.

On this perfect day, Patrick and I were alone, I said, "Willpower is a finite resource, it burns energy in the brain; then once you run out, you give in. So, for the love of God, we must stop what we are doing and take control of our home. We are not getting our main mission accomplished, Maggy's book."

Patrick stood up and loudly declared, "I totally agree! It's like running an athlete nonstop and then wondering why they can't sprint. So, I promise you, you have my consent to advise those who want to visit Thermopolis, they must contact Melvin at the Plaza. He has plenty of rooms."

A few months later, the aroma of Patrick's BBQ baby-back ribs baking filled my senses as I stood peering through the kitchen doorway at Humpy Back Haven. The smell of the saucy ribs and garlic bread baking made me wonder what the big occasion was. When Patrick cooked a dinner like that, he had a purpose. Closing the oven door, he turned exposing his apron that read Jambalaya with large dancing shrimp.

"I've got a surprise for you, Favorite Person. It's a special night for us.

I hummed while setting the dinner table.

Patrick yelled from the kitchen, "Be sure and place toasty warm, damp, hand-washing, towels. Must keep our hands clean."

I smiled as I placed the blue willow plates between the silverware and the crystal wine glasses knowing something good was about to happen.

I lit the candles while Patrick placed the food on the table. As we were eating, the murmurs and distant screeching echoed from an owl hooting outside. The sound was heard throughout the room, along with clinks of glasses and silverware as it tapped our plates. Patrick took a sip of wine and asked, "Did Leon talk to you about owls, what are owl's totem?"

I wiped my sticky fingers off with the warm hand towel and answered. "Owl totem represents a deep connection with wisdom and intuitive knowledge. It gives us the ability to see what's usually hidden too most. With the spirit of this owl, we are guided to see the true reality, beyond illusion and deceit."

Patrick sat across the table from me, leaned over and placed his hand on mine. "I have some news for you, Favorite Person. Thermopolis has a print shop. I have already talked with Kathy and her husband, the owners, and they assure me they have the expertise making a storyboard template for your book. Once I get it ready, which is Step One, everything needed is here in Thermopolis. Step Two is I have talked to Taylor Publishing Company in Dallas, and they will be your publisher. Are you ready to travel again? We will have to, for book signing tours, radio, and T.V. If so, I will start Step One tomorrow."

I gasped and looked at his face, "That was fast! I didn't know you had been working on this. I'm surprised."

Patrick, smiling, replied, "I wanted to surprise you. It's my job to help you get your messages out to the people."

We stood up.

I started, "But…"

Patrick placed his finger over my lips and said, "Shh." He whispered in my ear, "Relax and enjoy. Your dream is coming true."

I started dancing and yelling, "Maggy, your book is to be published. Oh, that means I need to get to my trunks where Maggy's pictures are. I have lots of them and Duke, I have lots of work to do."

Patrick and I made our daily schedule. Every morning we would swim in the mineral baths and do whatever we chose to through the rest of the day.

At 5:00 pm sharp we worked on the book. I had 1500 pages already typed making it necessary for Patrick to cut away stories. After our discussion of what to take out, I went to bed, while Patrick edited *An Angel with Muddy Feet*.

After reading my typed material filled with the crooked politician information during Maggy's mayor days and my law enforcement work, Patrick was concerned. He told me I would be sued for what I had written because it had politicians' real names and places.

"The congressmen, judges and attorneys will not allow this book to be published."

It was then I remembered Maggy saying because of the law enforcement information the book would have to be titled *The Biography of Maggy Conn as told to Shirley J. Smith.*

Patrick laughed saying, "That's good. You can't sue a dead woman. Now, my concern is your protection."

Shortly after we started the book work, I began having difficulty breathing. Patrick would go to Maggy's pictures and tell her "I will help Shirley release you Maggy."

My thoughts were always, 'What is he talking about? Maggy is working on the other side helping her book to be published.' In a few days, Annette, Maggy's New York friend, called saying "It's time to let Maggy go Shirley, she has work to do on the other side."

I told Annette, "Once *An Angel with Muddy Feet* is published, she will be released." That is when I started strongly gasping for air. Patrick came in from the other room and announced, "I've just filled the tub with water, you go soak and relax."

I jumped up and rushed to the bathroom. As I stepped in a tub of extra warm water, I felt my tense body struggling to breath, I knew the fear in my chest was wanting to take over. With closed eyes, I heard music, and I saw this music attached to colors, painting stairs in the same way grapevines grow - this way and that, in a beautiful chaos that was not quite random. I felt my body relaxing, my heartbeat was the steady drum to the melody, and I seeped into the moment, allowing myself to climb this rainbow staircase. Soon, Patrick came in and stated, "Now go to the bedroom, lie down and meditate. This is between you and Maggy. I'm told you have some work to do." He left the room.

I crawled into my bed, my cocoon, safe and cozy. I closed my eyes and immediately saw Maggy, and she was not smiling like she usually does.

Maggy spoke confidently, "Shirley, at the hospital when you looked into my eyes, I had gone through rigor mortis the death of my body, but my heart was still beating. The nurse told you it was up to me when my heart would stop. It was through our eye contact the energy connected our hearts. You must release our hearts connection. We need our freedom. I have Universal Love work to do, and you have your work to do. We are working for love and freedom. As you know freedom is only freedom for all when the earth has come to live through love."

I saw this silver cord attached to our chests, I visualized a pair of silver scissors and I carefully cut this cord. Once I did the final cut, her face exploded into millions and millions of stars erupting into a brilliant white light. I quickly opened my eyes felling extremely lighter, calmer, and yet energized. I knew Maggy and I had our freedom.

On this chilly day, the air could only come as far as the window-pane. Inside our home the fire-kept us cozy-warm. Patrick sat quietly while I told him about my experience with Maggy. I now have my own inner peace; and it created my inner world to become a place of tranquility. I thanked him.

Patrick replied, "I knew something had to be done. I heard Maggy telling me, "This is between Shirley and me."

"I'll have to say, my excitement began to dance when I realized my intuition had awakened. Sometimes I hear voices other times I feel a movement of energy before my senses tells me what it is." Patrick added.

Every day I looked forward to my walks. In the nature's hug of ever open arms of brown, cozy beneath the canopy of leaves, there is a welcoming spirit that calls. It is as if there is something in me the trees can feel and they chatter to it, my intuition perhaps. Every day during my walk, crows would fly in a circle over my head, some would land on the ground and waddle beside me. I had never seen birds walk with anyone; but they were always welcome.

Astonishing is what Patrick named it. To see those birds walking beside me each day with his naked eye and his brain open to the reality amazement comes.

Patrick said, "While you were walking, I have been mediating. Leon told me; I have connected with 'Iron Jacket.' Iron Jacket was a Comanche chief and medicine man whom the Comanche believed had the power to blow bullets aside with his breath. He's a Comanche spirit buddy of Leon's. He's been teaching me to work with energy and colors, showing me, they have magical powers connected with Universal Love. He says, with my engineer knowledge of how to apply the principles of science and math helps me to work the color energy connection. Iron Jacket says the Great Spirit directs the universal energy of colors; therefore, everything is of color. Another way putting it, what is up above so is below. The universe colors are extraordinary, so as they flow to planets, the colors become diluted and dimmer. Working the color energy, the universes colors connect to my colors inter weaving with what I am working with. Individually colors resonate vibrations of different frequencies and will help connect with humans and universal colors. These universal colors extremely powerful and will assist once the connection is made. Our working together, he says, this information will strengthen my power to heal people and earth. It is a great connection and I have been practicing what he says." Leon and I have talked several hours about this. I got up and gave him a hug.

Daily Patrick would take a chapter to Kathy for the storyboards while I gathered pictures and newspaper articles out of the trunks. Maggy had a diary and scrapbook about her Vaudeville days, UP and AP newspaper articles, years of Maggy's Corner newspaper, so many to gather for a strong story.

Early morning, the coldness of the snow-covered ground made us rush to the car, we were bound and determined nothing would stop us from our morning hot mineral water swim.

It was dangerously cold, thirty-nine below causing our car heater to take extra time to warm up. Huge snowflakes blew down the street in a horizontal blur.

Patrick turned up the heater and said, "The hot mineral water is going to feel extra good today."

I adjusted my soft knitted cap over my ears. "The ancient Romans and the Indians knew getting into hot water was a great healing idea. There is nothing better than soaking in a hot pool of water surrounded by mountains and fresh air. There's something decadent and delightful about sitting in a hot pool surrounded by snow."

Patrick laughed, "Soaking in the outside pool with below zero temperature is fun too, icicles hanging from our hair, yet we feel warm. The snow began to fall straight and steadily from a sky with a wind, in a soft universal diffusion more confusing than the gusts and eddies of the morning. It was a part of a thickening darkness, to be the winter itself descending on us layer by layer.

I swam to Patrick's side. "Look, Patrick, there is a momentary hint of blue sky. Even this bit of light is enough to release a flash of diamonds across the vast landscape. They say usually the snow stopped at that hour of the day, as if for a quick survey of what had been achieved so far."

The rare days of sunshine served much the same purpose. The flurries had died down. The sun's direct glare attempted to melt the luscious, pure surface of drifted new snow. It was a fairy-tale world, child-like and fun. Boughs of trees adorned with thick pillows, so fluffy someone must have plumped them up; the ground a series of humps and mounds, beneath which slinking underbrush or outcrops of rock lay hidden. It was a landscape of crouching, cowering gnomes in droll disguises, comic to behold, straight out of a book of fairy tales.

~~~~

Patrick announced, "Well it's springtime, Favorite Person. Our Indian paintbrush flowers are in bloom."

I looked up from my leather journal book, "Yep, spring has arrived. I love this time of year, the feeling I get when the weather is beautiful, and the flowers are blooming."

Patrick asked, "Let's go for a bike ride. We can ride our bikes outdoors, you know, that fresh country air has a way of releasing energy reserves, I never knew I had, I imagined it within me as an extra energy store only for use in the case of necessary fun."

I answered, "I like biking, that feeling of motion, the speed and the rise and fall of the path, the chance to go over grass, mud, or road… It is a freedom I will always crave. That sort of liberty is a gift, is it not?"

Patrick added, "It is a privilege of movement, to build the self-strong whilst having fun. And so, as I pass the cars that pollute, the passengers in the seats, I am the racer on my iron-horse and I take a turn into the park, enjoying the scenic short cuts and the song of the birds."

Patrick stood up and said, "One of the more unique things to do here in Thermopolis, is biking through the buffalo pasture. We can ride to the top of the pasture and view the surrounding area with the location of the buffalo."

We pedaled our bikes side by side; it felt so automatic. I thought, my legs remain in motion as my thoughts stay in the moment, admiring each blossom and bird. These wheels have touched so much of earth and always are so keen for more… this bike and me, we explore as if it were a migratory calling.

Walking into the house Patrick turned and said, "Go to our business table, we need a meeting."

I could tell by his voice he had something important to say. Patrick opened a folder laying on the table and held up a piece of paper,

"I have news for you, FP. I have a letter from Taylor."

I thought, 'This letter is on two cent papers, but the words are without price.'

Patrick continued, "Taylor has finished printing *An Angel with Muddy Feet*. I have scheduled you for a book signing, radio and TV in all states, so pack your bags."

I excitedly jumped up and yelled, "Maggy, I am fulfilling my promise. Your story is ready for the masses!"

Patrick gently held me close, running his hands up my bare arms, not slowly but fast, sending electricity that was a jump start to my heart. Love is sweet, in love we have our 'forever home,' and it gives us the ability to fly freely, returning when each heart calls for the other's touch."

Eating breakfast of scrambled eggs piled high on a piece of toast, bacon, hash browns all served with apple juice, is food fit for a king or queen. I always believed breakfast brought a serene sense of comfort that started the day so well. Sipping my green tea, I told Patrick "I had a lengthy dream last night…well, really I feel it was a vision with an important message."

Patrick grabbed his napkin and wiped his face. He asked, "Oh, yeah what message?"

He continues, "Favorite Person, there are times I don't know what to think about your messages. You have real passion in your soul, asleep or awake, your brain is always working on solutions. That's when your inner genius takes great leaps forwards."

He added, "That is why a person diverted from their dreams or vision waves farewell to their greatest potential of intelligence, to the greatest gifts God could have given us."

I interrupted, "In the dream, the sky was remarkable blue, the birds were singing, and I watched a bee on a clover nearby. I walked to a quiet stream running exceptionally clear, and it was fun watching the fish leap out of the water and land back in with a splash.

"Everything in the vision was vibrant, especially the colors. There in the center of a million multicolored flowers stands an old Oak tree. The Oak tree stood out with its branches reaching their limbs across the deep blue sky. I think of the branches as arms and that's why I love them so. Trees are deeply rooted stretching upward, drinking in both sunshine and rain in equal measure. The mystical magic of trees is represented by beauty, wisdom, and eternal life. I sensed there was a fraction of a moment between when my eyes smile and my mouth follows, and that anticipation is as exquisite a feeling as any I've ever felt."

I was looking up to the sky watching Maggy and Duke's smiling faces. You were standing as though you had an order to change the world. Even though you knew changing the world was never going to be a task for one person or one type of mind. Holding a strand of turquoise beads, you continued in a 'Stand Alone Mode' like warriors need to do from time to time.

The beads were the rich turquoise of the earth, the sort that speak of soul and belonging. Indians surrounded us. The Chief wore a brown fringe loose fitting cut shirt, with patterns designed in white bead work, brown pants and a long feather headband hang down his back. His turquoise necklace stood out hanging around his neck in various layers. I noticed the beads you held were the same as those the Chief was wearing.

The chief started slowly walking toward us, his soles moving upon such solid ground, as he made bold progress to great us. As he moved closer, I could see he was carrying a beaded stick with a feather hanging down one end and what appeared to be a little dream catcher on the other. Standing in front of us, he held the stick close to his chest.

We were watching him carefully and with a stern face, he spoke, *A Talking Stick is used in our culture. It is our powerful ancient "communication tool."*

"I Will Fight No More Forever. I am Chief Joseph of the Nez Perce Tribe and my words to you are not new. Patrick, I know you as 'Looking

Glass,' I speak to you, in another lifetime we have worked together on this planet. I am giving you my heart's permission to tell the truth about the history of my people and planet earth. It does not require a lot of words to speak the truth. You and Golden Mother are to spread the words of truth. Now remember earth is the mother of all, and all must have their freedom. Everything on Earth is alive and everything on Earth is spiritual. Treasure all spirituality for its energy is of divine power. Talk straight, be kind, treat and love all people alike, and definitely be strong hearted."

Handing you the stick, he said, "I give you the right to speak and all others must listen quietly and respectfully."

"In this vision, simultaneously we put our hands over our hearts looking at Chief Joseph and the other Indians standing behind him.

A young man, bare chested and bare footed wore a flute bag draped over his shoulder. He walked to us playing a wooden carved flute. The flute music was delicate and loving causing my heart to leap into the heaven, as if it had the power to transmit the real me."

Patrick spoke, "Flute music is my magic wand it conjures the best of me. I am thankful my cousin carved it for me. It is admired for its beautifully lyric. I think often of its haunting tone quality. No matter, the time of day, my flute is my light, no matter the season, my flute is my fire, no matter the silence or the roar of sound, my flute can always be heard in my soul. I have learned to live through my flute music, in a way other artists desire to resonate with."

I intervened, back to the vision, "Chief Joseph spoke again, 'We live, we die, and like the grass and trees, renew ourselves from the soft earth of the grave. Stone's crumble and decay, faiths grow old, and they are forgotten, but new beliefs are born. The faith of the villages is dust now... but it will grow again... like the trees. Every part of earth is sacred. Every pine needle, everything in the dark woods, every sandy shore, every meadow, and humming insect. All are holy on this great planet! I believe much trouble and blood would be saved if we open our hearts more. The love for planet earth must return. People are earth's living life cells. They must awaken their spirit and their souls to allow Earth to nurture and love them again. Love must prevail!"

Chief added, "Your power is your brain. Emotions are your actions, and your love will increase your energy for completion."

Chief Joseph turned and walked away joining the Indian group, he loudly declared, "Times have changed, I speak to you, throughout your travels spread the truth. It is truth that will open people's eyes. I say, opening people's eyes will open people's hearts. We fought for our freedom; we have spoken the truth, but the world's lies continue. People are still being lied to just as we were lied to. Truth is of the heart, it is golden."

Chief took his left hand patted his heart then waved towards the sky, and said, "After your lengthy travels, it will be time for you and Golden Mother to move on. It will be time to rest from the world's greed and lies. Wisdom in your heart, your intuition, will tell you to move high in the mountains. Mountains soak up the essence of your soul and returns it purified upon its reunions. Consider the mountains to be the center of the world, for they are a cosmic axis linking earth to the heavens. Mountains provide law and order to the universe. They contain divine inspiration, they symbolize constancy, permanence, and their spiritually signifies the state of absolute consciousness.

He nodded and continued, "To show your pure heart in a world that extols emotional indifference, to choose to resonate with heaven's vibes rather than those of the ice-cold world, is a strength one can train the heart to possess.

Patrick proudly proclaimed," Yes, history, truth and love is the answer."

Standing boldly Chief Joseph spoke forcefully, "Your loving heart was born to live out in the open, to sing from the eyes and speak in song. Your loving heart was born to protect and guide the thoughts to beauty and *true creative intelligence. For with the loving heart, you are trusted and trustworthy, honored, and honorable, noble, and brave. We will be with you willing to love and protect you forever. Our truth must be told and understood by all."*

The Indians including the Chief started fading; they were fading into what looked like a sunset. It was as if God graffitied rainbow-flame upon the evening sky, the sunset came in its boldest blaze. As I watched the Chief and his people disappeared into the glittering colors, The echoing words of the Chief were, *"Living high in the mountains will be your spiritual awakening enhancing earth's Enlightening Truth. It will give you mental strength to overcome any challenges. Mountains speak to you. It will be time for our Spiritual Warrior, and Golden Mother to respite..."*

We waved goodbye, yet I knew in my heart it is never a goodbye; its I'll see you later.

By way of his smile, I could tell Patrick was serious. He spoke firmly, "Chief Joseph has given us a mission! Once heaven spins a flashlight for a holy mission, I can assure you it will be done! And we will move...but to what mountains do we go?"

I quickly answered, "We don't know thus far. Laughingly I continued, "I think we need another vision."

His lips in their casual silent way, told me it was going to be alright.